# AS YOU DO

# AS YOU DO

## Adventures with Evel, Oliver, and the Vice President of Botswana

# RICHARD HAMMOND

Weidenfeld & Nicolson
LONDON

First published in Great Britain in 2008
by Weidenfeld & Nicolson

1  3  5  7  9  10  8  6  4  2

© Richard Hammond 2008

A CIP catalogue record for this book
is available from the British Library.

ISBN-13 978 0 297 85520
TPB ISBN-10 0 297 85532 3

Typeset by Input Data Services Ltd, Bridgwater Somerset

Printed in Great Britain by Clays Ltd, St Ives plc

The Orion publishing group's policy is to use papers that are
natural, renewable and recyclable products and made
from wood grown in sustainable forests. The logging and
manufacturing processes are expected to conform to the
environmental regulations of the country of origin.

Weidenfeld & Nicolson

The Orion Publishing Group Ltd
Orion House
5 Upper Saint Martin's Lane
London WC2H 9EA

www.orionbooks.co.uk

# CONTENTS

*Introduction*                                                    1

1. How to be an Arctic Ninja                                      4

2. Diary of a Brave Polar Explorer                               48

3. Diary of a Tired Polar Explorer                               67

4. You Don't Need a Land Rover in Surrey                        108

5. An Odd Week Part 1 – On Purpose                              138

6. An Odd Week Part 2 – Very Much Not on Purpose                156

7. Never Meet Your Heroes                                       192

   *Acknowledgements*                                           257

   *Index*                                                      259

# INTRODUCTION

There are two ends to every stick: the nice, clean one and the, er, well, the other one. That isn't so nice. And that's the end that I am regularly accused of getting in the course of the many and various TV exploits I have undertaken in the last year or so. I have tried all sorts of excuses to explain why it sometimes appears as though I must get the tough option, the hard route, when others I work with might get something softer, more comfy. I've put it down to the fact that I am relatively fit, at least compared to some, and therefore I am the natural candidate for the more energetic, physically demanding roles. But in the few moments I experience of clear, rational thought, I know full well why it happens. It is because I can't say no. I never have been able to. Another drink, a childish dare, a journey too far; anything that ever required a resounding no I have greeted with an enthusiastic yes and a smile. And I'm still doing it. Or, rather, I'm still not doing it, I'm still not saying no. And that, in a phrase, explains much of what happens in this book.

Every book has a theme. It's one of the things books have to have. Along with covers and those bits where you say thank you to people. And the theme of this one is, as it turns out, travel. The tales I tell in here are about journeys. They are journeys undertaken, mostly, in the name of making TV programmes. The programmes themselves can be about travel, but these are the stories of what goes on behind the camera, of what it is like travelling the world with a crew, a deadline and a vague idea of what you're there to film. When you get back, the TV show is cut together, goes out and, hopefully, is watched by more than five people. I wanted to tell the story of everything else that goes on. I could never, in the programme I was making at the time, tell of standing in a polar bear's dining room and enjoying a pee while a former member of the special forces and an Arctic specialist doctor threw polar bear poo at my back. But I can tell it here. And I have. Neither could the TV show I was there to film ever have revealed the truth about my ride with the Hell's Angels or my crime spree in Butte, Montana. But I have here. Every time I pack socks and a washbag and walk through the front door to go to work again, stuff happens. Cars get crashed, lions roar while I try to fix a carburettor in the dead of night and wild-eyed, manic salesmen corner me and my crew on railway crossings and forget, mid-sales patter, what it is they're trying to sell. And in this book I have had the chance to tell these tales.

So it's a travel book. But there's another theme here. Please don't be sick when I say this, but every tale, every story in it, has one other outstanding feature: friendship. These are stories about travelling with friends. The journeys may not always have been easy – we were chased by polar bears, I drove a car called Oliver into an African river, we were shouted at by a legendary superhero and I sank my camper van in the English Channel – but in every case, through every moment of fear, weariness or lunacy, I'm running, hiding or laughing with friends. This is my good fortune, the best thing about doing what I do every day and the most fun thing to share. Being lectured about the appropriate behaviour when you're attacked by a polar bear would have been no fun if one of our band hadn't suggested throwing a stick for it. Borrowing a pair of work goggles from a psychopathic Montana farmer to use as biking goggles on my Harley would have been merely terrifying if the crew hadn't been with me to turn it into something funny, special and memorable. And terrifying. Setting off on a mission to steal a new cue ball for a rundown bar in a tough American mining town just wouldn't have happened had I been there alone. It took an unhinged producer and a director who genuinely does not grasp the concept of fear to make that one a reality. We often know what sort of television programme we want to make, but we never really now what is going to happen to us in the course of trying to make it.

I shan't be publicising this book with a massive crash. Not again. The publishers did ask but, funnily enough, I did actually manage to say no. Just this once. The doctors weren't entirely impressed when I asked if I could run to the Pole with a dog team. They would have found it very easy indeed to say no. Fortunately, they didn't, and I went. They didn't say no when I drove across Botswana in a forty-five-year-old shopping car either. Although technically, I didn't actually ask them if I could. And this new tactic has helped immensely; they haven't said no to anything else since.

These are the honest, though not exactly predictable tales of what happened in a year in the life of a man who just can't say no. There are crocodiles and cue balls in it and there are honey badgers, floating vans, superheroes, floods, polar bears, collapsing tents and beard competitions, too.

# Chapter 1

# HOW TO BE AN ARCTIC NINJA

## (you'll need a really warm coat)

There are some pretty cool jobs in the world. You can save lives with lasers, run schools for underprivileged children, craft beautiful objects using natural, renewable resources, compose poetry, invent cures for things – these are wonderful, rewarding occupations in the pursuit of which you might choose to dedicate your precious time on this earth. Or you can do a job that will get you a business card stone-cold guaranteed to get you laid. There are many such jobs, probably more than you would think. And they can all be traced back to the same handful of jobs we wanted to do when we were kids. Spaceman, test pilot, matador, lion tamer – any of these will fit the bill. They all hold the same magical appeal they did when we were five. And some people grew up to actually do them for real. I met a test pilot in June while filming on a prototype passenger jet in France. He took me and the film crew for a flight in the multimillion-dollar machine. We sat on the flight deck with him as he confidently flicked switches and spoke smoothly into the headset to his test-flight engineers about measuring tolerances and checking systems. He told us that, yes, his job was a good one. Bathed in the intimate, warm glow from a thousand illuminated switches and screens in the console around us, he confided in calm, clipped tones that an exciting day was always marked by being given orders to wear a crash survival suit and parachute for a test flight. That was always a good day, one to look forward to. He pulled smoothly on a brace of levers that sent the undercarriage tucking itself away somewhere below us in the belly of this leviathan with distant rumbles and thuds.

'Wow. Cool. Have you got a business card then?' I asked. And he told me that, yes, he had. And looked slightly puzzled.

'Does it say Test Pilot on it?' I needed to know now.

Leaving his left hand resting on the joystick in control of the plane, our pilot leaned forward in his captain's chair and fished a smooth-worn brown leather wallet from his pocket. Placing it in his lap, he drew from it a plain, white business card. And, yes, it simply bore his name, his phone number and the legend 'Chief Test Pilot'.

'Christ on a bike. How do you stop shagging supermodels for long enough to actually test-fly anything then?'

He was a grown man, in his fifties probably, with steely grey hair and a lot of responsibility. Happily married no doubt, settled in a pleasant house somewhere in the south of England I'm sure. But he was also a test pilot and that demands a certain type of chap. So he knew what I was getting at, where I was coming from. He didn't look at me, but he suppressed a smile, lowered his eyebrows and tended to some distant dial in a corner of the console away from me. The TV crew giggled, because we're not test pilots, and so we can.

I invented a game that day – it's one of my very best. Business card poker works simply but it takes dedication and forethought to be a winner. The culmination of the game is a simple round of poker. I say 'culmination' because it is the months or years spent gathering the business cards you bring to the poker table that will make or break you. And the cards must have been gathered personally, received by hand from the individual named on the card and not picked up from telephone kiosks or sent off for on the internet. When the big day comes, players sit at a table, each holding a clutch of five business cards. There's no messing about drawing further cards to enhance your hand, it's straight to the chase; the lead player – who must be decided beforehand, usually by a game of paper, scissors, stone – announces a first bet. This is a figure that must reflect his confidence in his own hand without scaring off holders of lesser hands who might take their cash with them. To encourage his fellow players, to keep them in the game, he might show them one card from his hand of five. This might be an especially impressive one, against which other players can measure their own and devise a strategy. Equally, the lead player might show a weak card, lulling the others into a false sense of security. It's a moment laden with heavy strategic significance. As bets are placed and the stakes raised to stay in, so the money must be placed on the table, in the pot, because we are all lying, cheating bastards and it will never turn up otherwise. Lose confidence and it's time to drop out, leaving your cash in the pot. Or you could try taking it away with you if you're bored with having your arms bent just one way.

Ultimately, through a process of drunken boasting, shouting and boredom on the part of those who have dropped out, a moment will come when it's time to find the winner. The remaining players then declare their hands. Each is measured, not just for the impressive nature of the individual business cards but for the artistry of the gathered hand as a unit. So, a test pilot beats a small animals' vet, yes. But not when the vet is accompanied by a senior Member of Parliament, the poet laureate, a foreign aid worker and an assassin for hire. Such a gathering possesses a breadth of intent, integrity, moral variance and rarity that makes it almost unbeatable. Of course, the holder of the test pilot card might then reveal the accompanying cards featuring the president of an obscure African country, a vanished English lord, the inventor of a cure for malaria and a former Nazi war criminal turned warrior monk. And if he did so, he would win. Though not, I suspect, before some pretty rousing protestations concerning the genuine or otherwise nature of the business cards. It's a truly great game. There is always a fight, every single time. I thoroughly recommend it.

For me, though, there is one business card that tops the rest, one crowning glory to be clutched among your dog-eared hopefuls as you reach the climax of a particularly vicious round of betting in business card poker. And it is the card bearing the following: 'Arctic Explorer'.

Nothing else conveys the same romance, toughness and sure-fire shaggability as those two words. Dissecting the phrase in an annoying English lesson-type way only further strengthens its case. Take the two words individually: 'Arctic' evokes barren wastelands; sounded phonetically it rings out, hard-bitten and clipped. But the brutality of the idea is tempered by the perceived purity of the white, frozen cliffs, the ice fields and the pale, translucent snow that it conjures up. There is an innocence, an unspoiled, virginal simplicity and a loneliness to it that calls to your soul along echoing millennia of icy quiet. 'Explorer' is, in stark and immediate contrast to 'Arctic', a warm, rounded concept. It triggers thoughts of Victorian heroes struggling manfully to open new and wonderful vistas to the waiting eyes of a more innocent world. It speaks of moustaches, hastily painted watercolour renderings of new and marvellous findings, ruined temples in leafy clearings, desperate battles through jungles, heroic deeds and self-sacrifice in the interest of your friends. The wispy hint of a suspicion this brings with it of the subsequent commercial exploitation of the very landscapes and peoples so discovered only lends a top note of raciness and sexy caddishness to an otherwise noble and romantic role. Write them on a business card together, 'Arctic Explorer', and you had better carry a very big stick around with which to beat away the advancing waves of panting supermodels. In my world, anyway. And so when the chance came not only to acquire the card of an Arctic explorer, but be qualified to carry one myself, I bit hard.

## *Upping the Stakes*

We've become quite well known for our big races on *Top Gear*. The first one we ever did featured Jeremy racing to Casino Square, Monte Carlo, in an Aston DB9 against me and James travelling by the French TGV train that travels at 200 mph. The origin of this race was when we were discussing if one was taking a holiday in the South of France was it quicker to drive or go by train – and so started the concept of our massive races across Europe. The whole race thing sort of caught on and so, naturally, we did it again. And again. And again. And so the races grew in scale and ambition. The previous year, 2006, we had raced to Oslo; James and me via the ferry and speed boat against Jeremy driving a Mercedes SLR, and so we really needed something big for this year, something to top the other races. There was only one answer: the Pole. We had a big meeting – in the pub – and all agreed that, yes, we must dash for the magnetic North Pole. After a bit of research and a lot of deep-rooted and passionate but entirely unfounded conviction from Jeremy, it was reckoned that it might be possible actually to drive there. This had never been done before, people might well be killed trying, but as we are a car show we all agreed that something involving a car would be the best thing to do.

We needed to make this a race and so we needed a mode of transport for the car to challenge in this dash for the magnetic North Pole. Clearly, there are no trains or buses up there, so public transport was out. In fact, there turned out to be only one form of transport normally available in that neck of the woods: the dog sled. Yes, there are purpose-built snow machines that look like jet skis running on caterpillar tracks and go like hell. But where would be the fun, the challenge, the hilarity at someone else's misfortune in that? No, the dog sled had been in use around the polar regions for millennia and was, it was agreed by all, the perfect benchmark against which to measure the car in this, its biggest ever challenge.

Jeremy would drive the truck, obviously. But we quickly encountered a complication beyond that easy first decision. Usually, these races are done with me and James competing against Jeremy. But the dog sled could only carry two people. It needed an experienced handler to drive the dogs, otherwise they wouldn't go anywhere at all. So there would only be room for one other. And another thing was that travelling by dog sled looked, from the internet pictures we found, to be quite energetic. James is a man of many attributes – he is a talented musician, a knowledgeable car expert and has long hair – but physical fitness really is not one of them. He is robust, yes, and quite tough in a gristly, wiry sort of way, but would, we feared, collapse and die from the effort required to climb on to the sledge. And so I drew the short straw, got the shitty end of the stick and the raw end of the deal. I would go on the sledge while James and Jeremy took the car together. Bugger.

## Throw a Stick for the Bear

They sent us to Austria to learn how to be polar explorers. We were to spend a week practising our skiing – which they wouldn't need to do in their car; putting up tents – which were different from the ones we would be using on the real trip; learning how to live off the land – you can't: there's nothing to eat except polar bears, and they want to eat *you*; and generally arsing about in the cold. The arsing about bit, though not a formal element in our carefully constructed training course, would be quite handy. As it turned out.

We were sent to a ski resort and this was my first ever trip to such a place. I grew up in Birmingham and we didn't go skiing. Skiing to us back then was like going on aeroplanes, something only for James Bond. We went camping once a year in the Forest of Dean. And there was no skiing there. As it turns out, skiing trips are pretty bloody annoying anyway. It's mostly about queuing, skiing. You queue to get your breakfast in the stupid wooden hotel, you queue to get on the minibus or find a taxi to take you to the stupid skiing place at the bottom of the stupid hill. You queue to buy a pass, which you lose later in the day and then you get down to the serious queuing, at the point where you get on the lift at the bottom of the mountain to take you to the top. This, technically, isn't queuing, it's something more akin to fighting, so I preferred this bit. You hang around in a big crowd on a sort of train platform. Except there are no tracks, just a big wire overhead. Eventually, the cable car device lumbers into view and disgorges a load of really annoying people with stupid smiles under their stupid hats on to the other side of the platform.

The car never stops; it just swings around the bottom of the platform on a huge, horizontal wheel until it comes up the side on which you and several million Germans are loitering, ready to get on board. Then there is a really massive fight, lots of shouting, some vicious pushing and, the next thing you know, you're on the cable car, face pressed to the frosted glass, staring through it at crying kids back on the platform, disappointed mothers and bereft lovers waving mournfully as the other half of their life is transported away on the carriage that someone, usually you, prevented them from getting on by elbowing them in the face and jabbing a ski pole into their groin. It's really rather good fun. But only that part is fun; the rest of it is terrible.

We had been allocated three specially trained, ex-special forces experts to turn a ragtag band of TV softies into a hard-bitten, close-knit force of Arctic Ninja. They had a bit of a struggle. The hotel was nice, though, we all agreed on that. The pillows were soft, the water warm and the bar was well stocked, if a bit costly. On the Arctic Ninja front, however, there was still much work to be done.

It was the third day and we were excited. The daily ritual of skiing, lectures on frostbite, lectures on skiing and lectures on skiing with frostbite was about to be broken by the appearance of something different on our agenda: we were going to do polar bear training. Some of us were still having trouble concentrating since we had, in an earlier lecture, been shown a picture of a frostbitten cock. Not a boy chicken which had stayed out of the coop too long, no, but a man's willie, frostbitten. The image, projected on to a wall in front of us so that the grizzled and blackened remains of the poor soul's old fella stood some six feet high across the wall, was disturbing for a great many, complex reasons. Every member of the team had reacted the same way: jaws dropped, eyes bulged then snapped shut, legs were crossed and right hands thrust protectively into their rapidly retreating groins. Our lecturer told us solemnly that doctors had been left with no choice but to trim — note the use of the deliberately neat and inoffensive word 'trim' to describe an act so brutal it turns your guts to ice — but to trim they said, nonetheless, the first two inches off the man's penis. There was a lengthy silence while we all thought exactly the same thing. So I said it:

'Holy shit, at minus fifty degrees, that first two inches would account for the whole of my knob and the first inch of my pelvis.'

It was not a nice lecture at all and some of us had not slept well the following night, leaving us feeling groggy and scared that day for the first of our lectures on what were to become close, if not especially welcome, friends — polar bears.

This, we had been warned, was essential stuff. The bears, portrayed in cartoons and Glacier Mint adverts as cuddly, amiable critters with big fluffy paws, cute black noses and posh voices are, as it turns out, psychopathic killers which hunt the Arctic wastelands for babies they can murder for fun. They would all want to kill us as soon as we stepped off the plane; some would probably be hiding in the overhead lockers ready to fall out and kill us when we opened them. So it was important that we learned how to tackle a bear, should we meet one. Which we almost certainly would.

We had spent the morning in the lecture theatre where the experts explained earnestly that the bears are not frightened of us because they are the top predators in their world and have never encountered anything to be scared of. They actively hunt humans, sometimes for days, and wait for their opportunity to strike. We would learn more about them in the afternoon but had finished our morning lecture with a quick run-through of the procedure we would go through if and when we encountered a bear. Our trainer produced a shotgun. It was a Remington semi-automatic, black from stock to muzzle and as sinister looking as an Apache gunship. He showed us the shells he was loading into it. They were shotgun cartridges but, instead of containing dozens of tiny shot, the plastic shroud held a single, massive piece like a plumb bob. It was a 20-bore shotgun and could stop an elephant, never mind a bear. The gun took five cartridges, our trainer explained, and he slammed the pump-loading mechanism back and forth, just like on the films. One of our team giggled at the Rambo moment. Our trainer ignored him and pressed on, explaining that with one 'up the spout', loaded into the breech, there were now four in the magazine ready to go.

Then he grew very solemn indeed. It was very important that we didn't kill a bear; it meant a lot of difficulty for the mission and a lot of very upset locals completing a lot of paperwork under very close and uncomfortable attention from all sorts of organisations.

'So why have we got a shotgun then?' A reasonable enough question from the back of the room.

'We could throw it and give the bear something fun to chase.' A soundman's contribution found favour with junior members of the team. And me.

'They'd like that.'

'Fetch!' a mime was beginning at the back of the room with

one bloke throwing a stick and another, as a bear, panting after it.

Our trainer explained that it was there just in case. We would go through this later, he told us, but basically the idea of the shotgun was to scare the bear off, not to kill it. Before we ever used it, we would try everything in our power to scare it off.

'Oh, right, we try and scare the two-tonne killer bear off without using the gun. How do we do that then, shout boo?'

As it turned out, pretty much, yes. Arctic travellers had found that standing their ground when they came across a bear and directing as much noise at it as possible could have a remarkably potent effect. Clapping, shouting, banging pans together, making noises familiar enough to us but alien and subsequently terrifying to a polar bear had been found to scare them off. Without having to resort to the gun. If all that failed – and there was much speculation among our little group as to the many ways in which it might – then it was time to break out the weaponry.

There was a strict order, predictably, governing the manner of firing the gun. We would fire one warning shot to the left of it, one to the right, one overhead and one into the ice just in front of it to kick up fragments and scare it.

'What, so it's scared of ice? Why? It's a polar bear, it's not like it's never seen ice before.' Again, reasonable stuff from the back of the room. And, again, our trainer stayed calm and patient and explained that the bear would never have heard a gun before or seen ice suddenly dance up in front of it and would be scared.

'Well, it will have seen and heard enough shotguns if it's come across other explorers blazing away like twats trying to make ice dance.'

'Yeah, won't that have taught it not to be afraid of shotguns? They just make a noise.'

'If the fourth one doesn't scare it, hit it in the chest with the fifth. That'll blow the back out of it and then it'll stop.'

There was an uncomfortable silence. Something about the way

our trainer had said it suggested he knew only too well what shotguns could do to living things.

'Right, lunch.' He clapped his hands and we stood up, ready to file out of the bland, cream-painted lecture theatre and into the busy ski resort for lunch.

We would all have a go at live firing the weapons and running through the bear procedure as part of the day's exercise.

Half an hour later, we were gathered in the café where lots of skiers in unnecessarily gaudy hats were talking rubbish and trying to cop off with each other. Of course, we were different; we were there to prepare for our polar mission and we enjoyed feeling superior to the holidaymakers. In order to prepare ourselves for the primal shock of coming face to face with a creature which, for the first time in our sophisticated, modern lives, had no fear of us and viewed us only as prey to be hunted, killed and eaten, we had bought one. Well, not a real one – they're quite tricky to get hold of – but Jeremy had slipped off to the ski resort shop with a pocket full of whatever the local wonga was and returned proudly bearing a bear. A fluffy, white, cuddly toy polar bear about a foot high. We sat it on the metal bistro table and confronted our fear over a frothy cappuccino.

'Doesn't look so bad really.' I slurped my coffee through a straw and tried to imagine what the bear would look like if it were fourteen feet high and running towards me faster than a racehorse, desperate to disembowel me with its ten-inch claws and eat my purple innards as they lay cooling on the ice in front of me. The stuffed bear looked back at me, its beady glass eyes failing to transmit the wild fury I needed to complete the picture.

'How many shots do we get in that shotgun thing again?' I asked no one in particular.

'Six.' Camera assistant Jay had coffee froth dribbling down his chin as he answered and didn't look too convincing.

'No, five. And one up your spout.' Soundman Darren.

'No, up *the* spout, you twat. Not *your* spout.' Cameraman Iain May laughed as he spoke and made a gesture with his hand like a doctor examining a prostate to indicate what he meant by 'your spout'.

'Right up yer spout, mate.'

'Ooyah, that's gotta hurt, doctor.' Jay winced as he spoke in a fake New York accent.

'You wouldn't want to sit down too hard with one of them up your spout, would you?'

'Christ, no. Blow your balls off from the inside,' Iain was warming to his topic now. A few of the smarter skiing types were looking round at our rowdy bunch, dressed in drab, functional Arctic gear rather than the more common, brightly coloured clobber of the skiers.

'Lads, really, I need to know. How many shells? Five or six?' I held an imaginary gun in front of me, squinting down the imaginary barrels at the toy bear.

'Four,' Jay grinned.

James and Jeremy came back from the coffee counter.

'Five.' It was a gun question. I trusted them on that one.

'Right, five it is. Thank you, James. So we fire, what was it, one to the left, one to the right, fuck me, it's complicated.'

Jeremy had a brilliant idea. We would do our own polar bear drill practice. He dropped to the floor of the café, grabbing the bear off the table as he went. Snaking through the table and chair legs, he retreated around the corner. And then he began advancing with a menacing growl.

'Wow. Bear!' one of our team shouted as we had been instructed. And, without hesitation, we all swung into our polar bear-scaring noise-making routine. We banged on tables, hit plates with spoons, banged our heads on windows, shouted, swore and clapped. The other diners, perhaps not quite appreciating the importance of rehearsing your polar bear routine prior to an Arctic adventure, looked round and stared.

One of our group was singing 'Eye of the Tiger' at the top of his voice for reasons best known to himself. It was quite a frightening noise, though, and certainly alien, even to human ears.

'Oh, God no, please don't let the bear get me. I'm still a virgin.' A squeaky, falsetto voice from the back of the group.

'Mate, it's gonna eat you, not hump you.'

'I want to see the Taj Mahal before I die. And shag Natalie Imbruglia.'

And through it all, Jeremy growled menacingly, advancing on the group as fast as he could, shuffling on his belly, pulling himself forwards with his elbows as he gripped the toy bear in front of him and stared around its fluffy white head.

'Oh, for God's sake, why bother?' I stood up and mimed the pump action of loading the shotgun, levelled it at the bear and cracked off five imaginary shots, all straight into and through the bear.

'Right, that's done, who's for coffee?'

Yes, we knew there was a long way to go before we were ready to tread in the footsteps of Scott, Amundsen and those who had gone before into the Arctic wilderness. But we knew, too, that we would be ready one day and that day would come soon. So before all that, another frothy cappuccino and it's my turn to be the bear.


## If It's Yellow . . .

There was an incredible amount of planning to be put in before a trip like this one. Logistics, backup plans, contingency supplies – everything had to be planned and marshalled with immaculate precision and care. We didn't have to do any of that, though; it was all done by the team in the office. I just packed a really big jacket, bought some massive thermal pants and set off. The plan that had been so cleverly devised in the office called for me to travel out before the rest of the team and spend ten days in Iqaluit, northern Canada, learning how to drive a dog sled. I was very excited about this, being a bit of a dog lover and all that, and so set off with my bag, my massive thermal pants and a happy heart. I would stay, not in some bland hotel, but in the house of Matty McNair, the seasoned polar traveller, who would be my guide, companion and safety net for the trip. Matty McNair is the most experienced female polar guide in the world. In 1997 she led the first ever all-female expedition to the geographic North Pole. She has since guided three expeditions to the South Pole. In 2003 she crossed the Greenland ice caps with her children, Sarah and Eric, by ski kites and with dog-sled support. The dog team we would use on the real trip was hers, as was the sledge, and so my time spent training in Arctic know-how would be in the company of the very person, dogs and kit that would accompany us in a couple of weeks' time when we set off on our race to the Pole.

## 11 April

It's a lengthy flight to Iqaluit, in fact it's several lengthy flights. I slept through all of them. Having arrived at many airports across the world in the last ten years, I was ready to take Iqaluit in my Arctic Ninja's stride. And it was easy – all the usual airport stuff is there: trucks to carry bags around, shops full of brightly coloured gee-gaws bought by fathers to compensate for spending too much time away from the kids and bored people in cheap corporate blazers sitting behind check-in desks waiting to spend forty minutes tapping into a computer after you've told them your name only to then ask you to spell it for them. But everything is smaller, closer together and a lot colder. It's an airport, though, and surprisingly well equipped for such a remote place. In fact, the place is only there to support the airport. It was built as a staging post for early passenger jets that couldn't manage the long leap to Europe without stopping for fuel. It's a kind of Arctic motorway service station on a particularly remote stretch of motorway. The M50 perhaps, running from Birmingham to Wales. Iqaluit is, as it turns out, pretty damned northern, though, and the car park beyond the tiny terminal was filled only by pickup trucks, each bearing a thick glaze of grimy ice. My bags turned up on the conveyor belt – just like the belts in Heathrow, only smaller – and I grabbed a ride to the address I had been given.

I had whiled away some of the few conscious hours I had spent flying here, imagining my way around the home of a genuine Arctic explorer. Matty's home, then, had become in my mind a sort of ice castle, bedecked with memorabilia from her many trips. I saw paintings of strange, antlered deer and huge bears standing in stark silhouette against landscapes that would be lunar but for the haunting, blue ice softening the contours of the mountains under a dark, star-strewn sky. There would be, I felt sure, a few flamboyant touches, perhaps to honour fallen colleagues or to mark feats of endurance no longer discussed but never forgotten. Trophies, perhaps, ski poles or ice axes treasured now as icons commemorating past, never-to-be-repeated journeys.

Matty lives in a rather pleasant orange-brick bungalow not at all unlike my beloved, late mother-in-law's. The view beyond is as breathtaking as I had imagined; the sea at that time of year is frozen and stretches away from the icy shore in a solid, white mass of polished flats the size of football pitches edged with threatening borders of jagged ice like shark's teeth. She invited me in. Which was good, because I was cold and in urgent need of a piss. Her breath frosted in the cold air outside the front door. I looked at her face, quite flat, small-featured, free of the lines and deep crevasses of experience and toughness I had expected, but somehow a face that spoke of resilience and strength beyond what most of us would ever have to see or prove.

We walked into the bungalow. It was warm, unnervingly so. There was carpet. There was double glazing. There were ornaments on shelves and pictures on the walls – photographs of her son and daughter, together with Matty on what was, for them I suppose, the equivalent of a family holiday, except it was at the South Pole.

'I'm really sorry, Matty, but do you have a loo I could borrow?'

She looked round to see me following her along the short hallway, reached out to open a door ahead of us and said:

'These are just a few of my friends, Richard. We're a tight-knit little bunch here in Iqaluit.'

Her living room was filled by five or six people of various ages, smiling politely and looking at me.

'Hi.' I waved a hand and stepped into the room to stand next to Matty. I'm not a good house guest. I can't bear being in other people's houses, in fact. I feel self-conscious and worried that I might be breaking some taboo or piece of etiquette peculiar to the household. I'm the sort who, as an overnight guest, will awake and lie in bed for hours, frozen with fear, waiting for the householders to wake and make a noise rather than venture forth from the guest bedroom and see if I can find them already up.

'Erm, Matty,' I tried to whisper, bending closer to the wiry, auburn hair shrouding an ear that I now noticed was lightly freckled. 'Matty, I wonder, do you have a lavatory I might borrow? Only it was a long flight and, well . . . er, do you? Is there?'

'Yes, of course, Richard. Just there.'

She waved an arm towards a door immediately to my left, opening directly off the living room where she and I, together with her assembled friends, were gathered.

'Oh, right. Thanks.' I slipped through it and straight into a small bathroom. Beyond the plasterboard walls, the lightly muffled voices of Matty and her friends renewed their easy chat about the weather, the TV news and the local shop while I stifled a shaky sigh and tried to direct my torrent towards the porcelain sides of the bowl for discretion's sake.

Moments later, with the lavatory still flushing loudly behind me, I opened the door and stepped meekly back into the room.

'Ah, Richard,' Matty greeted me at the head of her group of friends. 'Now, we do have a little rule here.' She looked around to her suddenly solemn-faced accomplices and continued, sounding like an air stewardess as she announced, 'If it's brown, flush it down, but if it's yellow, let it mellow.'

It took some moments for me to digest her words and conceive the horror behind them. Her friends looked on expectantly.

I drew a shallow breath and held it for a moment.

Matty stood, calm and impassive, pleased at having pointed out, albeit too late, this important piece of information.

The lavatory cistern hissed loudly behind me as it refilled, finally stopping with a clunk as the ballcock floated to the top of its mountings.

'Ah. Well, it's okay,' I stared past them all to the frozen sea through the window. 'I had a massive shit.'

I would be staying in Sarah's room. She was away at university right now, so it was free. There was not much space in the little bungalow but Matty made it clear, walking around the place once her friends had left, that it was all open to me. Sarah's room was half filled by a pretty double bed with white railings at the head and foot, a cupboard, open to reveal a TV and stereo, and, across the floor, bags of clothes all designed for surviving tougher trips than I had ever experienced. I dropped my bag down; it sat alongside those already there and looked too new, too unused next to them. Stretched over the bed and humped over the pillows at one end was a bedspread made up of brightly coloured, woollen patches knitted together. It looked comforting, warm and simple.

I liked it and knew I would be fine in this room. I knew, too, that Mindy would have packed a small teddy bear, called Gribble, into my bag without me knowing – she always does when I go away in the hope that my bag will be searched in front of everyone else at the airport and I will die of shame when the bear is produced and I am asked, 'Is this yours, sir? Pack this bag yourself, did you?' by a massive customs officer with a moustache and a raised eyebrow. I decided that Gribble would look good perched on the small white table beside the bed and I would put him there later, when I unpacked.

Matty chatted about the days to come, about how we would spend time learning to run the dogs, learning about how to look after them, what they needed to be happy and how to get the best from them. They were her babies and needed treating properly. We were going to win this, yes, sir, we were, we were going to show them what doggie power could do. We stood a real chance here and Matty was not going to be beaten. I admired her confidence, and tried to share it. I couldn't. After a light supper, I sloped off to bed.

On the other side of that window, just feet from the end of my bed, lie the frozen fringes of the Arctic Ocean. Beneath the thick, concealing crust of ice, the dark, slow waters pulse and bulge with Arctic life. Pale whales and narwhals cruise and monitor the blue-black depths. Lying in my bed, head cushioned by soft pillows, body as smothered with warm bedcovers as the sea is crusted with ice, I smile and imagine I can hear the whale's call from below. The ice can make loud cracks at night as the tide beneath it pushes and pulls. I strain my ears to hear them, but cannot. The quiet is deep and profound. Arctic. And I sleep.

At 2.30 a.m., local youths fire up two snowmobiles, their two-stroke, dirt-bike engines shrieking into the night, and race them up and down the coast beneath my window. They are not hunting or carrying out mystic missions of tribal significance; they are being teenagers, arsing about. They live here, they have a right to be young, a right to push the rules and a right to get into trouble. I hope they fall through the ice and freeze to death. Soon.

## *Finding My Place in the Pack*

# 12 April

The first day of my personal Arctic survival and dog sledge-driving training course. Gotta think of a better name for it.

I really hadn't thought Matty would be a 'lie-in' kind of person. She wasn't. Up at 6 a.m., breakfast on cereals and tea, brisk hike out to her sheds to collect the dog harnesses and tackle and down to the ice to meet the team. This was it then, the moment when I would come face to muzzle with the dogs. I am, as has been noted, a dog lover. To meet and spend time with a team of working dogs bred specifically to survive and thrive in an environment so hostile to other, less specialised creatures that it may as well be in space was a unique life opportunity. Under a heavy, white sky, we marched out over the sea. I considered the water beneath us, the ice we walked over. I wore a heavy coat, borrowed from Matty, and my massive thermal pants nestled comfortably beneath waterproof outer trousers. I wore two pairs of gloves and wondered if my hands, so encased, could be of any use when it came to whatever work awaited us out there. Wherever we were going.

Matty was cheerful and excited. She was off to see her beloved dogs. We heard them long before we saw them. And they had smelled us long before we heard them, which is why they began a furious howling and barking as we approached across the ice. Matty chirruped and clucked back at them. With Matty's bungalow and the shore-bound detritus of sheds and oil drums dwindling into the distance, we came upon the lines. Tied between two stakes, these are the lines to which the dogs are chained at night. We were surrounded by fierce peaks and spikes of upended sea ice. But on this small plateau of level snow, the dogs had their home and it felt happy, even cosy out here, under a pale, diffused Arctic sun. Watching as Matty looked around her team, as the dogs looked up to her for approval and love, the night's snow and ice falling from their coats as unheeded as chalk dust, I knew that this would be a life-changing experience. And I stepped in a dog turd big enough to come almost up to my knees.

Scraping the glutinous mess off my boot, I wondered why it wasn't frozen. And as I wondered, I saw the dogs were all going about their morning ablutions. They were tied to the line, each on an individual chain about four feet long. This gave them freedom to move around, but kept them in order along the line itself. Several were stretching and looking about them. Others lay curled on the ice, noses tucked in tails, deep-set eyes looking up from under bushy brows. Behind them, barely ten yards distant, the wooden sled lay, close to the ground like a heap of broken wooden pallets. It was clear that the animals were the important ones here and the machine, the sled, took a very lowly second place. And rightly so: what use would it be without healthy dogs to pull it?

'Matty?' I wanted to ask the right questions, ones that revealed to her that I liked dogs, understood them and cared about them. 'So are they tied up in a special order?'

She was busy petting and patting, growling and snarling in play with an immense black dog whose coat looked dense enough to lose lesser creatures in.

'Yes, of course, Richard. They all have their special places. Don't you, Raven? Yes, you do. You do.' And she wrestled Raven to the ground. With his huge shoulders and dense coat, the dog looked like an actor in a bad werewolf costume for a 1940s film. I sidled up to her, surrounded by bouncing, baying dogs. The length of their chains was such that they could interact and greet us, and they did, with vigour. Well, they greeted Matty. She stood now, hand resting on Raven's huge head; another dog, a brown one I would later learn to identify as Bartlett, leaned against her leg adoringly.

'They're happy to see you,' I observed, pointlessly.

'Of course they are, they're my babies. And I love them. All of you guys.'

She turned to shout to the whole pack, gloved hands cupped to her mouth. As I watched, I felt a pleasant, warm sensation course through me. Specifically, it coursed through my right leg. The lower half of my right leg. I looked down to see a pale grey and white dog lifting its own leg to better facilitate the lengthy and drawn-out piss it was taking against mine.

'Bloody hell, Matty.'

She turned towards me, hands dropping to her sides to rest on the heads of the two dogs next to her. Three sets of eyes looked at me.

'Hey, he's pissing on you. Marvin, stop that.'

The torrent continued, spattering against my not entirely water-proof trousers with a deep, liquid rumble that would have been satisfying had I been the originator of the flow rather than the recipient.

'Is this a pack thing then?' I wanted to learn about the dogs, to learn everything about living, working and surviving out here. 'Is he asserting himself? So hang on, this guy's top of the heap right, a high-ranking dog, and he sees me as a newcomer and wants to say, "Hey you, I'm the boss round here." Yes?'

'This is Marvin. Actually, he's the bottom of the pack. The other guys all beat up on him and he has a pretty hard time of it.'

'So this is the lowest dog in the pack, taking a piss on me. Not good then, I s'pose?'

'I think he likes you.'

I looked down at the broad, grey face, framed by thick white neck fur. Marvin's deep-set, brown, almost amber eyes looked up at me. He grinned a doggy grin, black lips stretched back to reveal startling white teeth and black gums. He panted and rubbed his back end against my thigh happily. I'd found my place in the pack, and it was second to Marvin. The lowest of the low. I decided to like him.

Matty showed me how to fix the lines to the front of the sled ready for the dogs to be attached. This was not the line we chained them to at night, but another, lighter line made from nylon. From a thick, central core sprang seemingly dozens of other, equally brightly coloured lines. These lay tangled and twisted and would, I was told, need to be untangled and straightened ready for her dogs. She showed me, too, that to work you shed your outer, protective gloves, being very careful to put them together into your pocket as you took them off.

'You drop one of these on the floor and it blows away out here and you will die.'

I was left wearing just a pair of green, woollen, inner gloves.

'Take those off and put these on.' I peeled off the woollen gloves, waiting for the blast of cold to hit my exposed hands.

'It doesn't feel that cold actually. How cold is it?'

''bout minus twenty. Not bad, but it will get colder today.' Standing in front of me, the brightly coloured traces on the floor between us, Matty glanced around at the sky overhead and then back to her own hands, and she threw across to me a medium-weight black glove with plastic dimples across the palms, presumably for gripping and manipulating tools.

'These are our work gloves, see. Put those on and you can use your hands. That's for your left, there you go.' She threw the second.

She spoke constantly, issuing instructions, offering suggestions, giving me information, on everything we did.

'I have real, authentic old Inuit lines we could use if you like. They're made from untanned leather. I'll show you them later.'

'How long have people travelled like this?' I fixed one end of the blue nylon line to a carabina clip hanging from a trace at the front of the sledge.

'Thousands of years. It's how people got around, before those things.' She pointed out to the edge of the sea where a snowmobile was buzzing along the shoreline carrying three youths, huddled together in brightly coloured anoraks. The noise reached us as she finished talking.

'They ran one of those last night. Late. That happens a lot round here?'

'Every night.'

We finished unravelling and laying out the lines in silence. When we were done, the blue, red and yellow ropes lay stretched in front of the wooden sledge. The dogs, whose barking had slowly settled as we worked, sensed that we were ready for the next phase and stirred into an impatient riot.

'What now?'

'We tie 'em on.'

'What can I do?'

'You fetch 'em over, one by one. I'll show you how to put the harness on and tie them on and get 'em fixed up and ready to roll.'

'Right. Who's first?' I scanned the stretched-out line of bouncing, barking dogs.

'Start at that end of the line and bring them over, one at a time. You start with the lead dog, so bring me Raven.'

'Great. Er . . .'

'The big one, there, at the head of the line. Yes, you Raven.' His massive, shaggy head rose up from resting on forelegs like wooden beams.

'Who's my baby then? Huh, my little baby.' She spoke in the high-pitched, girly voice of dog lovers the world over.

I walked across the polished ice, my efforts to find a grip making my footsteps awkward and wooden. The massive dog, its black fur long and thick enough to look like a solid lump, stood by the chain, clearly trying to control itself. This was the dog that Matty had petted and made a fuss of. He looked like he might tear my arm off as an aperitif and burn out my soul with his eyes.

'Good boy, Raven.' I used a calm, steady voice. I thought Matty would be impressed with my ability to calm and get on with her dogs.

'Go on, don't be scared of old Raven, he's a pussy cat.'

I'm not generally scared of dogs. I'm lucky, I guess, I've never had a really bad experience with one. But walking into this group of them, penetrating the closed bubble of their pack, was intimidating. I felt every movement being analysed, processed and studied by critical brown eyes. A dog's position in the pack is everything and that position is decided and kept according to a strict and comprehensive code. Body language has as much to do with it as actual fighting ability or fierceness. Raven, clearly, was not going to be intimidated by me.

'Now then, boy, time to get you hooked up.'

A blue nylon collar was almost lost in the thick fur around his neck. I slipped my hand behind it, barely finding room for my fingers between the rough collar and his muscled neck.

'Just unhook the clasp and walk him over here. Steady, though, or he'll pull you over on the ice.'

My gloved hand struggled to shift the tiny metal clasp, but eventually it slid forwards. I unhooked it from the collar's 'D'-ring and braced to feel the pull of Raven against me. I could half stand with my hand still tucked behind the collar and my fingers grasped tight around it. And I felt the power in Raven's thick legs straight away. He didn't leap forwards or bounce around but he moved steadily and mechanically towards the sled and his mistress while I, with no choice in the matter, followed. I recalled my father shouting at our family border collie when we were kids as she pulled against the lead, choking herself on her collar. I have inherited my dad's deep dislike of being pulled around by dogs and I now discipline mine at home in the same way. There was, though, it was plain, little point in shouting at a sledge dog for pulling; that's what they are bred to do. And perhaps, then, there was no need either to be surprised at the fact that they really can pull like tractors. It was a smooth, relentless power that surged, seemingly without effort, from Raven's compact, shaggy form. This was not him acting up or taking the piss out of me. This was what he did.

It had to happen and, of course, it did. My left foot hit a recent and therefore unfrozen dog egg still steaming on the ice. I lost my grip and slipped. And I knew straight away that it would not be a pleasant experience. Raven plodded on towards the sled, I twisted and began to fall, but my arm stayed where it was, my hand gripping his collar. Technically and, I suspect, medically, my arm should by now have been facing the other way in relation to my shoulder. As I hit the floor, it was clear that, yes, my arm was now the wrong way round and it hurt. My legs flailed, sending my feet slipping round on the ice and turning me further in the wrong direction for my shoulder. I hit more turds. And more. I slid through some more, Raven's direct line towards the sled seemingly deliberately coinciding with as many doggy deposits as possible.

'You okay there?'

'Well, er, shit, dammit, no. Be all right. Raven, wait, good boy, wait.'

He didn't wait, why would he? And the two of us pitched up at the sledge moments later, him handsome and dusted with snow, me tangled and covered in dog shit.

Matty took me through the delicate procedure of threading a powerful and sometimes recalcitrant sledge dog into a tight-fitting and complicated harness. With Raven in place, we ran through the same procedure with the rest of the pack. Which meant a further nine trips back to the line and a further nine battles through many hundreds of piles of shit until the ice between the sled and the chain line was uniformly brown like a muddy rugby pitch.

The day was a long one. As I lay in bed that night, Gribble looking at me with concern from the bedside table, I reflected back over the ten hours we had spent running the dog team across the ice. It is a magnificent mode of travel, the dog sled. Though not, to modern eyes, entirely practical. There is some steering, though it is achieved only by shouting loudly and the results are, it would seem, entirely random. In my mind, preparing for this adventure I had seen myself riding heroically on the sled, swathed in Arctic furs, smiling manfully into the sun as the solemn, ice-clad mountains drifted serenely by. In the event, it turned out to be rather different. I spent the large part of my first day as a dog-sledder running behind the sledge. Matty half lay on the body of the sledge itself, riding on a complicated system of rugs, straps and fixings ready for the luggage that we would, eventually, be loading for the trip itself. In her hand, she carried an immense whip, some thirty feet long and made of bright, pink-tinted rope. She kept up a constant stream of chirruping and clicking to encourage the dogs. They trotted about the place, flicking glances at what little there was to look at on the snowy plains we crossed and generally not really seeming like they were putting their backs into it at all.

I was allocated the only other place on the sledge, which is mostly, as it turned out, off it. There is a backboard running across the width of the thing just behind the upright handlebars at the back. Not so bad, I thought, I could at least hold on as I stood there and perhaps try and rest one leg at a time. Very quickly, though, I learned that in certain conditions I would be forced to hop off and run behind. These conditions included deep snow, shallow snow, ice, broken ice, ice and snow and snowy ice. It was like being given a skateboard for Christmas and being told it will only work on the moon. Essentially, then, I was to run to the Pole. Top. And then came another shock: the boots that I had been told would be awaiting me in Iqaluit were not there.

Matty runs a sort of Arctic kit shop from the garage of her bungalow, and very well stocked it is, too. The garage doors had been fixed shut so we entered by a side door and inside were the usual trappings and fixtures of a shop selling outdoor equipment. Posters showed people snowboarding and skiing, racks held torches and windproof lighters. On shelves and rails, I admired her collections of thermals, special socks, hats, fleeces and insulated trousers. Everything, in fact, except the boxes of special Arctic boots I had been promised by our office. It didn't matter, though, because Matty had some ready for me. I anticipated a serious box opening up to reveal a pair of modern, technical boots with special straps and fixings and materials that breathe, insulate, keep out the water and make you look like an extra from an *Aliens* movie. She produced a pair of old, blue walking boots with red laces and nylon over-gaiters to keep out the snow.

'These are great. Tom wore them when we went to the North Pole, I think. I think it was these.'

She picked at the frayed gaiters and turned the boots over to reveal smooth-worn soles.

'Oh, look, these are coming away here, we'll have to fix 'em up.'

The waterproof over-gaiters were coming adrift along one side. Clearly, whether to the Pole or elsewhere, these boots had been worn somewhere by someone – for a very long time. And so, it turned out that I was to run to the Pole in a pair of second-hand boots.

I slipped outside for a while and did some swearing while Matty rifled through kitchen drawers looking for glue and sang a John Denver song.

*Tunik Time, Whatever That Is*

# 13–17 April

We had other trips out during my stay in Iqaluit. Every day we would trek out to the lines where the dogs barked and howled for us. We harnessed them up, got on board the sledge, set off and, invariably, fell off. We flipped the sledge on its side running down ice valleys like bobsleigh runs and hit ice boulders that brought it to a complete stop and sent me sailing over the top like a missile. On the second day, I fell off and caught my flapping boot gaiter in the runners as the sled hissed by. I was dragged across the snow, the ice beneath rasping angrily at my waterproofs. And every day I waited and waited for that magic moment, that moment when the majesty, the mystery of the place would overwhelm me and carve an indelible memory into my lifetime. And every day, when the moment never came, I would prepare myself for its arrival the next day.

Matty had other lodgers in her little bungalow. I met them on my second day there. A French–Canadian couple, they were taking a year out of university to learn how to drive dog sleds. Small, intense, earnest, they were ideally suited to each other and enjoyable company. And on the third day, they bundled into the living room breathless and excited. I wondered if perhaps they had been engaging in practices more normal for twentysomething students but no less physical than dog sledging. But no: they were excited because today marked the start of 'Tunik Time'. Obviously I was delighted, thrilled that my visit should coincide with Tunik Time. What a stroke of luck. What was Tunik Time, by the way?

It turned out to be a rather folksy local festival in which residents of Iqaluit join together to celebrate their local customs and history. Visitors come from far afield to hear local musicians, see exhibitions of artwork by local artists and see displays of old-time crafts by local old-time craftspeople. We were going to join in. I resisted the opportunity to visit a sort of hybrid drinking/singing festival, having made up my mind to kill myself should I find myself railroaded into the village hall where this was taking place. We agreed then to visit and, who knows, maybe even take part in, the igloo-building competition. On the way, I wanted to drop in to a hall to see an art exhibition and a display of traditional Inuit clothing and tools.

There was something haunting about the Inuit-inspired artwork. The muted colours, the naïve representations of people and creatures, the hunting, eating, fishing being depicted; all paintings showing people engaged in activities essential to life in a place that, really, just doesn't want us to be alive. There were no happy paintings of people strolling about in well-tended gardens looking relaxed, playing lutes and trying to chat up birds in big frocks. The broad-faced people in the pictures worked, they battled to stay alive. They fought to land huge fish, went whaling with a narwhal tusk as a weapon and gave birth to babies surreptitiously in hidden, cold corners on storm-lashed nights. Looking at the wall-mounted examples of Inuit caribou coats and tiny hide slippers, I felt a bit rosy-cheeked and hopeless. I asked Matty about the coats; they were selling them to tourists like me.

'Yeah, well you can buy one. Sure, I'll find out how much they are. They're great, though, never get cold in one, tell ya.'

'Will I get it through customs?' Thinking about how I might explain a peeled caribou in my luggage at Heathrow.

'Yeah, sure you will. Have to keep it in the freezer, though.'

I laughed, 'Why, doesn't it like the warm?'

'No, sir, get it warm and all the hair falls out. Have to keep 'em outside here; mine lives in the sheds. Can't bring 'em in, all the hair falls out, see, untanned, that's what you get.'

Running my fingers through the coarse, grey fur of the coat, I pulled away a dense clutch of hairs – spending time in this heated hall was already taking its toll. I wanted the coat and knew I would regret it when I got it home. I tried to picture stuffing it into our freezer, clearing out the plastic drawers of their bags of frozen chips, Cornetto ice creams and pizza. I tried to picture walking down our local high street, my head poking through the hood of the coat, leaving a trail of grey and white caribou hairs behind me. I wondered what my dogs would make of this arrival from a very foreign land. We left for the igloo competition, me still wearing a very ordinary down jacket, the caribou coat still very much on the wall, surrounded by tiny slippers and pictures of strange people trying to kill whales by moonlight to survive another dark winter.

The igloo-building competition was to be held in the grounds of the school. Posters advertising it were to be seen clinging damply to boards outside the feed store, the knife shop and the small supermarket that, together, made up Iqaluit's commercial heart. I watched people walking the ice-covered pavements, gravitating in groups towards the school that was sited on the side of the hill that overlooked the town of Iqaluit and the sea beyond. For some strange reason, the scene made me think of 5 November in any of a thousand British towns where families and friends come together to share sparklers and hot dogs round a huge bonfire in the grounds of their children's school. And the school we were headed for turned out to be disappointingly familiar. It was a standard, minor municipal building, red-brick with prefabricated additions and brightly painted metal poles supporting eaves that covered the walkways and paths linking one part to another. It looked like a polytechnic college anywhere in Britain, except it was pinned halfway up a snow-covered mountain, overlooking the frozen sea, surrounded by icy peaks that you knew didn't give way just over the horizon to a grassy pasture or a busy motorway. And, in the fields at the front of the school, preparations were underway for the great igloo-building competition.

It wasn't a complicated set-up; the competitors gathered in a circle, six teams in all, and were given a countdown and told to get on with it. Groups formed around the foundations of each igloo, people helped in cutting out chunks of the snow to form bricks, carrying them to the slowly growing circle of the igloo itself and setting them on to the wall. A proper igloo is built in a spiral; there are not courses of bricks as such, rather, the blocks spiral upwards from the ground, the second layer twisting on top of the first in a seamless run. Some of the groups knew what they were doing, some igloos were being built by solo builders. One guy, with a weathered Inuit face and clearly the local champion igloo builder, raced ahead. He was nearing the top by the time other groups, some including three generations or made up mostly of young children, had completed their first circle around the igloo's base and begun the next.

I took photographs and stood in the background while Matty joined in with a group of friends. She took the role of the person standing inside the igloo as it is built. Her friends cut the blocks and passed them to her to place in a spiral formation, growing the igloo like a giant crystal. We spectators now stood around the event some ten deep; I watched people gathering in familiar groups, sharing comments about how this year's competition compared with last and cheering on their favourites to win. Matty was now completely encased in her team's igloo. It was nearing completion and would soon be a perfect dome of snow under the heavy, grey-white sky. The last job was to cut the doorway in the side of the igloo and, until this was done with the long ice knife still busy rasping out chunks of hard-packed snow to complete the igloo's smooth curve, Matty would be entombed within its blank, doorless form. Her voice was muffled by the thick snow, but still I heard her calling for more bricks to finish the dome.

The old Inuit man had finished his igloo. He stood back to admire its even shape, broken only by the single door, surrounded by extra bricks to give shelter from the snow-laden wind to those entering and leaving his creation. A spontaneous round of applause broke out; he had won last year, too, and was a popular winner this year. Another group finished and we applauded again. The tip of the ice knife was visible now through the walls of Matty's igloo. Her team-mates had passed it through to her with the last section of snow to be fitted, completing the igloo's wall and her entombment. And now, like some giant bird breaking its way out of its egg, she was battling to escape. They shouted and laughed encouragement, it was close – another team was at the same point in building their igloo, but it was a rather sad, lop-sided and shrunken thing compared with Matty's symmetrical, even bloom of snow and ice. Her knife completed its trace of an arch-topped doorway and Matty's boot burst out from inside, kicking away the snowy remnants of a door that could never have hinged open. She climbed out now, red-faced and excited. Her team shouted, the youngest member, a girl of six or seven, ran up to Matty's side and held her hand and I took a photograph of them all, standing and kneeling proudly in front of the igloo as the onlooking crowd applauded mildly in the weak sun.

And all the time I knew that the day of our own competition was getting ever closer. Not long now and I would be setting off into the proper Arctic wilderness and for me, anyway, the unknown. The knowledge of it hanging there, waiting for me, made these few moments of simple fun all the more bittersweet and precious.

## *A Race. Not the Big One but . . .*

Race day: an important feature in my otherwise blank calendar. But this is not the big race that has brought me out to Iqaluit, this is another race. Matty has entered us in the local dog team race, one held every year as part of the Tunik Time celebrations. Six teams, all based in and around Iqaluit, will be racing for five or six hours across the sea ice fringing their town. It will give us a chance really to shake down as a team, to bond and learn about each other. Matty won it last year and is, unsurprisingly, very competitive about winning it this year. She wakes me with a cheery knock on the door at 6 a.m.

'Race day, fella, let's get on it. We've gotta be in it to win it and . . .'

I pulled the handmade bedspread over my head and bit my knuckle to choke back a string of expletives strong enough to turn the ice outside my window back into sea water.

I wasn't leaping out of bed. After three days of intense sledge training, the pain was now concentrated mostly in my lower back, upper back, middle back, arms, legs, trunk, torso, head and fingers. Everywhere, in fact.

Groaning, I heaved myself off of the mattress and on to the ground. In my baggy thermal long johns, I padded out and across the narrow hallway to the bathroom, feet disappearing into the suburban shagpile.

'Hi there, soldier. You ready for the big day then? How're you feelin'?'

'Fuck off, stop talking to me like I'm a moron, wipe that stupid, happy grin off your stupid face, stick your head in that pan next to you and fucking boil it' is what I wanted to say at that moment. What I actually said was, 'Morning, Matty. Yup, I'm ready. Just need to, er, get dressed.'

'Okay. Tea?'

'Oh, God, yes please.'

And Matty, one of the world's foremost explorers, a woman of physical and mental toughness and resilience that leaves the rest of us trailing so far in her wake it's difficult to imagine we are of the same species, pottered around the galley kitchen in her bungalow, placed a mug with big, primary coloured spots on its white flanks on to the counter and flicked the kettle on to boil. I wondered just how such a person can make the leap from battling alone through Arctic storms to the South Pole to pottering about on the linoleum knocking a cup of tea together for a visitor at home.

We worked our way through the morning ritual, gathering together our kit and, on the way down to the dogs, stopping off at the storage shed to collect our day sacks – home-made nylon bags that we clipped on to the handlebars of the sledge to keep our extra gloves, face masks and essential snacks handy. In another moment of the domestic nicety that makes such a strange counterpoint to her legendary toughness, Matty had made the bags herself, buying the orange and red ripstop nylon from a catalogue and stitching the bags and zips by hand. She had ordered sufficient material to make a third, giant version to sit on the sledge itself, fastened to the handlebars behind it. In this one, we stuffed extra jackets and over-trousers, flasks of soup and further sacks of the nuts, chocolate and dried fruit we had to nibble constantly to keep up the reserves of energy sapped by our bodies as we battled not only to cope with the sheer physicality of dog sledging, but to generate enough heat inside our layers of thermals, windproof and waterproof clothes to stave of hypothermia and death. Once outside the warmth of Matty's bungalow, we were like two central heating systems running on full power constantly to heat a house with no roof.

The dogs began their usual chorus as we approached the lines, our boots breaking through the hard crust of ice to grind into the powdery snow beneath. We would have been visible for miles, Matty and I, two figures in orange parkas carrying bright orange and red bags standing out vividly against the uniformly white ice and a softly diffused white, snow-filled sky. Today, I felt a new sense of purpose as we made the now familiar trek; we were marching down to harness the team and set off, but not on yet another trip to familiarise me with the team while Matty, like some Arctic resort tour guide, spoke endlessly about the ice formations,

the hills, the local people and the town's features. We were there
with a job to do, a race to win.

'Matty, what's this?' I pointed to the place where, every night, we
dragged the unhitched sledge and made it fast to the weighted oil
drum that served as an anchor for the end of the dog lines. But instead
of the now familiar sledge, with its long, blunt runners of splintery
bleached ash, there was a different one. It looked altogether flimsier
than the reassuringly sturdy thing we had been using. The wood was
cleaner, brighter, the handles made of thinner pieces.

Matty explained that this was her racing sledge. We would be
using this today and, all being well, in the big race to the Pole.

'What makes it different? Apart from the colour?'

'It's faster. It cuts through the snow better, it's a lot lighter, too.
We'll need to haul the thing around and it makes it easier. Now
let's get 'em tied on.'

I looked at this new, strange sledge. In a landscape with so little in
it, what few things there are to look at take on an increased significance. I had spent many hours looking at the old sledge, studying
the way it was held together only with ropes, lashed around the ends
of the crosspieces that made up the bed of the sledge and through
holes in the top pieces supporting the runners. Matty had explained
that the ropes were there to give it flexibility; it needed to be supple
to cope with the sometimes violent twists and shocks of travelling
over broken ice harder than steel. A rigid sledge would shake itself,
and its rider, to bits in seconds. And I had watched ours twist and
flex as we wrestled it through fields of ice boulders bigger than cars.
And now this new one had entered our world. I didn't like it. It was
different. I wanted the old one back.

We harnessed the dogs. The last to join the line was always
Sigloo, a lunatic who would wait until the moment he was harnessed in and then just set off, whipping the rest of the team into
a frenzy so that they followed him, taking the sledge and everything
we needed to stay alive, with them. The only way to counter this

problem was to leave the sledge anchored to the oil drum until we had finished harnessing the team. At the last moment, when all was ready, I would then pull a rope, releasing a snap toggle that freed us from the anchor and we would bolt off across the ice for the first, and usually the last, big sprint of the day. It was important not to give the dogs any sign of encouragement as we reached the end of harnessing them up. The slightest indication that we were off would have them tearing away, straining at their harnesses and risking disaster, even with the sledge tied off.

Anything could be the trigger: picking up the whip in too positive a way, sitting on any part of the sledge and especially using the wrong words. Rather like shouting 'walkies' to your friend's Labrador, the wrong words could lead to disaster. And it wasn't just the words themselves, though clearly calling out 'let's go' or, worse still, 'hike!' would end in catastrophe – it was the intonation and the way we said anything at all. If it sounded remotely like an encouraging word or one commanding an effort from the dogs, then that effort would come and we would be chasing a driverless sledge across the frozen sea. It was while we harnessed up and got ready for the day that I got the best sense of just how much the dogs love their work. Pulling sledges together with their friends and enemies is what they do, plain and simple. They are never really happy when they are doing anything else.

It was an especially cold morning today, minus thirty or there-abouts, and we had struggled to get them all hooked up. Sometimes the metal clasps fixing the dogs to the static line could freeze up overnight, usually because the dog wearing it had fallen asleep with its head near the clasp and drooled on it. And frozen dog drool is, as it turns out, harder than a diamond. I spent a long time kneeling on the ice next to the line, holding a dog's collar clear of its woolly neck with one hand, using the other to hit the tiny, frozen metal release button of the clasp with the butt of my heavy Leatherman. The cold interferes with your precision and coordination. So it's easy to miss the clasp and hit your hand. The cold then makes the resulting impact hurt more. I did some spectacular swearing and the dogs, perhaps sensing that this wasn't the time to goof around, lay still while we freed them from their line and fixed them to the sledge.

With the team ready and waiting on the most delicate hair-trigger imaginable, we moved slowly and calmly around the sledge, making last-minute preparations. We spoke softly, too, as a gentle fall of snow blurred the outlines of the dogs, standing tensed and quivering in their harnesses.

'So, Matty, is there anything new I need to know about this sledge?' I made my way cautiously around to the back, ready to pull the release toggle and stand up on to the backboard as we set off. Sigloo whimpered, sensing that we were getting ready to leave and then cringing as I stood over him and made it clear that we weren't going yet.

'No. Yes, this one has no brakes.'

'What?'

I took another few steps to reach the back of the sledge and looked down at the board running across between the handles, where I would stand when we set off. On the old sledge there were simple metal ice brakes fixed to the back. Nothing more than metal blades, hinged so that I could stand on them and set their teeth into the ice below to stop us. They were useful to bring the sledge to a gentle stop without running into the back legs of the team, but they were more useful as a comforter on long, icy descents when the sledge gathered speed and momentum which, unchecked, would have us careering into the dogs and crashing into whatever lay ahead, at the bottom of the slope.

'Well, what do I use? How do I slow it down?'

'Oh, don't worry. This is how we race them, we don't use brakes. And I've got these.'

Standing at the front of the sledge, though careful not to get between it and the dog team – people have been badly hurt by a dog team setting off and simply running them over, trapped in the lines – Matty stooped down to the storage boxes tied on to the very front, just behind the final, upwards curve of the runners. She reached out and, from the top of the boxes, pulled two dull, black loops of material about an inch wide and maybe a foot long. They had been held in place by elastic bungee cords which snapped back down on to the plastic lid of the box with a dull rimshot.

'You see, my brakes.' And she pivoted round to reach forwards and throw them over the tips of the runners.

'They're actually old snowmobile belts. Rubber. They get dragged down on the runners and slow us. See.'

The loops sat over the ends of the runners, resting on the ice. I could see how they would be dragged backwards by the sledge's forwards progress and might just dig in to the surface a bit, adding drag to the runners and slowing us down. At best.

'And they work?'

'Well, yes. They'll slow us. Sure.'

I had lost not only my one piece of comfort and security, but also, it occurred to me then, my only job. As brakeman, standing on the brakes at the back of the sledge, feeling the surface of the ice beneath kick up through the metal levers under my feet, I had a job, a function. On long slopes, Matty would shout back to me to stand on the brakes. As we headed towards a big drop or the edge of a plateau, she would call for brakes and I would pride myself on always being there, ready, anticipating the need for my brakes to bite into the ice and stop us before it was too late and we pitched over the edge. And now, I was made redundant by a pair of old, rubber belts which, I was certain, wouldn't work.

'Matty, would they have stopped us yesterday on that really long run off the island?'

We had made a lengthy trip up and over one of the many islands dotted around the coast here. On the way back down off the island to the sea, we had slid down a huge run of sheet ice. A kilometre or so long and polished by the wind until you could see the rock through the sheen of ice on top of it, the run headed off the top and dropped a few hundred metres over its length down to sea level. The dogs sprinted to stay ahead, but the sledge kept getting faster. I stood on the brakes, feeling every ridge of steely ice pulse through the metal levers as the teeth below shrieked and squealed, carving narrow grooves as we went. Thankfully, the slope had levelled out gradually and that, together with my brakes, had helped us slow to a gentle stop after a few moments of heart-racing terror. Afterwards, standing by the sledge to eat nuts and fruit before we set off again, we had agreed that it had been a bit of a close one and we should avoid those long slopes in future. Matty had given away not one hint of the fact that she had doubtless faced obstacles a thousand times more daunting on her travels and had spoken earnestly with me, while I panted and gasped, breathless and exhilarated. When she travels with someone else, she is in a team. And few people, I guess, have a better appreciation of the importance of working together as a team than a dog driver. So she must have been only too aware that our team could only go as fast or as hard as its weakest member – me.

And now, we were going to set off on to the ice again, but without the safety and comfort mechanism of those simple brakes. I was unemployed, then, and sure to be killed in a hideous slither down an endless ravine into a mess of pointed ice spears and rocks.

'Are you sure, Matty? I just wish I had the brakes, that's all; they make me feel . . .'

'We'll be fine. Let's go. Ready with the rope?'

'Er, yes, but what if . . .'

'Okay, release it then, and we'll go.'

I pulled the release rope automatically and, I suppose, obediently and felt it slacken. We were free.

'Hike!' She yelped the command in a high-pitched but powerful voice, and cracked the huge pink whip above the heads of the dogs. There was no need for further encouragement. They surged ahead, barking and yelping with delight. And immediately I could feel the difference in the sledge. It was faster, the reduced weight helping the dogs get off the line and the runners, seemingly, biting into the snow less, reducing friction and giving us more speed. Matty yelped and encouraged the team and they pulled for all they were worth. We cleared the flat compound and headed along a wide path, flanked by lumps and bumps of broken ice.

'You see, much faster.'

Matty was happy, we were sprinting away.

'It's lighter, we can go much faster.' She shouted, the words barely reaching me behind her as they were thrown out into the freezing wind.

'Yes, but Matty, what about the boulders at the edge?' I bawled back.

Waiting for us at the edge of the clearing of smooth ice where the dogs lived was a fringe of broken ice, thrown up by the tidal action of the sea still moving around beneath us into broken lumps and boulders. It was riddled with sharp drops and twists and had been a great place to practise crossing rougher terrain, when we had the brakes. Now, though, without them, I felt a knot of fear at the thought.

'Don't worry, we'll be fine. Relax.'

I concentrated on balancing on the backboard, enjoying the brief chance to ride the sledge that the dog teams' initial burst of enthusiasm and energy gave. Before long, I knew, I would have to hop off and run alongside or behind, giving the sledge a better chance of floating over the top of the surface, keeping the runners clear of gripping, slowing ice and snow and giving the dogs a better time pulling it. But right now, they were going like the clappers. I bent my legs, flexing my stiff thighs, feeling the bounce and rush of the sledge as it ploughed on towards the boulders.

Maybe it really would be okay. Matty is one of the world's foremost experts on dog sledging and Arctic travel, so she should know what would work for us. Yes, it would be okay. I breathed a gentle sigh and flexed my hands in their gloves, gripping the handlebars. And then I was in the air, looking down at the sledge. We had headed straight into a deep rut and the back of the sledge had kicked up as we dropped over the ridge. I was thrown just a foot or so up and forwards off the sledge and came back down hard on to the ice where, luckily, a large boulder connected with the exact base of my spine and, as further luck would have it, catapulted me straight back on to the sledge. I got one foot back on to the backboard and, with one hand, grabbed the crossbar running horizontally between the handlebars.

'You okay, Richard?'

'Yeah, still on.' I felt the bruise beginning to grow immediately, joining its legions of friends and colleagues scattered about my carcass.

'Well done. Neat move.' Matty looked back and smiled, her face drawn tight against the rushing cold. 'We'll make a driver of you yet.' She turned to look ahead, 'Left!'

I tightened my grip on the bars and dipped my left leg off the back of the sledge, sticking my foot hard into the surface and throwing my weight to the right, slewing the bars round and turning the front of the sledge left to avoid an oncoming wall of ice facing us end on. We missed it, Matty cheered, the dogs yelped and I felt, briefly, good.

We drew up to the start line. It had taken us an hour to get there under heavy skies and the dog teams, sledges and drivers stood out stark and black against the snow. We were directed to a spot midway along the strung-out line of competitors. This is the bit where, in a *Top Gear* film, we rev the engines and stare steely-eyed through the windscreen, gripping the wheel and doing our best to unnerve our competitors. But this wasn't a *Top Gear* film, the others weren't here and, anyway, we were separated from the competitors either side of us by a hundred or so metres, making it tricky to pull off the usual sidelong, intimidating glance. I guessed that we couldn't start any closer to the other teams because it might get a bit tricky with the dogs. I would learn later in the day just how tricky it can get when one tight-knit pack of working dogs meets another.

Matty was looking up and down the line, seeking out familiar teams.

'There he is, next to us on the left.' She pointed a gloved hand to our left and I saw the low-lying collection of shapes that indicated another team. I could hear the dogs barking distantly. Matty raised her whip in salute and I saw the figure next to the distant sledge do the same in return.

'Well, he made it then. I bet he's soooo excited.'

And the penny finally dropped. Jean Pierre, Matty's French-Canadian lodger, was competing in the race. We had discussed it at length on previous evenings and I had completely forgotten because I wasn't really listening. He had been working with another dog team for weeks to get ready for today; it was important. And I made the right noises to indicate that I wished him every success but hoped we could win through in a noble and brave battle to a richly deserved victory. At least, I hope that's how my various grunts and nods were interpreted.

The race started with a disappointing honk from one of those annoying little aerosol can air horns people take to football matches. And straight away it became obvious that dog-sled racing is about endurance rather than sprinting. The difference in pace made that clear. A couple of teams hared away from the line, sprinting like their tails were on fire. Matty tutted and shouted back, 'Short-distance dogs, see. They're smaller, lighter but they don't have the endurance. These,' she nodded forwards to her team, happily plodding onwards, 'are heavy-duty boys. They're stronger, they can pull more and for longer.'

The power in some of the faster teams was starting to fade already and they dropped back into view ahead as they slowed. I guessed there would be a lot of that smug hare and tortoise stuff before the race was over.

We never really stopped. For five hours we battled across surfaces changing from plains of wind-blown snow that whispered under the runners like crêpe paper to the craggy, broken borders where the frozen sea meets the coast and the tides tear the ice into crevasses and jagged peaks and we both had to get off the sledge and wrestle it over, around and through an endless variety of obstacles. And it hurt like hell. I am not an unfit man; I run daily and keep myself in, what middle managers call, 'good shape'. It's something I pride myself on; it's important to my self-esteem to be able to get out of bed and run for an hour or so without it hurting later in the day. But out here, I learned, it demanded a different type of fitness. Nobody here went off to the gym, mincing about the place in special 'technical' clothing and worrying about the origin of their mineral water. Fitness out here meant getting up early, getting out and doing stuff, all day.

Watching Matty out on the sledge, she just didn't tire. She could run alongside when the snow got too sticky for even the driver to stay on board, wrestle the dogs back into line when they got tangled in their harnesses, work to tip the sledge back on its runners when it lay on its side yet again, perch for hours on the front of the sledge, whip in hand, willing the dogs on with probably more energy than it would take to get harnessed up and pull the thing herself. And, watching her, I understood that she and the people out here were fit in a different way. It was something closer to the way we are fit when we were kids, when we could get out at first light, cycle round to a friend's house, have a running race, try to build a bike ramp, climb a tree, build a den and run to a field to play British Bulldogs for an hour before stopping for a quick lunch and then doing it all again until Mum made us come inside when it got dark. This was a grown-up version of the same thing. It's the same endless stream of activity; they use their bodies as tools to do stuff they want or need to do.

We didn't win. One of the younger, lighter, fitter teams of short-distance dogs took the trophy. We crossed the finish line a half-hour or so later, our grand moment rather overshadowed by a snowmobile race yelping and screaming around a narrow loop half a kilometre away across the ice.

Back at the bungalow that evening I had my first attack of sledge-sickness, where the rocking, bucking motion of the sledge carries on long after you've got off it, tied up the dogs and come home. Sitting in Matty's living room, feeling the sofa sway and lurch under me, I drifted in and out of the conversation. I was flying up to Resolute Bay the next day, to begin the race that had brought me out here. Matty, Jean Pierre, Sarah and another visitor, Tom, laughed and joked about the flights they had endured across the Arctic.

'Just make sure you never get on one of those Twin Otters. That's all,' Tom was laughing and joking. Another explorer and a friend of Matty's, he had arrived that day. He was English, young, in his late twenties maybe, and a genuine, steely-eyed hero of the ice. He has been everywhere you can go, battled through unbelievable hardships to get to places where human beings really just don't belong. He was very much a modern explorer.

'Don't go on a what?' I stirred from my nauseous reverie

'A Twin Otter. Ugly little plane, looks like half the wing's dropped off. They're awful. Rough as hell. And crash, constantly.'

I drifted in and out. The conversation ranged into areas too terrifying to register. As the sledge-sickness abated and the swaying slowed and stopped, I sank into the warm embrace of a suburban sofa and tried to figure out if I really was about to set off on a dog-sled race to the magnetic North Pole or wake up in my mother-in-law's bungalow having dozed off during a Christmas day visit with the kids.

# Chapter 2

# DIARY OF A BRAVE POLAR EXPLORER

*There Isn't Anything Else to Do in Igluik*

'**S**o what sort of plane's that then?' I squinted through the greasy glass of the tiny terminal building to watch a stubby-winged aeroplane drop down out of yet another pale, Arctic sky and land lumpenly on short-legged landing gear.

'Twin Otter.' The man standing next to me spoke through the ruffled collar of his enormous parka without looking away from the plane and I watched it too as its twin propellers freewheeled and slowed to a stop.

'Bollocks.' I muttered it under my breath. Didn't want my fellow passengers thinking I was scared. Or, worse still, joining in with my apprehension and fuelling it with their own. What was it Tommy Cooper said? 'Isn't it amazing; scream in a public library and everyone tells you to shush. Do it on an aeroplane and everyone joins in.'

'They any good?' I nodded through the glass at the grey and white aeroplane being tended to by two blokes in parkas even bigger than my companion's.

'Sure.' He didn't speak much, my new friend.

We had met at the check-in desk. And it really was a desk – a small, low wooden one with pencils stored in a narrow cardboard box next to a reporter's notepad with a curling, brown cover. It was jammed in a corner next to the door that led out on to the airfield itself. There are proper check-in desks at Iqaluit airport, but our flight was to Resolute Bay, a settlement too northerly even for the hard-bitten Canadians of Iqaluit to venture to regularly. It wouldn't be a direct flight. The solid, sturdy woman holding the fort at the desk by the door had raised a pudgy eyebrow and displayed a subtle smile that could have been sympathy when I asked where we would be going to Resolute via. Or it might just have been wind.

'Oh, there's a few stops along the way. You touch down at . . .' and she listed names of places that sounded like obscure album titles '. . . and then you'll stop off in Igluik . . .' her voice faded in and out in a monotonous Canadian drawl '. . . stop for fuel in Pond Inlet, but you can get coffee there . . .' she had thick, grey hair that crouched on her head as a solid lump '. . . another one and a half hours and you'll land in Resolute.'

Another traveller arrived, the door from the main body of the terminal swinging open and banging against the bare wall of our corner. He was a big man in a huge, black parka and I retreated from the desk as he strode up, handed the woman his passport and asked if the plane would be on time. The check-in woman beamed.

'Yeah, sure, of course. Always is.' And she handed him a blue slip of paper.

'Oh, sorry,' I leaned around a corner of the man and looked apologetically at the check-in woman, 'do I need a boarding pass? Sorry, I forgot, should I . . .'

She looked away from the man and studied me.

'No, dear.'

'Okay, er, sorry.'

The newcomer smiled.

'No, this is just something I've got to take to Igluik.' He waved the piece of paper at me as he passed it from one hand to the other and stuffed it into one of the huge pockets in his cavernous jacket. 'You don't need a pass on this flight. There'll only be, what, eight of us?' He looked across for confirmation.

'No, only five this trip.' She beamed as she studied the manifesto on a wooden clipboard.

I thanked her, nodded to the man and retreated to the terminal.

I had some hours to pass before the plane arrived and I mooched about. With no crew to join in, Airport Shopping Dare was out of the question. I looked around. The building was, not surprisingly given its remoteness, small and on one level. The interior was decorated with the rough, grey, unfinished texture of the concrete that formed its walls. Posters were pinned to display boards along the centre of the room. They showed faded blue and white paintings of Arctic scenes. It was early, yes, but a drink? Maybe. There was no bar.

'Hey, Hamster, wow, how are you?' A man in a red parka and matching trousers strode towards me by the rack of bright yellow payphones and introduced himself. Grey-haired and slim, he was smart, apart from the parka, and looked like he was missing his business suit.

'Oh, y'know, great.' I dropped my heavy bag to the marble-effect floor and shook his hand, glad to hear an English accent.

'What are you doing here then? Where's the rest of them?' He looked around, expecting, no doubt, to be pounced upon by Jeremy and James and a camera crew. 'Another of your races? There are no cars here, though, unless you count pickups.'

'Oh, just here on another daft trip. Y'know, messing about. It's work but . . .' I rambled and stuttered. It had been drummed into me that it was essential that no one knew what we were there to do because it would almost certainly then get out and people would be cross if news of our trip hit the papers before it hit the telly.

'And you?'

He was there to take part in an Arctic race and it sounded a lot more exciting than my trip. The tannoy shattered our comforting talk with its nasal blare. His plane was soon to depart and he hurried off, lugging a huge, orange rucksack. Most of the other occupants of the building followed him to the door in the corner leading out to the airfield.

Suddenly, in the now quiet terminal with just a half-dozen fellow travellers lounging about waiting for flights to obscure, cold places, solo Airport Shopping Dare seemed like a good idea.

There was one shop and it had about it an air both hopeful and hopeless. A short, weathered man stared at me from the counter, his hand hovering expectantly next to the controls of a hefty coffee machine. His shop sold Slush Puppies from another ancient machine surrounded by racks of postcards showing polar bears with funny captions and pictures of sunsets over fields of ice. I looked at a small display case of jewellery and an alarm clock. There was a touch of comforting familiarity about the rack of magazines. Out-of-date gossip rags and copies of *Cosmopolitan* jostled for place. *Top Gear* wasn't on it. I cruised the central aisle of shelves. And there, perched on the end at head height, a plastic figurine caught my eye from the confines of its gaudy cardboard box. Something about it rang familiar. It was a plastic Jesus doll and it was the doll's mournful face, narrow beard and thorny crown that had drawn me to it. Next to him, in a brighter, shinier box, stood a Barbie doll, her legs extending below a bright pink miniskirt. The two made an odd couple. Had the crew been there, we would have been in perfect Airport Shopping Dare territory with these two. I tried to convince myself that a plastic Jesus doll accompanied by a brash representation of a physically impossible tart would be just the thing to cheer me up and banish my nervous mood. I couldn't trick myself into the purchase, so I left and stood by the window looking out over the runway. And there I found my fellow traveller bound for Resolute. We stood in silence until the plane arrived.

There were indeed just five of us on the flight, discounting the pilot and co-pilot who also doubled as the baggage handler and air steward. One of the five passengers was a baby, perhaps six months old. The baby and her mother sat, predictably, behind the seat I had been allocated. I struggled to lower the metal base of my seat to a horizontal position.

'Hey, that's thirty-seven years old, don't kick it.' The co-pilot, built like a plane tug, grimaced at me as he chucked the last of our bags into the baggage hold at the back of the cabin.

'I'm thirty-seven, too, so don't fucking kick me.' I tried to growl it menacingly. And blushed as I wrestled into the cramped seat and struggled with the narrow, canvas harness. In the seat next to me, silhouetted by the window's bright light, the plane's fifth passenger, a young guy with a thin, wind-tanned face pulled out a book and settled back to read. His eyes shifted nervously up from the pages to look around the cramped cabin and I averted my gaze to avoid being confrontational. Something about his manner, his look, his presence, spoke of toughness. He looked, I decided, what women of a certain age would describe as 'shifty'. My amiable friend from the terminal had settled into his seat up front and nodded off, seemingly immediately. For once, I was envious of another person's ability to sleep on aeroplanes and I stared miserably at the bulging lumps of parka oozing over the top of his seat as he slumped comfortably and snored.

As we droned our way towards the first of our stops en route to Resolute, I made my own resolution. Assuming I wasn't killed in this plane, I would begin a proper Arctic explorer's journal to record this incredible adventure. It would be a romantic, epic tome, reminiscent of the explorers' tales of old. I pulled out my black Moleskine notebook and a biro from my canvas shoulder bag and began.

*Diary of a Brave Polar Explorer*
*16 April*

*They spoke for hours last night of the terrors of travelling to Resolute Bay in a Twin Otter. I'm travelling to Resolute Bay in a Twin Otter. And I'm a bit scared. It's cold and getting colder and the baby behind me keeps screaming. The thin man next to me keeps staring at me and he's reading a survival manual. I think he has a gun. It's noisy and the hostess is a bloke who shouted at me for adjusting my seat. I will sleep.*

I didn't sleep. We landed in Igluik. We were disgorged down the icy steps and sent into the shed that served as a terminal building while men tended to our ugly aircraft's needs. Once back on board, I picked up the biro and rejoined my Diary of a Brave Polar Explorer.

*Diary of a Brave Polar Explorer*
*16 April, cont.*

*We just stopped off in Igluik. It's a small village. It has been inhabited since 2000 BC. Apparently it still is. Don't know why. Polar bears' fur can conduct ultraviolet light to the black skin below where it is absorbed as heat. I read that on a poster in Igluik. There isn't anything else to do in Igluik.*

*Stopped for fuel again at a place called Pond Inlet. It's got a shed, some snow and a coffee machine. The coffee machine doesn't work. Spoke to Mindy on a payphone. She's got Dan and Jenny round and sounds happy.*

## . . . and Dreamed of Polar Bears

Eventually, after a couple of months or so, we landed in Resolute. The building there was smaller than the one in Iqaluit. The mother and baby had left our flight in Pond Inlet. The co-pilot hauled the passenger door open and beamed in: 'Welcome to Resolute.' The frostiness of our first meeting was clearly behind us. Or perhaps he hadn't heard me muttering behind his back.

Two young guys were playing frisbee in the airport building when we walked in. They were the airport staff and they stopped playing as we entered. The green plastic frisbee bounced loudly off a large, seemingly heraldic crest on the end wall and clattered to the black, stone floor where it caught a slant of watery sunlight seeping rather than pouring through the panels of glass making up the wall overlooking the airfield. The frisbee players laughed and joked with the crew of our plane. They looked like surf dudes and distinctly out of place but they were friendly, confident and chatty. I was met by a representative from the hotel where I would be staying alone before being joined in a few days by the rest of the team. Outside the airport building, I was shown into an ancient, grey van that smelled strongly of petrol.

On the way to the hotel, I looked around at the few, narrow, snow-covered streets of Resolute. Prefabricated buildings and huts, sheds really, served as homes and crowded up to the edges of the road. Most boasted a snowmobile in place of a car outside. A few children, shapeless in their layers of coats, hats and gloves, played in the streets, amazingly, on bicycles. The primal instinct to get free and ride around and explore the world extended to children even in a place where the bicycle, clearly, was not a first-choice mode of transport. The overall effect was that of any other small suburb, only encased in ice and snow. Perhaps our basic, human needs, once fulfilled in the most convenient and easy-to-live-with way, lead to similar scenes the world over. It's just that here the streets were feet deep in snow and ice, the cars had skis on them, the pet dogs were huskies – seen here and there, skulking in the gaps between homes and feasting on raw seal meat – and the horizon led straight to the North Pole. Gazing out of the yellowed windows of that van, I imagined that, if ever we do populate Mars, we will do so in neatly ordered rows of pressurised domes arranged along tidy streets travelled by postmen in tiny spaceships hoping not to run into trouble with the pet alien at number eleven again.

In fact, Resolute has more in common with a frontier space settlement than it does with Milton Keynes. A small Inuit hamlet on Cornwallis Island, Nunvut, Canada, it is one of the coldest inhabited places on earth with an average yearly temperature of minus sixteen degrees. The tiny population of just over two hundred people enjoy a school, a gym, a police station. From the end of April to mid-August, Resolute experiences twenty-four hours of sunlight. It is the gateway to the North Pole.

The hotel turned out to be an entirely wooden construction with flat, double-glazed windows punctuating its blank, utilitarian walls. It looked out over plains of ice that ran on until the curvature of the earth took them from view. In a lino-floored ante-room I was told that the place had a strict policy of requiring residents to remove outdoor footwear before entering the building. Somehow, this came as a disappointment; it was like going round to a posh mate's house as a kid and being told to take off your shoes before you went in. Perching on a low, wooden bench to undo my bootlaces, I looked around. The bulk of the massive jackets hanging from workmanlike hooks above crowds of boots as big as horse-boxes told me that this was not one of those boutique hotels you read about in in-flight magazines. There probably wouldn't be afternoon tea. On the plus side, there probably wouldn't be some numpty plonking about endlessly on a piano in the bar playing cheesy renditions of tunes nobody really liked in the first place. I was too tired to take in much else, but something about the place reminded me of childhood youth-hostelling trips in the Lake District.

The ante-room gave straight into a small, cosy living room complete with television, sofas and a coffee table bearing magazines and remote controls. It was homely and welcoming. And it was the private living room of the owner of the hotel.

'This is Osi,' I was told and the man escorting me waved an arm towards another who rose from his armchair in front of the TV and put down his magazine on the table.

'Hi, good to see you. So you're with the BBC?' Tall, balding and of Asian origin, Osi spoke with a cultured Indian accent as he extended a warm handshake.

'Er, yes, I am. Great, er, great place you've got here.'

'Best in town, my friend.' Osi looked at my escort as he spoke and smiled. These two had clearly welcomed many bewildered, tired and disorientated travellers to the hotel in their time and there was probably little I could do or say to surprise either. I liked Osi immediately; his sparkling eyes and ready grin gave him a roguish, lively air. He was a natural survivor, that much was immediately apparent, probably a tough guy to do business with but someone to trust all the same. But I was tired, falling asleep on my feet.

'We must get you to your room, Richard.' Osi handed me back to my escort and I was shown through into what turned out to be a canteen.

'We eat here,' he pointed out needlessly as I took in the shiny, school tables and tea urn perched in a corner by a large food hatch.

We walked through another room, long and narrow, lined with tables supporting a computer almost buried under piles of orange rucksacks bulging with kit.

'Getting ready for the race. They're off day after tomorrow.' He waved at the rucksacks and I took in the serious-looking straps and lengths of rope. This must be the Arctic race the guy in the airport had said he was competing in. Judging by the kit, it really would be tough.

'If you need the internet, you can use that.' He pointed to the computer, the keyboard just visible under a rucksack. 'Check e-mails and stuff.'

I didn't need the internet, I needed sleep.

I was shown to my room. It was large and without ornaments. The low dresser, narrow chest of drawers and bedside table were built of shiny wood and stood on a thin, green carpet the texture of toast. There was a small bathroom, a sturdy rail to take heavy, Arctic clothing and a double bed with a pastel pink bedspread. I climbed in and went to sleep and dreamed of polar bears crowding round the walls.

## The Resolute Corner Shop

The next few days would blend seamlessly from nervous antici-pation into boredom. The rest of the crew were not due to arrive until the end of the week. Until then, there was no gang to hang out with, no mates to loiter with in dark corners and make sarcastic comments. I was alone. Not a good place to be right now. I was left to my own devices to entertain myself as best I could. There were other residents in the hotel, the people getting ready for their race across the ice. Their race, though, was on foot and very different from the one ahead of me. I mooched about the bare, functional rooms, chatting to people who wanted to talk and staying out of the way of those too busy to break off from their preparations.

Desperate for a purpose, I made tea in the canteen and helped clear the tables and trays when people had finished, scraping leftovers into the huge plastic bin and passing the emptied plates through the hatch to a huge, flamboyantly downbeat chef for cleaning. It never got dark, the effects of being this far up the northern hemisphere meaning the sun never quite dipped out of the sky. The days would have seemed long enough, even without the twenty-four-hour sunlight. The crew would arrive in a few days but before then, the plane carrying the truck that James and Jeremy were to drive would land and disgorge its precious contents on to the icy runway. I had to be there for that.

In the event, I was late. I had gone shopping. There is only one shop in Resolute and it stands, perhaps not surprisingly, on a corner. Patrons of the Resolute corner shop can buy tinned food, bottles of methylated spirits, pots of butter, thermal socks and even leaf through a selection of magazines in a shopping environment that feels every inch like any other high street general store and newsagent, but for the windows being boarded against the elements, the three-foot icicles overhead as you cross the threshold and the sacks of frozen seal meat being hauled out through the door by people stocking up for their huskies. Each product line must be flown in, of course, so it's best to check the date on any purchase being considered. And that includes checking the year as well as the month. With this in mind, I avoided the dairy section, which was kept, unnecessarily I thought, in a standard shop refrigerator, and mooched along the busy shelves.

I treated myself to a knife. It's a symbolic thing for a chap to buy, a knife. Whether a clasp knife with a bone handle, a small bowie knife with a thick, shiny blade or a complicated penknife with a thing for digging stones out of horses' hooves, it is always, for me anyway, crammed with childhood associations of *Swallows and Amazons* and the Boy Scouts. I associate knives like the wooden-handled, stainless-bladed sheath knife I bought in the Resolute corner shop with whittling sticks to make rudimentary tent pegs, skinning a trapped rabbit for the pot or carving the name of your Scout patrol on to a wooden sign to hang at the end of your tent – innocent pastimes indeed compared with knifing strangers for their mobile phone outside your inner city school. It's a terrible shame that these symbols of early independence and basic, human capacity for ingenuity and survival have been hijacked

A Very Brave Arctic Explorer.

Scene of our *Jurassic Park* moment.

OPPOSITE PAGE TOP  Plane failing to collect us. 45 minutes of solid swearing followed.

OPPOSITE PAGE BOTTOM  They can do this at minus 80 degrees.

TOP Bartlett doing
what he does best.
On the ice at minus
40 degrees.

LEFT A brief stint in
the driving seat,
Matty behind. We
crashed shortly after.

'What sort of plane is that?' A twin Otter, nearly 40 years old and the pride of Arctic Airways, refuelling on the way to Resolute Bay via Igluik.

ABOVE LEFT  This hurts. But it kills time.

ABOVE RIGHT  Running 10 miles at minus 40 degrees will do this.

MAIN PICTURE The best sight in the world. More moving than the Taj Mahal or St Paul's Cathedral.

ABOVE 4 Men in a Tent. Climbing out of our frozen sleeping bags.

TOP  Another day dawns, another battle with ice and snow. I think I'd rather be in the Lake District.

RIGHT  A chilling sight: a polar bear this way came...

and demonised by a few deviant hoodies who could no more rely on their grubby little switchblades for survival in the wild than they could rely on their wits to argue their way out of trouble when they are finally nailed for pushing drugs to ten-year-olds in the park.

I reflected sadly on today's misguided youth as I pocketed my newly acquired knife and strode out of the Resolute corner shop, screwing my face up against the deepening cold. I fingered the knife, nestling in its sheath in the depths of my anorak pocket, and secretly hoped to bump into a polar bear that needed slaying, skinning and presenting to Osi and his staff back at the hotel. Fortunately, my trip up to the airfield to see the pickup truck wasn't interrupted by marauding polar bears. It was not interrupted, in fact, by anything at all. I arrived at the single, large building and presented myself to the cargo handlers. They showed me to the back of the building and into what they called, rather ambitiously, the cargo-holding area. Piles of purposeful, outdoorsy equipment filled the large room, some of it of a type definitely not normally encountered at an airport. Jerrycans, coils of rope, snowmobile parts, piles of shovels and unidentifiable machinery loitered around in the gloom. And through it all, I made out the red and gleaming flanks of the truck, hiding in a corner with its face to the wall.

It was beautiful. And I hated it immediately. Not because of its purposeful stance or its bristling array of specially fitted running gear, but because it wasn't mine. Running a hand along the top of the load bed, I paced the length of the creature, taking in the shining aluminium flight cases mounted behind the cab, the huge, balloon tyres fitted specially for helping it float over snow and ice. Inside the cab, I saw extra dash fitments to allow controls of the specific off-road features fitted to it in faraway Iceland by legendary glacier-driving specialist Arctic trucks. Looking back down its length, I saw the gun case jutting out of the side. And I had seen enough.

## Always Trust a Military Moustache

I shifted my weight and the row of blue plastic seats acting as my temporary bed squeaked and complained, their upturned edges digging into my ribs and thighs. Looking around the room, I tried to stop myself checking the time yet again on the plain, black and white clock and failed. Another forty-eight minutes to go. Damn, I wasn't supposed to check for another eight minutes and this unscheduled time check was beyond the number I had rationed myself to and now, knowing that it had only advanced three minutes since I'd last checked, I had drawn out the time to wait even further. I was loitering in the one building at Resolute airport. Very soon, in just forty-seven and a half minutes – damn, checked again – the plane carrying the rest of the *Top Gear* team would arrive. I would have friends to play with again and there was a chance, just a slim one, that I might regain my sanity. Assuming I didn't lose it entirely in the next forty-six and three-quarter minutes – got to stop looking at that clock – and eat the seats while waiting for them to arrive.

Hanging around in Resolute with nothing to do had taken its toll on the already tattered remnants of my mind. I was aware, though not entirely in control, of a raft of facial tics. I glanced obsessively once more at the clock, fiddled with my lucky pencil in my jacket pocket, touched my lucky bangle made out of twined pieces of blue string I had found in the canteen bins and practised rocking backwards and forwards in my seat. I made up games involving peculiar, repetitive sighs and winks. I tried to read things from as far away as possible, marking the furthest point from which I could read the safety warning peeling off the side of the single, rust-streaked fire extinguisher leaning against the wall by the entrance to what I imagined must be the office. Or the room where they grind you up for polar bear food and throw you out of the window for their pets. I tried to avoid imagining things. I counted things instead: polystyrene ceiling tiles, floor tiles, wall tiles in the gents, coins in my pockets. I tried to sleep, failed and tried not to sleep. And I fell asleep.

And they arrived. I have spoken to Jeremy, James and the crew since and they claim that I ran up to each of them as they entered the building from the snowy airfield, grabbed them by the hand, peered into their faces, studying them closely as a dog might study its master's face made unfamiliar by a new beard after a long trip away, and grinned with a manic ferocity and intensity that left some of them wondering if I had been drugged. Others claimed that I grabbed hold of their trousered legs and humped them wildly, shouting out their names like a warped roll call. I think they exaggerate, but probably only a little. I was, in short, very pleased to see them all. To have contact once again with the group was like, well, it was like having contact once again with fellow shipwreck survivors having been cut adrift alone on a flat, calm but terminally dull and lifeless ocean for a couple of weeks.

And now the work could start in earnest. We would leave in two days, setting off on our voyage into the unknown. James and Jeremy went to inspect their truck, I stayed in the hotel and laughed wildly at every joke the bewildered crew made. We readied filming kit for the ordeal that was to come and rehearsed our polar bear drill over dinner. In the evening we learned more of the skills that would keep us alive in the Arctic winds and temperatures that could drop to minus fifty or sixty. On the way to our simple – far too simple for some – dinner in the hotel's youth hostel canteen, our instructor marched us all outside and into what turned out to be a surprisingly mild evening. Our breath still frosted in front of us, but it hung about like clouds, undisturbed by the howling gales and shrieking storms of our collective imagination. We walked past a simple, white canvas tent slumped on square-edged, wooden poles next to the bins and a pile of, presumably old, gas bottles. This tent, he pointed out, would be our home for the next week or so. It would be all that stood between us and certain death in the jaws of a polar bear or the teeth of an Arctic storm. He spoke of these horrors with a touch too much relish for the taste of some.

'Bloody hell, had one like that as a kid.' A crew member, skulking at the back of the group reached out and rubbed the coarse cloth of the tent between gloved finger and thumb.

'No, it was better than this.' He dropped the canvas with disdain, letting it fall back and hang limply.

'And that was to go to Cornwall.'

'Will it stand up to, y'know, to it all?' I waved my arms in the direction of the crowding Arctic terrors extending beyond the hotel as I asked the question we were all thinking. The tent hung impassive and slack from what looked, now we were closer, like a roughly made timber doorframe.

'Stand up to anything. These things are proven, they'll still be standing when you're long dead.' Our instructor barked his defence of the kit. 'We've tried all that fancy modern stuff, but these old Prospector Tents' – he surveyed the pile of canvas and wood with what probably passed for affection on his strictly military face – 'you just can't beat 'em. Just what you need, no carbon fibre, no Gore-Tex crap.'

'No fucking chance either.' A low voice from the back murmured it too quietly for the instructor to hear but loud enough for the rest of us to appreciate the sentiment. But he did hear; probably specially trained.

'Not out here, mate. You can keep all the fancy stuff. This is what you need. You'll see.' He had a jet-black, military moustache of immense presence and bristliness that looked like it could, on its own, outweather even the toughest Arctic storm. It looked, in fact, as though it might actually provide an easily portable emergency shelter for its owner. On those grounds, I chose to believe him and trust him with my immortal soul.

After dinner, having feasted on glutinous chicken bathed in

watery gravy, we marched back past the tent. It had fallen down. It lay in a pile, the two upright poles, made as we now saw from standard four-by-two builder's timber, jutting out from under the snow-drifted cloth. Nobody said anything. There was no need.

What we liked to refer to as our 'expedition' had taken over a large social room in the hotel and converted it into a sort of lecture theatre and kit-assembly point. Tables had been lined up around the walls and were strewn with boots, socks, ice axes, cameras, lenses, socks, bags of peanuts, more socks, orange spades with collapsible handles, gloves, a selection of inappropriate hats and boxes of hand warmers. These were our 'stores' and, surveying them, the image of the tent heaped like something found in the back of a builder's pickup still fresh in my mind, they didn't amount to much. Our instructor joined us. None of us had the nerve to tell his moustache that the tent had fallen to a wind gentle enough to leave a birthday candle untroubled and he marched around confidently, showing us how to erect one of these lifesaving shelters for ourselves.

We learned how to wedge the two vertical poles into wooden jaws fitted to the ends of a third, longer pole that lay horizontally across the top, forming a ridge for the cloth to lie against, and I began to appreciate that, for all its apparent fragility in the eye of a gentle breeze, the tent did possess some finer qualities. Firstly, it was indeed a simple thing, made up of only two raw ingredients – wood and canvas – making it easy to repair 'in the field'. As long as you had access to ready supplies of wood and canvas. And the tools to work them. None of which we would have. Secondly, it was, aesthetically, a rather pleasing device: the coarse-textured, thick, cream canvas creasing itself comfortably against the unfin-ished timber made an earthy but satisfyingly light and natural collage that spoke eloquently of enjoying the great outdoors in a simple, time-served way. If I hadn't just seen one fall over in conditions we would have been lucky to enjoy on a summer's evening at home, I would have been buoyed up by the rugged purposefulness of it all. At least the name of it was good: 'Prospector Tent', redolent of images of old, white-bearded miners travelling the scorching plains of America, panning for gold and dreaming of hookers. An exciting, romantic image, but not much use in an Arctic situation.

'It's not much, is it? Not when there's bears out there.' We strained our eyes to see out of the windows. The sun had dipped as far as it would dip towards the white horizon before beginning its slow climb back to mark another Arctic day. The low twilight it now cast on the icy plains warmed them in our imaginations, but hid legions of polar bears sharpening their claws in the gloom and arguing over whether small and stringy beats plump and fatty when it comes to humans.

'Yes, but we'll have the gun.'

'Yes, now, is it five shots or six?'

'Shut up. It's five.'

'Don't forget the one up your spout.'

'How could I, it chafes like a bastard, especially in these pants.'

We bickered and joked in the warm room as the sun completed its downward slide and began hauling itself back up the frozen sky.

*Diary of a Brave Polar Explorer*
*25 April. Two days before we leave*
*We learned about the tents we would be using on our expedition today. They're not very good but they are made of very nice canvas. They reminded me of village fêtes. The man with the moustache did a lot of shouting and marching about. We just sort of hung around and looked at stuff. His tent fell down. Not sure we're going to get much sleep on this one.*

*Didn't sleep too well last night because of the bloke snoring in the next room. Again. He's a big, fat American and is here, I learned from the guys in the kitchen, to go hunting. The local Inuit are granted permission by the government to sell a controlled number of tickets each year to people who want to hunt polar bears. You pay your money, bring your gun and hunt them.*

*I don't blame the locals; they've got bugger all money here and tourism opportunities are, not surprisingly, pretty thin on the ground. They have got plenty of polar bears though, so . . . But what I don't understand is why anyone would want to come and shoot a polar bear. I'm not against hunting per se; it's what we do as humans. We are predators. You can't eat a steak without first a cow being killed. Even my little girls know that chicken comes from chickens. But polar bears are an endangered species. And they are not killed for food, but to feed the bloated, voracious egos of whatever fat-bastard hunters want to come up here and compensate for whatever miserable little deficiencies cower in their waterproof hunting trousers by shooting a bloody great bear on its home territory.*

*And it can't make any sense to the bears; they are the top predator here and always have been. They are not scared of anything, because there has never been anything they have to be scared of. Being preyed upon is just not part of the gig if you're a polar bear. I mean, if you're a rabbit and you get eaten by a fox, well, fair dos, that's the sort of thing that happens if you're a rabbit. It probably happened to your parents before you and will almost certainly happen to your kids after. It's what life generally deals rabbits. There must be compensations for being a rabbit. The sex, I suppose . . . But the bears have roamed around here for millennia with no one and nothing to fear. They have evolved techniques for hunting and killing their prey, which is anything that moves really, so that they can feed it to their young. That is just what they do. Who the hell could get any pleasure at all from hiding behind a lump of ice with a bloody great gun and waiting to get sight of the prime predator, the king of all it surveys, the noble and deadly killing machine that has ruled these parts since time immemorial and then pulling a stupid little lever to kill it from three hundred yards away? Where exactly is the pleasure in that? All they must take home is a crap rug and, hopefully, a nagging sense that they have done a great wrong. And the same fat-bastard-polar-bear-murdering-American-hunter-shit in the room next door snores like hell and is keeping me awake every night. It sounds like someone left a diesel dumper truck running on the other side of these cardboard walls. I hope he chokes on his own flabby tongue. Better still, I hope he finally gets sight of the bear and runs out of bullets just as it charges.*

## Chapter 3

# DIARY OF A TIRED POLAR EXPLORER

*3.10 a.m. Kill Him*

**Diary of a Brave Polar Explorer**
*27 April. The day before we leave*
*We did our final preparations today; we leave tomorrow. I packed my rucksack at least fifty times and I know I've forgotten something. I just don't know what. Mindy gave me a packet of photographs of her and the girls to take with me. I printed off some extra ones of my cars to put in with them. I don't know what happens to photographs at minus fifty though, do they shatter? I've packed spares of everything: gloves, socks, fleeces. I've been warned a billion times about the importance of controlling my layers to control my body temperature. If I get too cold, I will die. If I get too hot when I'm running behind the sledge and sweat, the sweat will freeze next to my skin when I stop running. And I will die. Basically, dying seems to be the only thing on the menu out here.*

Later that night ...

*I'm ready to go. I rang Mindy and the girls and tried to say the sort of things you say when you think they might be the last words you say to someone but don't want them to know that until the time comes. Tricky that. Didn't want to sound like a prat, 'now remember, daughter, be a*

*brave girl as you grow up and have a good life . . .' all that sort of thing*
*would have been way too much, but I didn't want them to be left clutching*
*a last memory of their father shouting at them over the phone for not*
*brushing their teeth. Think I pulled it off. Very excited and nervous. Got*
*to sleep, though. Will need every ounce of strength I have tomorrow.*

In the event, I didn't sleep. And it wasn't because excitement or
fear was keeping me awake. It was the fat-bastard-polar-bear-
murdering-American-hunter-shit next door. He had long since
left the hotel, dragging his bloated carcass out on to the ice where
I secretly hoped it would be pounced upon by a bear, eaten and
shat out on to the frozen sea where he could spend all of eternity
as a mound of polar bear shit with a scrap of stupid plaid shirt in
it. He had left very early, obviously the sort of thing that polar bear
murderers like to do, making them feel dangerous and exciting.
Much like their pitiful attempts to make themselves feel dangerous
and exciting at the very specialised private sex clubs they like to
frequent back home in Pointlessville, Arizona.

I can see how it must be a bit like Christmas really, dragging
your hideous, lumpen body out of bed early in the morning,
gasping as the cold air hits your pasty, sagging flesh, pulling on a
hunter's shirt and hunter's trousers you bought from a catalogue
and scurrying out into the crystal-clear night with a massive gun
to hide behind a rock and hideously maim or, better still, kill a
beautiful creature that has for millennia been the proud and noble
ruler of its cruel territory.

Unfortunately, in the process of going through his hunting-day
rituals, the fat-bastard-polar-bear-murdering-American-hunter-
shit hadn't been strangled by his own neck fat or accidentally shot
himself in the leg. But he did leave his radio alarm on snooze. Ten
minutes later, at precisely 3.10 a.m., I was stirred from a sleep so
deep as to be barely millimetres from death by an insistent and
incessant honking. After flailing around my bare room opening

drawers and cupboards, rifling through my packed and repacked rucksack and stripping the bedclothes in search of the source of the noise that had dragged me to unwilling consciousness, I did eventually pin it down to the alarm in the fat-bastard-polar-bear-murdering-American-hunter-shit's bedroom. Standing in the corridor, unaware at that point that he had left, hopefully to be killed and eaten by his prey, I indulged in an early-morning fantasy involving kicking down the door and beating him up to, but not quite past, the point of death with the blunt end of his hunting rifle before covering him in dog-o-meat, enlisting the help of a passing forklift truck and transporting him out to the frozen sea to be staked out in his boxer shorts for a very, very close look at a polar bear. It was not by any means a gentle start to the trip. But then it wouldn't be, I was soon to realise, a very gentle trip.

## Gentlemen, Start Your, er, Dogs

It's one of those strange moments, the start of an Arctic expedition. You stand around and chat with the same mates that you have stood around with all over the world in far more ordinary circumstances. We spoke about the weather – it was snowy and cold, obviously; we spoke about how we had slept – very badly, thanks to the fat-bastard-polar-bear-murdering-American-hunter-shit. They all looked the same as they did standing around with me at the test track in Surrey or in the pub. Except they were rather more wrapped up in big coats and hats.

We readied the filming kit. Which meant it was finally time for me to see the provisions that had been made to capture on glorious Technicolor videotape the events and adventures that would befall me as I trekked my way to the Pole. I was shown a small video camera that had been fixed on to the right-hand side of the sledge, just above the runner.

'Er, I'll knock it off. It won't stay there. Watch.' I leaped on the sledge and sat where I would spend whatever brief seconds I managed to stay on board before being ordered off to help our progress through the wrong kind of snow – which included, as far as I had been able to gather, all types of snow. As I did so, my right foot knocked the camera on its mount so that it pointed down at the ground where it would be able to record for the television audience nothing more spectacular than the snowy surface passing slowly under the sledge runners, punctuated by the occasional dog turd left by the engine room up front. The technician assured me that it would be no problem and reached down to readjust the camera, fixing it back in its place and tightening whatever it is you tighten to make a TV camera stay put on a dog sledge.

'Yes, but look, when I get off again,' I hopped off and made ready as if to run alongside the sledge on the move. In the process of so doing I clouted the camera once more with my second-hand walking boot and it returned to its position monitoring the ground and waiting for the surprise arrival of a new dog turd.

'The audience aren't going to be happy with that.' It was okay, though, because a second camera had been fitted to the sledge for me to talk to and record my impressions and comments as we battled through the cold and driven snow. It had been fixed to a nylon bar curving up between the front of the runners from where it could look back along the sledge. It would encompass only the person sitting at the front.

'That will only be able to see Matty. She sits there to drive the dogs. I don't think she's expecting to drive the sledge, navigate, look after me and do all the TV presenting.'

I looked across to James and Jeremy's truck, gleaming red against the snow, and thought of the banks of remote-controlled cameras bristling around the custom-made interior. And I felt more than a little jealous. I felt, in fact, like a ten-year-old being handed an empty shoebox and a packet of crayons for Christmas while his mates next door are given the keys to a helicopter and a live tiger in a cage. Never mind, though, I was determined; I would carry out my half of this trip with courage and dignity. I would be tough, I would impress them all with my resilience, my newfound Arctic fitness and the finely honed sledging skills that my weeks in Iqaluit had given me.

There was more standing around, more chatting and more fiddling with kit. We were turning into a bunch of blokes standing at the side of a pool full of cold water putting off the moment when we must all jump in. Finally, though, even we ran out of ideas for procrastination and had to concede that, yes, it was time to go. Matty and I harnessed the dogs. The crew watched us do it. And they watched as I slipped in yet another dog turd and tried to persuade the dog that had pulled me over to get into his harness and sit quietly while I went back for another. Finally, they were all harnessed and Matty tended to our sledge bags while I wandered among the pack brandishing the pink whip and trying to suppress their excitement with my authority. Marvin pissed on my leg again and Bartlett bit K2, who howled and yelped.

'Bloody hell, do you have to do that every time?' Jeremy had watched us harnessing up the team.

'Yup, every single time. And if we stop for so much as a pee, they all have to be made safe and pegged down or the whole sledge could take off and we'd be left out there with nothing more to protect us than what we've got in our pockets.' I thought of Mindy's lucky charms nestling in my rucksack, strapped to the back of the sledge, and made a note to remove them that evening, or whenever we stopped, and put them in my pocket.

'Look, we're ready to go and we can't stand around for too long or at some point' – I waved an arm at the dogs, each one of them staring and panting, coiled and desperate to go – 'this lot will just take off.'

The moment came. James and Jeremy climbed aboard their

truck to flick switches and turn on cameras. They started the
engine and gunned it as we would at the start of any other race at
the test track. But back at the track, I would be in a Porsche or a
Ferrari. Instead, I climbed on to the backboard of the wooden
sledge and made ready with the release rope while the two on-
board cameras recorded my right boot and Matty's chin as she
readied herself for the off. Someone shouted 'GO!' and we went.
The dogs pulled as if the sledge was on fire and I felt their power
vibrating up through the vertical grab handles in front of me and
into my shoulders as I held on and braced myself against their
forwards charge. The truck's engine roared as it too tore away from
our improvised start line. I strained to see ahead, my eyes drying
out quickly in the cold rush of air, but I could still see the dogs as
they bent to pull their payload, their heads down and straining
forwards, their powerful back legs digging deep and their strong
hearts grateful for the chance finally to be away and doing what
they did best.

I waited to see how the pack would react to being overtaken by
a bright red pickup truck with engine wailing and two yobs
doubtless hurling insults as they overtook. But they never came
past. We were ahead. On our wooden sledge pulled by a handful
of mutts we could out-accelerate their custom-built, technology-
laden truck. My face was being lashed by the wind now as we
powered away and I twisted round, grateful of the shelter from the
freezing air, to watch as the truck dropped away behind. I could
still see James and Jeremy in their cab. And they weren't straining
to catch us up, their faces weren't pressed to the windscreen,
grimacing with premonitions of defeat at our dwindling dog sledge.
They had stopped. I would learn later that James had forgotten his
gloves. I turned back and laughed into the wind at seeing James's
hunched figure as he hurled himself from the open door to run
back to the hotel while Jeremy yelled abuse at him through the
same open door. And then the sledge hit a small crest in the ice. I

was thrown upwards and had time to look down and see my boots leave the footboard before I landed on my back on the steely ice.

There's little point in my telling the tale of the race, drawing out the tension until the last moment and then revealing the glorious winner while paying due respect, of course, to the plucky loser. Millions saw it on the telly and so the result is hardly likely to come as a surprise to most. And so, yes, I was, in the final analysis, that plucky loser. James and Jeremy were the winners, finishing the race soaked in glory and a bewildering sense of achievement. And their joy at winning was well-deserved and hard-earned. They endured a tough trip, hacking through ice fields with knives to clear a path for the truck when it could no longer clamber over obstacles big enough to stop a tank, let alone a pickup truck driven by two middle-aged men with – and they would be the first to agree with this, I am sure – no real training in the rare art of Arctic driving. And it is a rare art because no one has ever really done it before. They were the first people to drive there and were, therefore, breaking new ground all the way.

The fact is, though, they were very lucky not to break new ground in the literal sense, crashing through the frozen sea ice to die in the dark waters beneath. The tension of spending endless hours staring through the windscreen as the flat ice slid slowly by underneath, waiting for the sudden crack that signified their imminent doom as their truck plunged through, put them, as it would anybody, close to the limit of their endurance. The endless glancing to check the location of the window hammer clipped to the door pillars in case they fell into the sea and needed it in a hurry; the million times they were forced to stop and let air out of the almost frozen tyres to increase their traction and help them move off yet another snow-covered ridge of broken ice in the sure-fire knowledge that, five minutes later, they would be out again to re-inflate them – these and a thousand other repeated tasks that would, if we had to do them only once, have most of us crying out for it all to stop, took their toll on them both. But seven days after starting out, they arrived at the finish, checked their precise location with the help of satellite navigation and felt a rush of elation that few can hope to experience. I didn't do that. And so this is the brief tale of what befell me on my side of the race.


## How Do They Get In?

*Diary of a Brave Polar Explorer*
*Day 1*
*I'm in the tent. It's cold. I'm in my sleeping bag wearing everything I've got except my jacket. Which is outside on the sledge getting snowed on. This, apparently, is what you do – when you're a Brave Polar Explorer. You leave your coat outside so that it doesn't soak up all the condensation that comes off your body in the night and then freeze when you go out in it the next day. Everybody's obsessed with sweat, piss and where to take a dump out here. And, no, there isn't anywhere. You just wander out on to the ice with a bog roll and the gun in case of polar bears – the gun is there in case of bears, not the bog roll, which really wouldn't help. Actually, though, you would kind of need bog roll pretty quickly if a bear charged you, I imagine. There's nothing to shelter behind, no trees obviously, just flat ice. So you pick a spot, drop your trolleys and get on with it. While, presumably, your arse freezes, turns blue and drops off in minus bloody forty degrees. Me, I like a nice comfy lavatory miles from the rest of the world, a copy of my favourite* Land Rover *magazine and a spare twenty minutes. I'll get round the crapping problem by not taking one. It's better that than suffer the indignity of squatting on the ice in twenty-four-hour sunlight to crimp off a length in front of a film crew, the world's leading female polar explorer and ten dogs that already think I'm a prize twat. And taking a piss, well, I can't even begin to talk about it. It is, as I've recorded, very cold indeed; minus forty or fifty degrees. That has a less*

*than flattering effect on the gentleman's area of even the most steely nerved, testosterone-filled Brave Polar Explorer. I don't wish to go into details, dear diary, but bloody hellfire. Bit of a shock that one and not a proud moment in my life as a man.*

*We ate some dried stuff or other that I heated up on our primus stove. Not bad actually. Don't mind a bit of camping food. Although it's amazing I could fit it in – I spent the day eating enough nuts and chocolate to run a power station with their calorific-flaming-value. So I certainly haven't neglected my calorific intake so far. I might be the first Brave Polar Explorer ever to return from an expedition and have to go on a diet. And God alone knows what effect the nuts, chocolate and dried food will have on the crapping situation. Don't want to think about it. Going to try and sleep.*

The first race day had been tough. And a day of discovery. We didn't discover the North Pole, obviously; that was done years ago by men in massive hats with ships that got stuck in the ice and pit ponies that got eaten when they found there were no penguins. But we did discover that filming a dog sledge go past is very different from filming a car go past. And it came as a very large and very worrying surprise.

Compared with the team supporting and filming the truck, we sledgees were a small outfit. We were just eight-strong. Matty and I were on the sledge racing and then, to record our astonishing achievements or dismal failure and acts of astounding heroism or whimpering cowardice, cameraman Iain 'Flash' May and sound recordist Darren Tate. Grant Wardrop was with us, too. He works primarily as a producer, setting things up and making sure everything goes according to plan. On this occasion, though, he would be doubling up as a sort of director, too, keeping an eye on what we were getting and making sure we recorded everything we needed to. Matty's daughter, Sarah, an accomplished Arctic explorer in her own right, and veteran of trips to both North and South Poles, was travelling with us to help Flash and Darren as they filmed in an environment not always friendly and accommodating to the needs of a film crew. We had been given strict orders governing how we would work: standing around, even for a few moments, was to risk hypothermia, frostbite and a million other nasty things that don't happen to you filming at a racetrack in Surrey. The batteries that would power the kit were expected to last a fraction of the time they would in warmer climes and the simple business of taking off gloves to get the camera and sound kit out of their travelling cases to set up a shot meant risking the loss of one of those gloves to the constant, streaming wind and the subsequent loss of the exposed hand to frostbite.

Sarah would help the guys manage their kit and themselves as they struggled not only to make an arduous journey, but to record it with the high degree of quality and attentiveness that the show demands. To provide extra help for the camera team and, indeed, for us all, another Arctic specialist had been drafted in. An ex-special forces member, Gaz is a seasoned professional in the business of working under conditions such as the ones we were headed into. The only thing is, he is more accustomed to carrying out rather different objectives from ours and, well, frankly, he scared us a bit. An endlessly friendly, relaxed and easy-going guy, there was something quiet, unspoken and impossibly frightening contained within him. He would be just as at home walking into a chic party in a dinner jacket as he would be crashing into a room with a pair of sawn-off shotguns and one particular face fixed in his calculating mind. He would, we knew, be handy in a crisis and we just hoped we'd never need him.

The final member of our team would require no help from anyone. Ian Davis is a GP with a busy practice in Gloucestershire. But he is also a specialist in providing medical support in an Arctic environment. He has completed countless journeys across the ice and brought a breadth of experience of surviving out there, along with a comprehensive knowledge of just what happens to your body when it is subjected to physical exertion in unbelievably low temperatures, an atmosphere drier than the hottest desert and twenty-four-hour daylight. My doctors at home had been much comforted when they learned that Ian would be travelling with me. Actually, they sort of insisted. I was still very much in recovery from brain damage and the possible effects of living in temperatures of minus forty or fifty, allied with the stress of completing a physically demanding race while attempting to make a film about it, were not, if they were honest, predictable. Ian would be on hand if I should be taken ill in any peculiar and unforeseen way. On the many Arctic trips he has undertaken, Ian is always known as Doc and has evolved an entire personality to go with the nickname. He would provide a massive amount of entertainment and, we quickly learned, does more work as a medical man by keeping his team's spirits raised and their will strong than ever he does by waving boxes of tablets under their frozen noses.

Iain May and Darren Tate are tough old goats. Iain has filmed stuff pretty much all over the world and is a keen yachtsman in what spare time his work allows. So being cold, uncomfortable and inches from death is a familiar position for him to be in. He brings to his work not only his unmatched skills as a cameraman but a flamboyant and wild nature that makes him fun to be around. He is known to all of us as Flash, after the equally loud and rumbustious character of Lord Flashheart from the legendary *Blackadder* series. It suits him. Darren, too, has filmed pretty much everywhere and had recently completed a working trip to the Arctic, so brought with him a wealth of experience of the rigours of filming in a deadly environment. He had started to share some of these experiences with us the day before we left and was told pretty forcefully to shut up and stop scaring us. We would ask him later why he decided to come back. He never did answer that one.

We were aware that we would need time to get used to working here and had allowed for that in our expectations of the first day of the race. Flash, Darren, Grant, Sarah, Gaz and Doc would travel on three snowmobiles towing cargo boxes on sledge runners behind them like trailers. These boxes contained everything they needed to survive and work. Matty and I had our kit on the sledge. Soon after leaving the start line we veered off into rough ice, keen to press home the advantage that James's dithering with his forgotten gloves had given us. The truck could not, we were pretty sure, tackle the same terrain and would be forced to detour around the rough stuff, staying on flat ice for as long as possible. We wouldn't see the truck again for two days.

Confident that the truck was dwindling ever further behind us, we set up, as planned, for our first shots. These would be 'up-and-bys': shots where the vehicle being filmed drives up to the camera and passes it by, usually about thirty feet or so away, and carries on into the distance. We have filmed them a million times in car reviews. Only they are shot on roads. And I am usually in a car. Flash and Darren dashed ahead on their snowmobile with Sarah following in their wake. They would set up the camera and sound boom when they found a suitably scenic spot and film Matty and me as we slid majestically past. We wouldn't have to stop the sledge: the snowmobiles could go faster than us and our progress would be uninterrupted, essential if this were to be a fair race. As their snowmobiles buzzed into the distance, I settled on to the backboard of the sledge to compose myself into a manly pose for the camera. And I had to jump off again immediately as we hit deep, cloying snow that grabbed at the runners and slowed our progress to a walking pace. Although once off, I found it was more of a running pace and jogged obediently behind, as I would spend many hours doing over the days to come.

But I was glad to have started the race, even on foot. At last we were underway. We had cleared the ice-boulder fields that we hoped would force the truck into a lengthy diversion and hit smooth sea ice lying under a crust of snow. I was happier than I had been for weeks. My crew was up ahead getting ready to film their first shots of the race, the dogs were pulling strongly, not so strongly that they could pull me as well as the sledge, obviously, but pulling strongly nonetheless, and we struck out across the frozen plains under a heavy, grey sky with something close to joy in our hearts.

It turns out that the same snow that grabs at the sledge runners also grabs at your feet. If those feet are encased in huge, second-hand walking boots big enough to house a family of four, then running is, I quickly found, a pretty strenuous business. Every step meant, I knew, that I would in just a second be hauling that same foot back out of the heavy snow. Picking up my trailing leg was as much hard work as striking out with the leading. It doubled the effort of running. I measured my breaths carefully, feeling the cold shock as the freezing air poured into my burning lungs. As my muscles warmed up and my pumping arms and legs generated heat simply by the friction of my heavyweight parka rubbing against itself, the Arctic cold was beaten back from my body and I felt, for the first time since we had left a couple of hours ago, warm. Actually, I felt very warm and suddenly remembered the doom-laden warnings of the dangers of getting too warm, sweating and dying on the Arctic ice in a sci-fi movie cocoon of yellow, frozen sweat. The thought made me hot with rising panic. Which made things worse. But I was enjoying the freedom of running across a landscape straight from a childhood book and decided that I would risk carrying on and sort myself out when we stopped rather than admit to Matty that I hadn't got a clue what I was doing and wanted my mum.

As the dogs settled into their stride, the first, fresh burst of mad enthusiasm when they powered away from the line dwindled into a quiet determination just to keep pulling until their mistress told them to stop, and I settled into a gentle lope behind and wondered where Flash and Darren had gone to get their first shots. This would be quite a moment, I thought, as we tracked towards the distant horizon where mountainous towers of broken sea ice bit into the skyline and promised adventure and thrills enough for a lifetime. This would be the first time the guys had stood back and watched us do what we had practised doing, Matty and the dogs and me. And I hoped it would make for good footage and looked forward to talking it over with them when we broke at the end of the day.

Up ahead, a lump of ice the size of a small house was growing closer. I guessed that Flash would have picked it as a useful piece of foreground to give his shots some perspective and a sense of movement as we went past. And, sure enough, as we got closer I could make out their blue and orange jackets as the two of them stood out from the snow in a familiar filming pose in a very unfamiliar place. Flash was sitting on the snow, the camera braced between his legs in front of him; the low angle would increase the drama and give him the chance to include the sky that now broiled with wind-streaked clouds. Darren stood behind, his microphone extended in front of him on its boom; he hoped, no doubt, to capture the evocative crunch of snow as the sledge went past some thirty feet away from his carefully aimed rifle mic, with perhaps a trace of sound coming from the dogs' panting breath and scrabbling claws.

We got closer still and I could see Darren, craning to look around him, and I guessed he was just taking in the fact that he was doing his job somewhere very different from usual. Somewhere that he had visited before but now, unbelievably, found himself back again. Flash's face was obscured behind the camera, his right eye jammed into the suede pad of his eyepiece, focusing his energy on making the most of every shot. It would be a long trip and he could not afford to spend much time grabbing the shots he needed to hand to the editors at the end. He had to make it count every time he hit the button.

We got closer still. The dogs, settled now into the familiar monotony of dragging their load across a landscape devoid of features, plodded on with their heads down, their tongues out and their ears back. Raven, the lead dog, massive and shaggy-black at the front of the pack, saw Flash and Darren. They were easy to spot against the white ice, even if their smell hadn't reached the information-hungry noses of the pack. Which it had. More heads went up among the team. Glances were exchanged between them. Something new was out there, something unfamiliar, something interesting. It had to be investigated. And the dogs swung the sledge in an arc and headed straight for Flash and Darren like a comet streaking across the night sky, drawn, inexorably, by the gravity of a waiting planet. Flash never looked up, his eye fixed to his camera as he recorded every image.

From there, the pack of dogs, panting and straining at their harnesses, mouths drawn back into grimaces showing white teeth dripping saliva with their effort, must have looked magnificent. And quite big. Very big, in fact, and getting bigger by the second, and I was surprised when Flash still hadn't looked up as the dogs, the sledge, Matty and me and our payload of tents, food and Arctic clothing bore down on them. I threw myself on to the backboard, holding the handlebars, and dragging my feet behind, digging my boots into the snow to try to slow us. Darren hurled himself to one side, the cable between his sound kit and Flash's camera giving enough reach for him to clear the oncoming juggernaut as Flash disappeared beneath it. He was, I was perfectly sure, dead.

He wasn't dead. But he was quite cross. He was laughing, though, as he pulled himself out of the Flash-shaped hole the dogs had hammered him into, but it was the laughter of a bloke who always laughs at painful stuff, especially if it happens to other people but even if it is his own body being bruised and battered. Flash was fine, the camera was fine and the dogs, after thorough investigation from a concerned Matty, were fine, too. What wasn't fine, though, was our prospect of making an especially good film of the trip if every time we set up a camera it was going to be stampeded by the dogs and Flash brutally killed. And it was the prospect of us having to return to England with nothing more than a few videotapes of madly approaching dogs and shots of sky-ground-sky-ground-snow to the aural accompaniment of frenzied barking and even more frenzied swearing that was worrying Flash. And, indeed, us all.

We would have to devise a technique. But now was not the time to do it because we had already been standing around for too long. Our hands and extremities were chilling down rapidly and the dogs had to be untangled, the lines straightened out in front of the sledge and we had to get underway or risk being overtaken by the truck before the first day was over. For the first time, though very much not the last, we shovelled handfuls of nuts and chocolate into our greedy mouths, fixed on our goggles, made our various vehicles ready and headed off into the falling snow.

Later in the day we stopped again to try to solve the problem of filming the sledge. This was, after all, the object of the trip. There would be little point in returning to England having had a thrilling and memorable journey across the Arctic ice if we didn't bring with us the footage of it to make into a film. Someone would get very cross about that. We talked as we stamped around, keeping warm as best we could, our voices raised against both the wind and the layers of hats, hoods, face masks and goggles we all wore. And we devised a plan.

Sarah would go on ahead with Flash and Darren. As the sledge approached them, she would pick her moment and make a mad dash away from the film crew to distract the dog team. They were trained to follow her voice commands and both Sarah and Matty were pretty confident it would work. And, amazingly, it did. We repeated the set-up of earlier in the day and, as we bore down on Flash and Darren's lumpen forms standing in stark contrast against the white ground, a third figure broke away and ran in front of us, arms waving and voice straining above the wind and the hiss of the sledge runners. The dogs lifted their heads as one to inspect this new distraction from the endless monotony of dragging their load across the ice and they veered round to charge after Sarah's retreating form. Flash and Darren got the shots and Sarah finally stood her ground with her arms up in a signal that the dogs recognised meant they had to pass her and carry on their charge. Which they did. We had solved the problem and evolved a technique that would stand us in good stead for the rest of the race.

And so, in our various ways and facing our various challenges and problems, we made it to the end of that first day. We set up camp, just as we had learned back in Resolute. As it was the first day of the trip and we had a lot to discuss on the filming side of things, I bunked in the big Prospector Tent with Grant, Gaz and Doc. Flash and Darren shared a tent in which they could sort out their filming kit every night. There was a third tent, Matty's own, and I would share this with her later in the trip for filming purposes. This evening, though, she shared it with Sarah. When we had eaten, written up our diaries and made plans for the following day, we dispersed to our various tents gathered on the ice.

The wind had stirred itself into something more determined than the breezes of the day and it whipped around our tent now and pressed against the loose canvas, slung from its simple, wooden frame. It whistled around the snowmobiles parked in a group behind us. The dogs would be curled up in their line, noses tucked into tails, slowly being buried under the night's snowfall. In the morning, they would wake, rise up from their snowy blanket and shake it off, as we shake off a duvet. Their coats contain double layers of fur for protection and warmth. So effective are their defences against the Arctic cold that on some days their biggest problem can be how to stay cool. They can pump blood at immense rates down into their paws where it circulates through their huge pads and cools in direct contact with the ice as they run. They are quite happy down to minus eighty degrees. Indeed, they are at their happiest when it's coldest. Matty told me that they struggle with the heat if it gets as warm as minus thirty.

We were not worried about staying cool now, as we bedded down and made ready for our first night out on the ice. I shivered as my legs, still clad in two layers of thermals, made contact with the cold sides of my sleeping bag and I pulled my knees up to my chest, to preserve a hollow chamber of precious warmth where my body curled around itself. Of course, it would never get dark through this night. And the sun threw a thin, diffused light through the canvas sides of our tent. The stove had long since guttered and gone out after we had cooked, its warming glow fading to leave pools of shadow by the tent's doorway.

Every night, once we had chosen a suitable site and pitched the tent, we would dig a pit by the door so that whoever was on cooking duty might be better able to sit at the stove with their feet in the hollow trench. Now, though, the pit was crowded with our boots, lined up and ready for the next day. Their coloured tops peeped over the top of the trench, a visual and constant reminder of what lay ahead after a few hours' sleep.

The four of us, Grant, Doc, Gaz and me, lay in a row at the far end of the sagging tent. I drew the slot at the edge of the tent, lying close to the canvas, and stared at the sunlight through the pores of the thick material, each hole blurring into a pale, yellow flower barely an inch from my face. I thought of lying in the sun on holiday watching the sunlight do the same thing as it shone golden yellow through the holes in a straw sun hat pulled over my face. The sunlight was thicker then, richer, more generous. I felt no warmth from the thin, spiteful sunlight here. The tent material was cold and quickly damp from our combined breathing as it condensed against the frozen sides. We talked quietly, chatting through the day's events.

'Gaz, are polar bears really as dangerous out here as the people in Resolute said? Or are they just trying to make us nervous?' Grant asked the question, but it could equally have been me. It was a question that had rolled around my mind through the day.

'Yes, they're dangerous.' Gaz's voice was muffled by the material of his sleeping bag. He lay flat on his back, the bag pulled up to his nose and its hood tucked down over the top to meet it.

'Too bloody right,' Doc joined in. 'Mean things. Big as a racehorse and damned near as fast. Only they've got massive teeth and they want to kill you.' He knew his way around this environment as comfortably as a village GP knows his own patch and, I suspected, enjoyed watching newcomers into his strange, frozen world.

'You got anything in that medical box that can help if they do then, Doc?' Grant's voice, too, was muffled now; he had burrowed down into his bag in search, no doubt, of a scrap of warmth and comfort.

'Nah. Got plasters though. And I can give you something for constipation if you need it.'

'Oh, great. Thanks.'

'I could take your appendix out. Hammond can hold you down. All I need is a spoon.'

'No thanks.' We managed a few soft laughs and lay in silence for a while.

I broke the silence, timidly.

'But we're okay in here, right? They don't understand what tents are.'

'Course they know. Why would the tent stop them?' Doc rolled on to his back and spoke into the tent's tall, pitched roof. For a brief moment the wind leaned heavily on the canvas and it pressed down to brush against the hats and gloves hanging from a line in the apex of the roof before the breeze died away again and the tent hung slack and still.

'But the dogs will scare them away.' I tried to keep the pathetic, pleading note out of my voice. And failed.

'Er, no. You heard what Matty said. Some bears will be scared off by the sound and smell of the dogs. They'll stay away, sure. But some won't. The really big ones won't give a bugger if there's a few little doggies around the place. They'll see them as a nice snack.'

'Shit. So the dogs just act as a sort of filtering system then. They save us by scaring off the wimpy little bears that we could have got rid of with a rolled-up newspaper and then act as bait to get us killed by the big ones.'

I heard a soft rustle as Grant rolled over in his bag. I had got his attention, too. I went on, keen to press the point home. 'They make sure that if we do get attacked by a bear, it's guaranteed to be a big, mean mother who's scared of nothing.'

'Guess so,' Gaz joined in again. He liked this line of chat. I thought of the gun outside and wondered how quickly Gaz or any of us could get to it.

'So if we hear a bear, then, it's one that's come over to eat our dogs as a sort of aperitif, an *amuse-gueule*, before getting down to the main event. Us.'

'Nice.' Grant stirred again on the other side of the tent, facing away into the ice beyond, and laughed sarcastically at the thought of our dogs being able both to protect us and get us horribly killed.

'Yup.' Gaz sighed contentedly as he answered and moved further down into his sleeping bag.

'How do they get in the tent, though?' I needed to know but immediately regretted asking.

'They open the zip; really nimble paws they've got.'

'All right, Doc. Reasonable enough question, though. Sorry. I just wondered, y'know.'

'Waddya think they do?' Doc was having fun now.

'Well, I dunno. We don't get polar bears in Cheltenham. Never had to worry about it.'

'It's simple.' Gaz spoke from the depths of his bag now, his tones low and measured. 'They just tear through the canvas. They know we're in here. The tent doesn't scare them and neither do the dogs. They sniff us out; sometimes they'll track us for miles and miles over days and days. They pick their moment, walk up to the tent, stand up on their back legs and then stamp down with their front paws to get through. Then they reach inside and pull you out on to the ice and eviscerate you with their claws before eating you then and there.' He ran through the details for us as we lay, stunned into silence.

'If you smell fish really strong, then that's a bear coming into camp. You can smell them long before you hear or see them. And if you do see them, then it's too bloody late. They stink, though, terrible. It's what they eat. Like bloody fishing boats. If you smell fish really strong, then wake me. All right?'

Nothing came back. We concentrated on breathing slowly.

'All right?' He repeated the question.

'Yeah. Wake you. Fine.' I whispered the response.

And then silence. I lay and looked at the end wall of the tent just beyond my head. To my right, the canvas sides sloped upwards. I imagined what it would be like to see the huge silhouette of a bear rising on to its hind legs to smash through the tent. I could sense the others thinking the same thing. For all their bravado and sense of fun, Gaz and Doc both knew that it was very easy to die out where we were. They knew it better than Grant and me. I thought of the gun, lying outside where it was safe from condensation in the tent. And I wondered how we would get to it, who would open the front door and poke their head out into the night to grab the gun and then fire it out through the sides of the tent. And I marvelled at the irony of the predicament: the only place to keep the gun for our protection from bears was outside. Where the bears were.

I slept deeply at first, my aching body enjoying the familiar feel of sleeping under canvas on the ground. But I woke later in the night, conscious of a deep, primeval cold reaching up to me from below, reaching up through layers of ice that lay millennia thick to find a hot new soul fresh to its territory. I knew with each slumbering moment that nothing about this place would forgive my fleshy carcass for venturing into it, that I was physically and mentally an alien here, unable to last even a minute without my protective clothing, my thick canvas tent, my sleeping bag, my sacks of food and my gun. Stripped down to my essentials, down to what I brought into the world naturally and carried with me as an animal, I would be dead in a heartbeat. It was a humble sleep.

## Days Go Out of the Window

We all woke and stirred simultaneously. Once, many years ago, together with two friends, I made camp midway through a lengthy hike and our awakening then was rather different. We were walking through the night between the Yorkshire hills and the coast on the Lyke Wake Walk, the idea of which was to cover the forty or so miles within twenty-four hours. But out on the moors, in the screaming wind of a Yorkshire night, we decided it would be wise to stop and make some sort of camp for a few hours until dawn. We found a broken-down stretch of dry-stone wall and built a bivouac against it using the groundsheets and emergency blankets in our rucksacks. Once inside, we drank off the hip flask of brandy I had brought and bedded down, sheltered from the effects but not from the noise of the moorland wind and rain. We had agreed to rest for a couple of hours and get going again at first light. Within seconds we were asleep.

Later, I woke, opened one eye and saw a weak, watery daylight seeping timidly into our makeshift shelter. Beyond, past the dripping eaves of our bivouac, I saw a line of evil hawthorns crouching meanly in defiance against a hard, white sky. The wind had dropped from its earlier frenzied lashing and contented itself now with a constant, nagging rush. The rain, too, had settled into a surly, miserable drumming against the sagging sides of our shelter. I swivelled my eye around to try and see my two companions. Neither stirred. I thought of waking them, of getting up to pack the shelter, as agreed, and setting our weary feet back on to the cruel road. And I didn't do it. Instead, I remained still and slipped back into a deep and satisfying sleep where the wind didn't blow around my head and the road did not beckon to me like a sinister headmaster with a special punishment prepared. We all woke around ten o'clock. The day was several hours old already and our chances of finishing in a decent time were over. And I discovered later that each of the three of us had gone through exactly the same experience: waking early, seeing the day hanging bleakly around us, seeing that the others still slept and so slipping gratefully back into sleep to pretend later not to have woken at all.

This was not such a morning, though. We all stirred and shifted as we woke, confessing to our consciousness with grunts and moans, keen for company. I had burrowed deep into my thick sleeping bag and climbed my way out again now. As I pulled back the hood, I felt something wet and cold drag across my face. The opening to the bag was a frozen mass of white ice. It crackled and crunched as I crawled out of my own personal ice tube. I looked across to see the others also wrestling their way out of their frozen bags and I turned to Gaz and raised a questioning eyebrow at him to ask wordlessly if this was normal.

'Always happens. Your breath freezes on the bag through the

night. Nothing to worry about.' So it really had been as cold in the tent as I had thought.

We dragged ourselves out of our bags, still wearing our many layers of thermals, and we lay around on the layers of thermal bed rolls. Grant fired up the stove and we were grateful for the warmth.

'No bears then,' I announced gratefully as I pulled on an extra pair of socks over the two pairs I already wore.

'Nope.'

And the door was ripped open with a huge and fierce growl as Flash poked his head in.

'Raaah. Gotcha. Morning, girls, where's breakfast?'

*Diary of a Brave Polar Explorer*
*Day 2*
*Didn't sleep much last night. Bears on the brain. Didn't get eaten, though. We were told that we had to drink at least a litre of water in the morning because the freezing atmosphere takes away all our body's moisture and it's actually as dehydrating as the hottest desert out here. Weird really, there's water everywhere, but it's frozen, locked up as ice. We get our water from snow. You put the stove on, stick a massive cooking pot on it and shovel tonnes of snow into it. And it really does have to be tonnes. A load of snow as big as a Land Rover will produce enough water to fill an egg cup. I spent an hour and a half melting snow to make water for everyone. And the ungrateful bastards just trolled into the tent, filled their flasks and walked off with it all. Some of them came back three or four times. People fall out over stupid stuff out here. There are lots of tales of explorers on long Arctic treks wanting to shoot the bloke in front, just because he's in front. I wanted to shoot them all because they took the water I had prepared for them. Hope we don't all go mad and kill each other.*

*You're supposed to examine the colour of your pee every time you go, to see how dehydrated you are. If it's clear then you're okay. If it's the colour of straw when it hits the snow, you've got to drink more or you risk getting massive headaches in the day and being ill. Mine came out like sand. I need to drink more. I drank three litres of it and am sloshing about like a water bomb the size of a space hopper. On the subject of things toilet related: no, I haven't yet. Still can't face it. Did set off with the bog roll and the shotgun, mooched about for a bit looking for a suitable spot and couldn't find one. Kept bobbing up and down into a crouching position and feeling it wasn't quite the right place for it. Wonder if it's possible to drag a Portaloo behind the sledge?*

*Matty has told us that we're going to give up running our operation on a twenty-four-hour clock. The dogs can only go for so long before they need a break and it works better if we do what she calls 'rolling the clock'. This means we throw away the idea of days being twenty-four hours long. We get up, we harness the dogs and run them for six to eight hours, or as long as they can manage, then we pitch camp, have a short sleep, maybe four hours or so, and then set off again for as long as the dogs will go. It doesn't matter if we get out of synch with the days because it never gets dark. In fact, it's better if we do 'roll the clock' completely and end up running at night; it's colder then and the dogs prefer it that way. Sounds lovely. Colder. Can't wait.*

*We've got to get over Bathurst Island today. It's big, many miles long and easily discernible from the rest of the sea ice because it rises up into a huge, white mound. I flew over it before we set off and saw huge, icy slopes running off it and back down on to the frozen sea. How the hell we'll get down those without the ice brakes on the back of the sledge, I don't know. Might die. Again, sounds lovely. Before that, though, we have to go up on to the island through a wide valley. It's called Polar Bear Pass because the polar bears travel through it every year on their migration. There are thousands of them. And this is migration time. Once again, lovely. If the cold, the slopes and the bears don't get me, terminal constipation will. And people do this for fun? Bloody lunatics.*

*Oh, and Marvin still pisses on me every time we stop the dogs for a break.*

We hit the opening of Polar Bear Pass by what would have been early afternoon if we weren't 'rolling the clock'. With the sun never disappearing it was hard to tell the difference between three in the morning and five in the afternoon. As the day's traditional anchor points of meals and bedtime were taken away, we were all cast adrift on a timescale as bewildering and featureless as the eternal ice we travelled across. We stopped to drink hot soup from metal flasks. It had gone cold. We ate chocolate – it was like frozen rock and broke my crown. I walked around the sledge, taking in the landscape. In front of us, the valley spread, wide and forbidding, flanked by low-lying hills. In places, the wind had polished the tops of the hills until the ice glinted black. The wind had dropped again now, though, and the sky hung low and heavy. We were halfway up the valley side, our tracks stretched behind us, the broken, turned-over trails in the snow winding back through a gentle turn around a blunt headland. I walked further from the sledge and the snowmobiles to inspect our unlikely caravan. The crew milled around, swinging arms to get the blood flowing in them and stamping feet to ensure the circulation reached their extremities. The dogs were tied up and lay curled in the snow, contentedly asleep the moment they stopped working.

I picked out something ahead of me, a rare detail standing stark against the white, and I walked closer to it. A hole opened up in the ice, dark and a couple of feet across. The ice around the hole was black and crusted with lumps and stones. I looked closer. The black crusting on the ice was dried blood and the lumps and stones were bones and teeth. This was what the Inuit people call an agloo, a place where a seal had made a nest for her pups. A polar bear had smashed its way in and eaten the pups. I stooped to pick up a jawbone, the tiny teeth still rooted in it. Kneeling, I peered into the hole, poking my head through to examine the nest. And it crossed my mind that, had the polar bear decided to hang out on the offchance that the mummy seal might come back to inspect her offspring, it would get a rare meal of very shocked Brave Arctic Explorer today. No one was home, though. I saw the thickness of the crust of ice that the bear had smashed through and I imagined it rising up on its hind legs to lunge forwards with its weight and break through the roof of the nest to the tasty morsels within. And I realised how easily the bears could grasp the concept of a tent containing food. To other creatures elsewhere in the world, to lions or different bears, food comes as it is, naked and running away, not contained like this. But to polar bears, it is the most natural thing in the world to smell prey and then get down to the business of opening the tin. I made a mental note to share this thought with the guys in the tent that night and walked back to the sledge.

## Polar Bear Pass. Or Piss

There was no regularity to our days, but, freed from the confines of the clock, there was still a kind of rhythm. We travelled for as long as the dogs could pull. We strained up hills and dragged through endless patches of clinging snow. I ran and ran and ran, my boots never achieving the metronomic beat of running on a harder, more stable surface because the snow itself grabbed at them and broke their rhythm. But the process of running for a spell, riding briefly on the sledge when I could, and then running again was, in itself, a kind of rhythm. We stopped for short breaks to eat handfuls of dried fruit and nuts and to drink cold tea from our flasks. We set up shots of the sledge, Flash and Darren always going ahead on their snowmobile, establishing the shot, filming us pass and then catching up again on the powered machine. This way, we never interrupted the progress of the sledge and we kept the race honest and realistic. We managed brief updates with the other team over the satellite phone we carried with us.

It was strange to stand on a wooden sledge that could trace its history unchanged for thousands of years and use a device no bigger than my hand that could carry spoken words up into the sky and across the world in an instant. They were doing well in the truck. It worked better out here than anyone had predicted. We were going to struggle, we knew that now. The truck could run for twenty-four hours without a break. It didn't need to sleep, it didn't need to rest. They were battling through tough terrain, fighting to clear the ridges of ice that rose up from the frozen sea, but they were still moving. Matty pushed the dogs as hard as she dared, but we were at their mercy. They pulled and worked their hearts out, as only a sledge dog can. But they could only ever achieve the possible.

On yet another brief camp, we set up in a field of small hills and broken ice on the first slopes of Bathurst Island. With the tents pitched, we gathered together to take in the view. It was beautiful. The sky had cleared a little and shone now, a pale, watery blue. The ice hills around us clustered and gathered, their sharp peaks and ragged outlines breaking up the tedium of the flat, featureless plains we had been crossing. We would eat soon and then sleep for a few hours before setting off again. This was Polar Bear Pass we were moving through now and we didn't want to take our time here. And then we saw a bear. The shout went up. Flash saw it first and, typically, ran for his camera. We strained our eyes in the direction he had pointed. And we saw the bear. It was, as we had been told, huge. And it was yellow, not white. The shaggy coat was not the pristine, icy white of the cartoons; it was a more natural, earthy tone. It passed across in front of us a couple of hundred metres away in a rolling walk, its thick, furry body and limbs hanging from its shoulders like a rug thrown over two chairs. And behind it was another, smaller bear. Its cub. Gaz had pulled the gun from where it was kept, strapped to the sledge. The bears carried on their way; they walked across in front of us, covering the distance in a surprisingly short time. There was a heavy silence around us now. I felt suddenly aware that we were in a place that had its own order, its own rules and its own way of working. We were outsiders to it, invaders, and we didn't know our place. Right now, though, seeing the confidence in the bears, the measured, calm pace, I knew for sure that our place was not at the top. The mother bear lifted her head to look across at us and swung back to her walk, unperturbed. If she was curious, she hid the fact.

'They've been hunting us for a couple of days.' Gaz held the gun casually, gripped in one hand by the stock with the barrels rested in the crook of his other arm.

'They're beautiful.' I almost whispered it.

'Better keep them away, though. We need sleep tonight. Make some noise.'

And we did. We clashed pans, shouted and screamed as we had been taught. Gaz had a better idea. He leaped on a snowmobile. Doc had clearly thought the same; he leaped on another and beckoned to me to get on.

'Come on, we'll scare 'em off.'

We took off in a snarl of two-stroke engines and paraded around a circuit of our campsite. This was the first time I had been on a snowmobile and I gripped Doc's bulky waterproof jacket as he swung us around small boulders and patches of soft snow. He yelled back through the tearing wind: 'More like it! Nice to get a bit of speed on for once.' I saw his narrow face grinning tautly beneath his goggles and mask as he turned back to the front.

We stopped. The bears were gone, we were sure. My conviction came, perhaps more from desire for it to be so, but Gaz and Doc, as they surveyed the landscape from the low hill we had stopped on, drew on rather more extensive reservoirs of experience and knowledge to come to the same conclusion.

'They won't have liked that. Should leave us in peace now.' Gaz still carried the gun, swung now from one hand as he paced the hollow top of our hill, fringed by craggy pinnacles of ice a few feet high.

'Lads, gotta take a leak. Sorry.' I climbed off the back seat of the snowmobile and walked quickly to a pile of ice to one side of our small hilltop. As I walked, I saw bones and teeth like the ones I had seen earlier at the smashed agloo.

'These seal bones?' I shouted back over my shoulder as I released a torrent into the snow.

'Yes. This is a killing site. Definitely.' Doc had picked up a jawbone and turned it in his hand slowly. I decided to get a move on and tried to hasten the flow. Having stuck to, even exceeded, my recommended daily water intake, I could do little to speed things up now. I tried to relax, rolling my neck and letting my head rest back, looking up into the cold, white sky. I felt a dull thud between my shoulder blades. And another. And then another, lower down, near my legs. I turned to see Doc, his right arm flashing down to his side, as he turned to Gaz who was crouching on the ice, picking something up. He stood and threw it at me, a black lump the size of a cricket ball and laughed with Doc as it punched into my side.

'Bullseye!'

I looked down at the floor, where the missile had landed.

'Is that . . .?'

'Polar bear shit? Yes. There's loads of it.'

I smiled contentedly. And I stood in a corner of a hollowed-out hilltop used recently by polar bears to kill their prey and I finished my pee while a practising doctor and an ex-member of the special forces threw frozen polar bear shit at me and laughed themselves senseless. It was, without any doubt, the best piss I had ever taken or will ever take.

*Diary of a Brave Polar Explorer*
***Don't know what day it is any more – we've given up using them***
*We're in Polar Bear Pass. It's frightening. I had a piss today in a polar bear's dining room while Gaz and Doc lobbed polar bear shit at me. Very cool indeed. But now we've come to a really weird place. It's some sort of polar bear research station. There's an old building, all boarded up. But Matty had, apparently, arranged permission for us to use it, so we opened the boards and got in. It's bloody strange. The snow was piled up almost to the roof in places; we had to dig to get to the windows. Most of it is all frozen up inside. There are three small rooms, one of them has an old bed in, one of them a small desk and a filing cabinet and the other is a sort of viewing room with broad windows looking out over Polar Bear Pass. They were doing some kind of work here surveying the migrating bears, I guess. There are shelves of tinned food and provisions from years ago. Flash opened a tin of something or other and actually ate it. The pillock. But it's a chance to dry all our kit out and get straight. I'm sitting in an actual chair to write this. We're all playing cards and messing about round the big table in the middle of the room. We're going to stay here for a few hours, get some kip and then move on. Actually, I can't wait to go. This place is weird, it's giving me the creeps. It's like something out of a* Jurassic Park *movie set in the Ice Age.*

And it was. We knew it would be there when we came upon it. Matty had told us about it. We saw the low building from miles away, standing on top of one of the moody hills forming the edges of Polar Bear Pass. The broad valley swept past it but we left the valley floor at an angle and fought our way up towards it. The weather had changed again and we made our way through a steady fall of dense snow. Eventually, we arrived at the compound. Though it was, at first, barely possible to tell there was anything more to the place than a single, very lonely building hardly visible above the snow. Slowly, we made out the features that marked the place as some sort of scientific establishment not visited in a long, long time. Aerial masts leaned out of hunkered boxes half buried in snow. Piles of barrels and coils of wire were arranged in lines behind the building, covered with snow and ice.

We drew the snowmobiles together in a group and Matty and I unharnessed the dogs and made their line fast to an old oil drum filled with concrete that stood to one side of the building and had probably been put there, Matty told me, for this exact purpose. We scraped and dug at the doorway to clear it of snow. The door itself was obscured behind a metal panel put there, I guessed, for security. Though who would be passing this spot and likely to ransack the place, I couldn't imagine. Your average hoodie is unlikely to venture this far north. Their hatchback would have got stuck long back. Matty had some sort of metal key, though, given to her when she had gained permission to use the hut as temporary shelter if we needed it in an emergency. It wasn't an emergency, but sheer curiosity meant we had to check it out. And the possibility of spending an hour or two inside a real building with hard walls and a roof was too tempting to ignore.

The panel was moved and we opened the door. I kicked the snow off my boots and walked into a bare hallway and on into the hut's main room. It had a basic, functional table in the centre of it and workbenches running around the edges, under the wide windows. Little light came in through them, though; they were almost entirely covered with drifting snow. The walls were lined with wooden shelves. The place smelled of disuse. In one corner we found a heater of some sort and quickly set to packing it with whatever we could spare that would burn. We would be warm, for the first time in days.

The others' footsteps echoed hollow on the wooden floors. They fought their way out of heavy coats and hung them around the walls where they could find hooks, until the place was a riot of colour and textures. I studied the shelves and picked up some of the tins of food, turning them over in my hands. Coming so suddenly to a place where other people had been, that contained all the familiar signs of human life and activity in the middle of such a vast wilderness where seemingly everything, including the very ground itself, wanted to kill us, was unnerving. Finding things that we recognised and were comfortable with threw into heightened relief the strangeness of the place we were travelling through. Coming across these small, everyday human concerns all around us felt like finding a newspaper on the moon, and a strange melancholy descended.

As Doc and Gaz hunched by the woodburner with their treasure trove of splinters of wood and strips of cardboard, I set off with Flash and Darren to see if we could make any useful film from the place. We walked around the outside of the building. The wind and snow had died down again, the sky cleared to a thin, milky layer of constant cloud and, through it, a tinge of pink grew as the sun slipped down towards the lowest point in the sky it would be prepared to go before beginning once again its twelve-hour climb back to the top. It must have been about midnight then, though it could equally have been three in the afternoon for all my tired body knew of it. Flash shouted out when he found a ladder running up to the low roof and I shinned up it, my heavy boots slipping as they broke through the crust of snow on the treads to the ice underneath. The ladder led to a flat section let into the roof like an inverted dormer window. I lowered myself on to it and sat on the snow, looking out past the eaves to the broad valley beyond and watched the pink tinge in the sky grow and spread. The sun would be on the turn soon. Flash busied himself below, searching out static shots to give a flavour of the place.

'Flash,' I leaned towards the edge of the roof and shouted down to him. 'You know in *Jurassic Park*, where it all goes wrong and they hide from the Velociraptors in that scientific building thing?'

'Yeah,' he shouted back up. I strained my neck to look over the edge and could see him, hunched over his camera filming a snow-covered pile of oil drums.

'And then they get surrounded by dinosaurs and it all gets a whole lot worse for them.'

'Yeah.'

'Well,' I looked around at the hillside and to the valley beyond, 'I can't help thinking that this is a bit like that. We're in the middle of Polar Bear Pass, hiding from polar bears and, well, I get the feeling we're being surrounded.'

Flash laughed and carried on filming. I looked out for the yellowed, shaggy shape of bears circling us, all waiting for one to shout suppertime.

Later, we gathered around the table and, for the first time, hung out together and relaxed. The heater had taken the edge off the freezing air, and we could sit in our chairs without our heavy down jackets, although we still wore an interesting selection of hats, neck warmers and liner gloves. Flash decided that he had to try some of the tinned food ranked around us on the shelves. He was sick of eating dried stuff and wanted to taste something else. We protested, but it was no use. He pulled down a tin of curry-flavoured tuna, opened it and ate the contents with a teaspoon he found lying in a low wooden tray under the window. I checked the date on the tin later; it was 1984. They're a specialised breed, sailors.

Later still, maybe an hour or so, I went outside again for a walk. There was something endlessly fascinating about the place. Who had worked here? What had they done? Did they have families at home and did they miss them for the long months they spent out here, doing whatever it was they were here to do? As I walked around the building, I looked up and saw another, smaller structure standing in a bank of snow a few hundred yards away on the edge of the hill. And my heart nearly stopped. The shape of it was familiar; it chimed with something deep in my human heart. It was narrow, maybe only a metre wide, but tall; taller than a man standing. There was a single door to one side, the side facing away from me. The snow had heaped itself halfway up the other side of it and the little building seemed to lean away from it, as if struggling with the effort of standing up. The pink tinge splashed itself across the sky behind it and the hills rolled away into the distance for a thousand miles. It could only be one thing. And I had to run back and tell the team. Immediately.

'Bloody hell, guys.' I slammed through the door, not bothering to stop and shake the snow off my jacket before I crashed into the room, breathless and elated.

'There's a bog here. I've found it. Out there.' I pointed to the broad windows spanning the front of the hut. 'It's beautiful. I want to see if it's real. Give me the gun. And the bog roll. If I'm not back in half an hour, tell my family I died a happy man.'

And it *was* a lavatory. Of sorts. A basic wooden outhouse of the kind you might see gracing an allotment. To my eyes, though, it was more magnificent than a cathedral, more gracious and stately than Blenheim Palace. I would have swapped the Taj Mahal, the Eiffel Tower and the Sydney Opera House for this building any day of the week. The plumbing was rudimentary – there wasn't any. It was a sort of Arctic Glastonbury affair. But it worked. There was a seat and there was privacy. And I didn't care how many polar bears were dancing around outside sharpening their teeth and arguing over who wanted leg and who wanted breast; they could bloody well wait until I was out.

## Forty Minutes Straight

We left the research building after a few hours, our hearts lifted by the opportunity we had enjoyed to reorder our rucksacks and dry out our sleeping bags. But the slight melancholy that had descended when we arrived there was replaced by another, stronger sense of being very far indeed from home as we left it behind and set our faces once more into the freezing wind. There were more adventures to come. We got split up, we found one another, we saw more bears, we got lost, we found our way again and we got very, very cold. Matty and I were forced to take a short cut over a sheer drop falling away some ten metres or so into a narrow valley. With words of encouragement and comfort, Matty left me at the top with the dogs tied up and the sledge standing behind and threw herself over the edge to slide down the icy drop, coming to rest where it curved more gently to the bottom of the valley. Once there, she looked up to me above her and gave the signal for me to release the dogs from their tether. They cannoned over the edge, desperate to get to their leader. Then, following the instructions given by Matty before her sliding departure, I pushed the sledge over after them. And then threw myself down to complete the reunion at the bottom.

On some days we travelled under pale blue skies of a frosty intensity that rivalled those over the Mediterranean for brightness if not depth of colour. On others, we trudged under a solemn, brooding panel of uniform white that let through almost nothing of the constant sun. We camped by fields of broken ice boulders where polar bears hunted seal pups and we watched as they ignored the arrival and departure of these noisy strangers for the harmless, pointless creatures we were to them. We made short stops, standing huddled in the wind, making plans, changing them and then changing them again. We practised our shotgun routine late at night when we feared we were again being hunted. We monitored the progress of the truck as it and its drivers made their way across the frozen sea towards the magnetic North Pole. And we lost the race.

The news came as we burst out of yet another stretch of broken ice boulders lying in a chaotic mass, now behind us. Jeremy could not keep the joy out of his voice as he told me that he and his team were standing at the finish point. Their satellite navigation system had confirmed it. They were record holders. They had struggled through and done something no one else had ever achieved and were, justifiably, proud and pleased. I was struggling to compete against them using a form of transport that had evolved in this very place over millennia. I looked at the dogs, their heads up as they glanced round at me talking into the box in my hand. I wondered if they might resent me for letting them down, for failing to help them win a game that was played, after all, very much on their home ground. Bartlett smiled a doggy smile, his gingery fur thick on his broad head and his amber eyes following me for the slightest signal that we could move on again. And I guessed that, no, even if they were capable of such an emotion, they would not have felt it. They had pulled their best and would carry on for days, weeks, if we asked them. But we could not match the truck in its ability to plod on for hour after unbroken hour.

A plane would land on skis on the ice at the magnetic North Pole that evening and collect the truck team. Then it would land and collect us. And then we would begin the long journey back into civilisation, to a place where finding a tin of tuna on a plain wooden shelf doesn't leave you in a mournful state of melancholy deep enough to sink a ship. To a place where remembering your coat is a matter of comfort and not life and death. And to my own dogs at home, who would never display the bravery, dedication and endurance of the dogs in front of me now, but whose loyalty and willingness were equally strong, if expressed in rather more comfortable circumstances. And I would go home to my wife and daughters, the women who together make up the reason for my life, wherever it takes me.

We made our final halt. The plane would be with us in three hours, dropping in to collect the other team before flying over to us. We erected the Prospector Tent quickly as a basic shelter and made plans for what we must do. Before the plane could land, we had to prepare a landing strip. This was another skill we had been taught in Resolute and, although heavy hearted at losing the race, we were strangely elated at the chance to build our own airstrip. It's a simple enough task in concept, but a tough one to carry out in practice. First, we found a site, a long run on the flat ice free of drops and dips. We paced its length, checking for hidden holes or patches of thin ice. We unfurled a stock of black bin bags kept on the sledge specifically for the purpose of runway building. We used shovels and gloved hands to fill them with snow and formed a human chain to carry the filled sacks out onto the ice and place them in two long lines either side of where the runway would be. They lay like inverted landing lights, their shining black surface making them clearer than the brightest of beams against the snow and ice.

Using the three snowmobiles as graders and steamrollers, we made runs up and down the stretch of ice and snow between the bin bag landing lights to prepare the surface for the plane. They would be here in less than an hour now and, with our work on the runway finished, we retired to the Prospector Tent to drink cold coffee from our flasks and tried to stay warm. The call came soon after. The satellite phone's shrill alarm sounding louder and more artificial than any phone had ever sounded to me before. The voice told me that there had been a problem. The plane had landed at the magnetic North Pole and loaded up the truck team. But in landing it had broken one of its skis. It could now only land on its wheels. Which meant back at the airport in Resolute and not here on the snow, where its wheels would be useless. And that meant it would not be coming for us tonight. We would be staying on the ice until they could land back at Resolute, fix the plane and make the return flight for us. There were no other planes available for the trip. And they didn't know if they would need spare parts to repair the ski and, if so, how long they would take to get hold of.

I was told later that I managed to swear constantly and without repetition for forty minutes. While I suspect exaggeration on the part of those forced to sit and listen to my heartfelt outpouring, I am nevertheless proud to have found ways to express disappointment and frustration never before thought of or considered. We settled into the tent, accepting our fate with, perhaps, rather less bravery and equanimity than Scott and his team accepted theirs as they faced certain death on the ice nearly a hundred years ago. But, all the same, we made the best of it. We unloaded more kit and made the tent as comfortable as we could. We fired up the stove and left it running in the corner, unheedful now of the waste of precious fuel in keeping our home as cosy as we could. Doc produced a half-bottle of vodka he claimed to have kept hidden in his medical case for just such an emergency and we passed it round happily, enjoying perhaps more than at any other time in our lives the fiery warmth of its descent. With the pressure off, a lighter mood permeated our crew and we gathered in the tent as we would in a local pub, helped along by the fast-dwindling stash of emergency medical vodka.

Looking around, we were as ragtag a bunch as might be expected after our ordeal. We had not shaved, of course, and our beards varied from manly and bushy coverings worthy of a bear to my own, sad, wispy affair. A beard-shaving competition was declared. We must arrive back in civilisation in style and with a dash of manly, explorer's panache. A variety of shaving implements were produced from rucksacks and bags. We laid them out. No one had brought shaving foam. We had not anticipated a need for it. But we found that by holding your head over the steam from the now constantly boiling pot of water on the overworked stove, or even holding the shaver's head over the pot for him if he was unwilling to subject his chin to the onslaught of scalding steam, you could soften the beard at least to the extent that screams could be stifled and tears withheld as we scraped away whatever growth we had been able to muster over the days we had been away.

I lost, naturally. Though I thought my Shakespearean moustache and dangerous, narrow beard rather the part, Flash won, a magnificent set of sideburns complete with massive handlebar moustache clinching the deal. More time passed. We invented games. Darren produced the speaker he had brought so that he could listen to his iPod without headphones – it's the sort of thing sound recordists carry with them in case of what they would doubtless consider an emergency. Several of us had iPods: they had done sterling work keeping us sane through the long hours spent trudging or skiing across the icy landscape or hanging on for dear life to the back of a wildly leaping snowmobile until the next film stop. We invented iPod roulette. It's simple. Those playing must each bring their iPod to the game. A random letter is announced by an independent figure who has no iPod, and then a number. All players must then dial into their machine the relevant letter and assign to the play menu the track beginning with that letter that also corresponds to the number declared. If it's 'E' '7', then you play the seventh track beginning with E. It's bloody revealing.

There can be no cheating. If it's suspected, the other players must immediately leap upon the possible transgressor and begin punching him hard, all over, in anticipation of finding him guilty of foul play. Meanwhile, a single player forcibly removes the iPod from the cheat's wildly flailing arms and checks that the facts correspond with the punishment to which he is already being subjected. The point of the game is to throw up the most embarrassing, humiliating tracks possible, giving the other players the chance to laugh at, mock and abuse the player thus exposed for life. My advice is to insist on playing the game by using the letter at the start of the artist's name rather than the track. With that agreement in place, simply fire in the letter 'A' and watch how many big, tough blokes turn out to have an Abba track or two squirrelled away in what they thought was a private corner of their iPod collection.

The game kept us busy for another few hours. The plane would not arrive for many more. The vodka was gone, our iPod speaker batteries expired and our beards were trimmed and barbered to a magnificent degree. Solemnly, quietly, we bid each other goodnight and, for the last time, bedded down in our sleeping bags to pass the night sleeping on top of limitless depths of ice and frozen sea.

The arrival of the plane was a magnificent, heart-soaring moment. Its red and white fuselage touched down gracefully on skis that seemed pleased to kiss the surface of our carefully groomed landing strip. We greeted the pilots, threw in our kit and made ready to leave. The dogs would travel back the way they had come. Matty and Sarah would take them. To her, the entire exercise had been a pleasant stroll or a short drive in the country. We said our goodbyes, to them, the dogs and the desperate, cruel, beautiful place they called home. We took off in near silence, each alone with our thoughts in the cramped and crowded aeroplane as it banked and flew back across the terrain we had battled to cross as if it were in another dimension entirely. It left its mark on each of us; the place does. We had suffered and learned. We yearned now for home. I looked out of my small window as the ice boulders and jagged edges that had dominated our lives grew small and blurred into one smooth, white blanket. I waved goodbye, physically waving a gloved hand at the place that had terrified, elated and hurt me. I will go back. Just knowing it's there isn't enough. You have to go back and check it for yourself.

# Chapter 4

# YOU DON'T NEED A LAND ROVER IN SURREY

## Botswana

*Meeting Oliver*

The first time I met Oliver I knew two things immediately and with absolute certainty. The first was that this little yellow 1963 Opel Kadett was the car in which I would drive across Botswana. And the second, that his name was, indeed, Oliver. It wasn't sign-written down his rust-speckled yellow flanks or anything, and he wasn't sold to me by a little old man in a magical car shop who told me: 'Take good care of Oliver, for he is a special car,' as he might have done in a Disney film. I just knew Oliver was his name because, well, because he was Oliver.

I'm not actually in the habit of naming cars. Mindy is. And not just cars; she names motorbikes, bicycles, kitchen knives, hats — anything. But only those things she feels are deserving of names. They have to be 'special'. They have to move her, convince her to honour them with a name. It's not immediately apparent to less gifted 'name diviners' which vehicles will be worthy of the honour. It's certainly not based on material value. Our current crop of cars at home includes four Land Rovers: Buster, Lollipop, Molly and Gertie. They are all old, unreliable and leaky. And they have all been given names. But my Porsche, Morgan, Ferrari and vintage Mustang, though all fully functioning, desirable and valuable, have yet to be blessed with a name. It does indeed take some very specific qualities to move Mindy to bestow a name on a vehicle and, judging from those she has chosen from among our current collection, being a bit crap but strangely charming is chief among those qualities.

One of the great disadvantages of naming cars, quite apart from the shame when you refer to them by that name in front of your colleagues on the world's largest and least forgiving car show, is that it makes it a lot harder when the time comes to 'move them on'. You see, even now, this soppy anthropomorphism has forced me to resort to a euphemism for the simple and necessary business of flogging a car because it's old, knackered and costing a fortune to keep going. After a slight miscalculation involving Her Majesty's Tax Inspectors some years ago, I found myself obliged to look around for ways to raise a few quid rather quickly. We were, in short, bollocksed and about to hit the financial wall pretty hard if I didn't come up with the dosh to fill the hole we had accidentally left gaping in our tax funds.

My gaze, having alighted first upon and then discounted the idea of selling the dogs, any part of my anatomy, the house or the children, fell finally upon the car. At that time, our sole car and our family transport was an elderly blue and white Land Rover station wagon that leaked water in through the sunroof so that it was festooned with stinking green mould like Gollum's cave and let oil out from the bottom of the engine so that, wherever we left it, we returned to find it slumped in a black puddle of the stuff like an incontinent old dog. But it was called WallyCar. My eldest daughter had given him the name when she was three. It had stuck. And it made it slightly tricky when I had to announce to the family that, 'ahem, now listen girls, sometimes we have to think about who and what comes first and, well, money's a bit tight right now, we'll be okay, don't worry, but, erm, WallyCar has to go away.' From the tears, screams, stamps and tantrums, I might have just sold them all into slavery to pay for my drugs habit. It would have gone down better if I had.

As I drove WallyCar off to the dealer to be sold, my departure was accompanied by a trio of crying women draped on the front gate and howling after me like I was carrying off their long-lost brother to sell him for meat. My advice is, if you think you may have to sell it, whatever it is, then for God's sake don't name it. WallyCar's name is still spoken in hushed and reverent tones in our house, as one might speak of great ancestors long passed on. Along with him, the girls whisper of Rufus – a broken old Porsche who smelled worse than WallyCar; Cornflake – an ancient Honda motorcycle with the exhaust held on by a roof guttering bracket; and Boris – a huge BMW motorbike, uglier than a swamp donkey and heavier than the sun. One mention of LaBamba – old Fiat convertible that cost more to run than the Kennedy Space Center and worked only three times out of a hundred – is enough to reduce Mindy to a pile of wistful jelly with a pair of mooning, upturned eyes on top.

Nevertheless, even I, as an insensitive, shallow male, was immediately aware that Oliver was Oliver. And I knew, too, that he was coming with me. I didn't meet him in the flesh first time. We were in the process of researching and setting up yet another overambitious *Top Gear* feature in which the three of us would attempt to drive across what Jeremy dubbed, rather romantically, 'the Spine of Africa': Botswana. We were trying to prove to the people of Surrey that just because you've moved out from London and there is, from time to time, a leaf on the road outside your suburban house, you don't really need a massive 4x4 with the off-road capability of a lunar buggy and the engine power of a naval frigate to cope with transporting your kids two miles to school. We were, therefore, going to attempt this thousand-kilometre journey in two-wheel-drive cars. We could make our selection only from cars bought in or near Botswana and we had, as always, a budget strictly limited to just less than we needed.

In the course of, unusually enough, trying to get ahead of the game and do a little pre-preparation, we had jumped into the internet and splashed about to see if we could find information on the kind of cars we might find up for sale second-hand in Botswana when we got there. And, bugger me, one of the research team came up with the website of the African branch of *Auto Trader*. I vacillated between joy at the opening up of this simple route to second-hand-car happiness in Africa and absolute disillusionment as the mystery and magic of the trip were shattered by the realisation that it would begin by leafing through the same magazine I spent my teenage lunch breaks flicking through in a chicken factory just outside Ripon, dreaming of having enough money actually to buy anything. *Auto Trader*, for God's sake: it was like finding the jungle temples of the Inca had a McDonald's outlet.

But it did make it a lot easier to be sure we wouldn't arrive in Botswana complete with film crews and big boxes of tapes, only to discover that we could no more find a suitable car within budget than we could rely on buying a mountain bike in Manchester that wasn't stolen. There were fleets of old Land Rovers for sale and I drooled over an especially tasty dark green Series III station wagon with a safari roof and an extra spare wheel on the bonnet. But four-wheel-drive cars were not allowed. If this trip was to have any meaning, any scope for entertainment and any chance of making what is actually a pretty valid point, we had to stick to ordinary two-wheel-drive cars. And they don't come much more ordinary than Oliver. I still have his photograph from *Auto Trader*. One look at the four-square, tiny-wheeled, slab-sided little cartoon saloon car and I decided that this wasn't just an indication of the kind of car we might find to do the job, it was the actual one I was going to use. And so it was.

In Botswana, at a busy marketplace in a strange town by a major road, we arrived at the rendezvous point one by one and introduced our purchases. James had bought a huge Mercedes on the grounds that that is what people used out there, given the chance, and in the unlikely event that it broke down it could be fixed locally by engineers familiar with the car, drawing on a readily available stock of parts if necessary. And he was probably right. Jeremy had bought a Lancia Beta. Because he is, sometimes, bonkers. I arrived in Oliver and the other two laughed. A lot. They laughed a lot more when his name accidentally slipped out in front of them. We set off and, as you may have seen on TV, it was an astonishing trip. It made for a great piece of telly and, in the process of creating a half-decent piece of entertainment, we also made our point concerning how unnecessary most 4x4s really are for their suburban owners. But the business of making this bit of telly was an especially involved one.

We would stay every night in tents. We would eat together as a group round a campfire. We would be issued with canvas water buckets for shaving and washing. There would be opportunities to shower at two pre-arranged stops on the way. We would follow the route agreed with our guides and environmental monitors.

'Christ on a bike, we'll smell like a bunch of lepers after that lot. Two showers, in how long?'

The briefing was going with its usual professional smoothness as we gathered around the convoy of safari trucks and, of course, the second-hand cars of James, Jeremy and myself that would make the trip.

'It'll take about four years I should think, Flash. Maybe five.' The crew were lounging about, slumped on the wings of the safari trucks and leaning on their mountains of filming kit, all wearing khaki or green clobber of the styles and types they variously thought suited to the climate, terrain and task. We looked like the set of *Raiders of the Lost Ark*. If *Raiders of the Lost Ark* had been styled by ten-year-olds after too much Sunny Delight.

'These tents, how big are they?' Ben, a cameraman and veteran of a thousand filming trips all over the world, asked the question of our guides and guardians.

'Ooh, need room for all your clothes, do you, love?' They never got the chance to answer.

'Well, Hammond'll need room for his hair stuff.' Another voice from behind one of the trucks. Probably a camera assistant.

'Yeah, thank you. Whatever.' I couldn't help being pulled into the bickering.

'No, what I mean is, where do we keep the kit?'

'And those generators for charging the batteries, how much fuel we got?'

'I bought a cool Leatherman. Look, it's got pliers on it.'

'I've got a head torch, look.'

'Where do we take a shit?'

There were a lot of questions to be answered about a lot of things before we could commit this travelling circus to the road with any hope of being able to work and film across hundreds of miles of salt flats, jungle, desert and savannah. And there was a lot of kit to worry about, too. This was a big shoot. We were expected to return with a complete programme. That would mean shooting tens if not hundreds of hours of footage to get the stuff we needed. It was a mark of the scale of the undertaking that the boss, Andy Wilman, had chosen to leave his desk and editing suites and come with us to marshal the team and make absolutely sure that the budget that he, as the overseer of the programme, was committing to this film shoot resulted in a worthwhile bit of telly.

## Oh God, Vultures

Incredibly, we achieved everything we set out to achieve. We drove across the legendary Makgadikgadi Pan salt flats, crunching over a thin crust of dried-out salt that covered what local myth avows is a bottomless pit of ooze and slime. In fact, the whole area is an ancient dried-up sea. As the water was boiled off by the African sun over the millennia, it released its salt to lie in dazzling white plains on the surface. Underneath it, there lay, and still lies, the original sea bottom. An eternity of fish, algae and plant life rotting quietly into a primeval ooze probably not unlike the one from which our distant ancestors first crawled. Watching us walk about on the salt crust, competing to try and stamp through it and then wiping the green goo all over the back of each other's trousers, you might be forgiven for thinking it wasn't that long since we crawled out of it and lay blinking on the shore.

We had not made an especially impressive arrival at the salt flats. At least, not when compared with the one made by the vice president of Botswana minutes after our ragtag convoy rolled up and stopped on the edge of the seemingly endless plains of glaring white desert. As we stamped around in our new boots, asking our guides if there were tigers out here and listening to each other's skins sizzle and blister under the African sun, a lone voice called out to us to look up. We did. And in the distance, way back over the desert, we saw a cluster of tiny dots in the sky, seemingly hovering motionless in the heat haze over the surface.

'What is it, vultures?' The crew, sharp-eyed and observant as always, were quick to give their critical analysis of what this spectacle might mean.

'Oh God, vultures. We're gonna die. And they know it.'

'Shut up. No, look, it's something else. They're people.'

Every eye was on the horizon.

'It's people, flying.'

'Flash, get a hat, mate. Sun's shagging your brain up.'

'No, he's right. Look, they're powered hang-gliders.'

'Microlights, actually. Difference is that the canopy is attached to the frame and not the . . .'

'Yes, thanks, James. Whatever. Thing is, they're people up there and they are flying straight at us.'

And they were. The vice president of Botswana had decided he had better check out this team from the BBC in England who had requested his permission to drive their cars and trucks across his salt flats. He also happens to enjoy a spot of recreational micro-lighting, so I guess it seemed like a good excuse.

I hate microlighting. Why anyone would want to climb aboard a children's playground frame with a blender on the back and a bedspread on the top and spend their afternoon wallying around the sky being overtaken by fat pigeons and old crows is beyond me. The machines are shite, the speed is shite, only the views are good. But then you run the risk of, at any moment, becoming a close and integral part of that scenery when one of the bits of wire holding your stupid machine together goes twang and you paste yourself all over the hillside like a picnic rug. Still, the vice president of Botswana likes it, so bully for him. If you must have a hobby, it's better than collecting things anyway. Or morris dancing.

And, actually, it did make a pretty impressive spectacle. Being a vice president, he doesn't just strap himself into his sky moped alone and throw himself off some dreary cliff edge overlooking a mining town. He flies with a whole team of supporters. It wasn't clear which was the presidential microlight – it wasn't draped in a vice-presidential flag or anything – but then they are quite slow moving, microlights, and they would make a very big target in a part of the world not know for its placid and easy-going attitude to presidents, vice or otherwise But whichever it was, it was surrounded by a flotilla of other microlights – if that's the proper collective noun for a bunch of ninnies in crap mini-aeroplanes. These other microlights bore the vice-presidential friends and minders. Many of them were armed. I was surprised their craft could lift them. Maybe they left the bullets behind to save weight. Probably not.

But better, even than heavily armed airborne friends, he had a ground-based force tracking him across the desert floor. Plumes of dust were kicked up by a pack of howling dirt bikes and quads bearing yet more guards. And these were definitely armed. To the bloody teeth. They looked like something usually seen only in the rear-view mirror of Mad Max's *Pursuit Special*. But the overall scene had a more magnificent, romantic image to it than that. A fleet of tiny aircraft floating gracefully and, at this range, silently across the African sky while below stalked a hellish range of heavily armed guards on dirt bikes and quads, kicking up clouds of desert dust to billow and hang against the reddening horizon. Pretty cool, we all agreed. Not Mad Max. A James Bond movie. That's what approached us across the expanse of the salt flats.

We went into a bit of a gentle panic. Not a full-on, tear your hair out, froth at the mouth and soil your kecks panic – more of a stare around and realise you look like a bunch of sixth formers on a badly organised day out as you are about to be descended on by the airborne vice president of a major African nation kind of panic.

'Wadda we do?'

Good question. We could hardly be expected to know and adhere to the internationally agreed etiquette for greeting an African vice president on a microlight when he drops in on you unexpectedly as you are about to drive a shit car across his precious salt flats for a TV show made several thousand miles away. I straightened my cowboy hat and adjusted the many brightly col-oured beads and bracelets I had bought in a market on the way. James hummed a piece of Bach.

The descent of the airborne half of the vice-presidential arrival was slow and graceful. The roaring, smoke-belching, dust-kicking warriors below timed their arrival on the white salt immediately in front of and around us to coincide with the tiny wheels of the lead microlights touching down just behind our convoy of trucks, cars and huddled figures. And we just sort of stood there, hands in pockets, mouthing the words 'Fuck me, that's cool'. I decided then and there that I wanted to travel everywhere with just such an entourage and would do anything in my power to make it possible. Not managed it yet. But I did once hire a helicopter to arrive for an after-dinner speech I was hosting at a golf club. It scared the crap out of the ducks on their posh lake, blew all the golf balls away and covered the golfers I was there to entertain later in leaves and duck shit.

As the sun blistered the salt flats, we waited to meet the vice president and his followers. They were very polite and welcoming, for a bunch of people who travel like James Bond villains. Jeremy stepped straight into the role of ambassadorial representative of the British media. And, despite this, the encounter remained cordial and enthusiastic. We told them what we were going to do. The vice president laughed and said something to the effect that we would almost certainly die. He was a devilishly handsome man who looked exactly like the vice president of an African country should, right down to the bushy moustache, striking cheekbones, sunglasses and thick, gooey layers of braid adorning his magnificent military hat. He smiled a lot and talked about English public schools, world affairs and his country. He scared the shit out of me because he is important, powerful and strong, and I am not.

What we were about to attempt had never, as it turned out, been done before. We were the first. I'm not sure that the vice president understood entirely why we were going to try and drive across the lifeless, drought-ridden, death-stalked plains of his sun-baked salt flats in cars more suited to tootling around the backstreets of Eastbourne in search of a loaf of bread and a newspaper, but he managed at least to wish us well.

He was, he told us, travelling with many of his friends, confidants and family. Along with the heavily armed guards. We said hello and goodbye to them all, impressed upon them that we were happy and, indeed, privileged to be there and that we hoped they all had a smashing time flying about the place. The vice president repeated his concerns for our survival and wished us well once more, despite the peril he feared awaited us. And then they left. Their departure was as stylish as their first appearance. I waited for death to arrive next to me with a winning smile, cough politely and strip me to a pile of bleached bones on the hungry desert floor.

We had to make some preparations. That's the sort of thing people do when they are about to undertake a terrifying mission. To stand a better chance of making it across without cracking through the salt and sinking into the primeval goo below, to spend all of eternity preserved like one of those peat bog men that turn up in Denmark or wherever, only entombed in an old Mercedes, Lancia or Opel Kadett, we had to lighten our vehicles, giving them a better chance of skipping across the surface. I say 'we', but actually that's not strictly true. James's Mercedes, weighing in at a couple of hundred or so tonnes, had to shed some weight to drive on tarmac, let alone cross a three-inch-thick crust of prehistoric salt. So he cut off the doors, the boot lid and the bonnet, threw out the back seat, most of the windows, the bumpers and the spare wheel.

Jeremy, never one to miss out on a good game when he saw it going on, performed similar surgery on his Lancia. With the help of his favourite tool, in fact the only tool I've ever seen him wield – a hammer – he quickly reduced it to little more than four wheels held apart by a rusting Italian chassis garnished with a steering wheel. I stood next to Oliver with a screwdriver and a hacksaw, listening to the assorted crunches, bangs and grindings as the other two worked on lightening their cars ready for the salt flats. And I couldn't do it. He had survived out here in Africa for more than four decades and I was not about to be the straw that broke this tough old camel's back. So I claimed that he was light enough already and that, actually, given his simplicity and the absence of unnecessary luxuries and features, this had been part of my plan all along. It hadn't been, of course, but then neither had it been part of my plan to form a faintly unnatural bond with a heap of rusting metal, rubber and vinyl to the extent that I was prepared to risk jeopardising our film and even my own neck to preserve him. Sorry, 'it'.

We made it, of course. Despite James's Mercedes breaking through the crust to lie on its fat belly on the salt and paddle fruitlessly with its wheels at the goo underneath like a bear swimming through trifle; and despite Jeremy's Lancia, with the new 'Superleggerra' lightweight racing format he had given it, proving to weigh more than the country of its origin, we got to the other side. On the way, we spent a night by Kubu Island. A genuine island stranded in the midst of a sea turned into a desert by a slow-changing, elemental destruction that had taken millennia to find its form and yet bit into the soul of the visitor with a visceral immediacy that would hold a lion at bay, Kubu Island was a place of such haunted beauty and heartbreaking desolation that it, briefly, silenced even us.

The mound of the island stands proud of the salt flats, as it would have stood proud of the original sea when it was formed. Its gentle curves are broken by low-lying brush and baobab trees. Thousands of years old and tens of feet wide, these trees have stalked my imagination since I studied pictures of them in my *Encyclopaedia of Nature* as a kid. Hungry to experience a childhood fairy tale made real, I touched one, stroking its gnarled, wrinkled skin as I might stroke a living dinosaur. They are blighted on the island, falling prey to a disease that is killing them by the dozen. All around us in the soft, pink light of sunset, lay the shattered carcasses of baobabs that had succumbed to a disease supposedly brought in accidentally by a visiting tourist a decade or so ago. Kicking at a detached chunk of baobab wood lying close to its splintered parental trunk, I was surprised and slightly disappointed to find that it has the weight and consistency of cork. Or of a polystyrene model from a

*Star Trek* film set. I had anticipated a wood more ancient and dense than mahogany or lead.

And all the while, over every mile and through every long hour, Oliver pressed on. He sat on the fringes of the mystical Kubu Island as we wandered among the stricken baobabs. And when I returned to the shore and climbed into the driver's seat for the final stretch of the day to that evening's camp, he lifted my troubled mood with his simplicity and willingness. Sure, it was just a collection of nuts and bolts obeying the immutable laws of physics to turn fossil fuel into forward motion. But he wanted to do it. At least, in my sun-saturated brain he did. Every time I returned to the little yellow car, whatever I had been doing and however much it had pissed me off or dragged me down, Oliver would pull me back up again. It's just a knack he has. He waited patiently while we dug the other cars out of the oozing desert floor and cheered me up when I got back in. Sitting in the driver's seat, hands resting on the narrow-rimmed, white steering wheel, eyes scanning the simple, metal dashboard studded with only enough dials to keep you informed of Oliver's essential needs, a smile just sort of arrives and unfolds on your face.

## Honey Badgers Go for Your Nuts

### Diary of an Intrepid African Traveller and his Faithful Sherpa, Oliver

*We saw baobab trees today. Wanted to see them since I was nine. They're bloody big. And they're all dying on this tiny island in the middle of the salt flats. We camped not far away and James and Jeremy were starting to regret taking the doors off their cars by the time we got there. The dust here is finer than talcum powder and they looked like proper twats by the time they arrived, caked in the stuff until they were a uniform grey with pantomime-dame red lipstick round their mouths where their ever-flapping gobs had washed the dust off their lips. I shat myself laughing. And then ran away.*

*Oliver is doing well. He never broke through the salt crust and he never even threatened to break down. My only complaint is the vinyl seats: who the bloody hell decided that the best material with which to cover the seats in a car bound to spend its life under the baking African sun was vinyl? It heats up until it's hotter than that same African sun and then, when you sit down on it, assuming you are wearing shorts – which you will be, it's Africa and it's quite warm out here – there's a smell like a barbecue and the flesh on the back of your legs and arse is instantly welded to the seat. When you stand up again, you leave a human hide seat cover in the shape of your arse stuck to the seat. Why? Why vinyl? Why not velour, canvas, paper? Bloody anything but vinyl. The rest of the car is perfect.*

*Still not seen a crocodile.*

Later, we would cross a corner of the Kalahari Desert. James and Jeremy's enthusiastic weight-shedding measures came at a cost. And it was a price paid here once more, as storms of dust so fine it ran like water when it collected in the footwell billowed into their doorless cars and threatened to choke, blind and deafen them. I can't say I managed not to be smug, tooling along in Oliver with the doors not only still on, but firmly shut with their windows up and the dust still very much on the outside. The resulting footage of James and Jeremy in their authentic local headgear, but barely visible to the camera a couple of feet away in their own personal dust storms, made for one of the best bits of the film.

We made camp every night, enjoyed eating round the campfire and agreed that we did, indeed, all smell pretty damned bad. And we made some good telly. I did, eventually, see an elephant. In fact, we saw giraffes, hyenas and elephants when we got to the

Okavango Delta. And we saw creatures we really hadn't expected to see. At a watering hole one evening, as the African sun reddened and slipped below the tree-lined horizon and a family of elephants dipped their trunks gratefully into the still water, we saw a tourist with the best comb-over the world has ever, ever witnessed and we pissed ourselves laughing until he turned round and looked quite cross. Not as frightening as the honey badger, though. This critter is one of my favourites in the world and I was, once again, blessed on this trip by getting to see one for real.

It was at the same watering hole as the comb-over made its appearance that I got my first sight, not only of the best hairdo the world has ever known, but of yet another creature from my childhood *Encyclopaedia of Nature.* The honey badger is not, it turns out, so named for its attractive, golden-yellow colouring. Nor is it so called on account of its sweet temperament. It is, in stark contrast to everything the name suggests, a psychopath. The honey badger lives on a diet consisting mostly of – and herein lies the origin of its name – honey. Honey is made by bees. And bees get quite cross if you try and steal their honey – they sort of need it. They don't make it for fun and it really pisses them off when people just mince up to their front door, tear down a wall and steal the home-made provender they were rather hoping to raise their children on. And so the bees get together, form a swarm and sting the living crap out of anyone nicking their honey. They are especially ferocious and dangerous in Africa, because most things are. These African bees make our English ones look like a bunch of poetry book-toting little mincers at a garden party. The African honey badger, on the other hand, couldn't give a shit.

I've seen one swagger up to a hollowed-out log, housing about a million rock-hard bees all jealously guarding their precious hoard of honey, stick its grizzled little snout straight in, emerging from the log with a face full of madly stabbing bees and a gobful of honey, and just stand there, licking it off the end of its nose while

ABOVE Sailing a VW camper-van towards France, as you do.

FOLLOWING PAGES It sinks just outside the harbour wall and James and I are rescued by a gloating Jeremy in his pick-up.

Johnny Vizor and I rescuing Zog and Jill
Ziegler from the Severn floods.

A Very Brave African Explorer scanning the saltpans of Botswana for polar bears.

Oliver. It was love at first sight. And I have him still.

Oliver doing his best to look like a rally car. The locals are distinctly unimpressed, as is a giraffe.

Ollie in the river. Yes, there was a croc nearby, but they didn't tell me until I had been rescued.

the bees went mental and stung the shit out of everything and everyone for a hundred miles around. And it's not that the honey badger is somehow immune to the stings; it isn't. The badger I saw ended up covered in huge red lumps and bumps like someone in the *Beano* who has had their head shoved into a bees' nest – which of course, the badger actually had. But it just licked its lips slowly, realised it had room for perhaps another little dab of honey, and stuck its head straight back into the log. Probably mouthing 'all bees are nancy boys' as it did so. The bees went absolutely berserk, but he never even flinched. If he had had a napkin and opposing thumbs, he would have dabbed the corners of his mouth politely when he finally finished, belched quietly and said thank you. Well 'ard.

Of course, I didn't see all this for real. Honey badgers are actually quite rare in Cheltenham. I saw it on the TV some years before I made the trip to Botswana. And I read about them in my *Encyclopaedia of Nature*. This, I should say, was my bible. I harboured a strong desire to follow in the mighty footsteps of David Attenborough himself and dreamed of the day I, too, would get to visit orang-utans in the jungle and deliver an intense and knowledgeable commentary as they did orang-utan stuff in front of my TV crew. I made a right bollocks of achieving that particular ambition, obviously. But it was a serious one that started young and stayed with me for many years. I entered a competition when I was eight to win a trip up the Amazon with David Bellamy on a nature expedition. You had to keep a nature diary for a month, detailing the birds, hedgehogs and butterflies that frequented your garden, what they did and why they might be doing it. My mum bought me a set of coloured pencils specially for the task. I was convinced I would win. I loved nature and my best subject was art.

I spent hours drawing pictures of the stupid birds hanging out on the stupid bird table and splashing about in their stupid birdbath – I didn't really like birds, I thought them a bit soft and considered bird watching to be like stamp collecting, only less dynamic. I drew hedgehogs that had no more arrived in my suburban Birmingham garden than a wildebeest might. I sketched in the huge array of feeders, home-made bird boxes, bat boxes and bloody owl boxes that I didn't actually have dangling off every branch and trunk in the garden. I sent my diary off and made plans for what best to wear when exploring the Amazon with a famous wildlife commentator off the telly. And nothing came back. Not a bloody thing. He never even wrote back. The bastard.

But my childhood love of the natural world had forearmed me with a ready enthusiasm when I finally came face to face with the honey badger in the wild. Actually, getting face to face with a honey badger is surprisingly difficult. They are blessed with the unique and, I should imagine, bloody surprising ability, if you've just caught one by the scruff of the neck, of being able to turn around inside their own skin. Grab one by the neck, look it in the eye and you'll quickly find that that's not its eye you're gazing into any more and its turned round in its skin so that it can stick its teeth out of its own arse and bite your nuts off. And they do enjoy a reputation for doing just that: tearing off the gonads of anyone foolish enough to provoke them. It might be some sort of bitter reaction to their diminutive scale compared to many other creatures – and, boy, can I empathise with that one – or it could just be that they've learned over the centuries that jousting with sinister curved horns, snarling, pawing the ground and banging your chest are all well and good if you're a big, impressive animal and want to signal your potency to an enemy, but if you're a small and irritatingly cute-looking thing and want to be taken seriously in the seedier end of the jungle, tearing someone's bollocks off with your teeth does get your message across quickly.

Our honey badger arrived on the scene at the watering hole as we were still sniggering over the tourist with the comb-over – it was brilliant, though; you should have seen it, every black strand separated and scraped across a shining, sunburned dome. Perfect. Those final sniggers ended pretty abruptly, though, when someone hissed that they had seen a honey badger. We had sat by enough campfires with our guides and environmental minders over the past few days to have heard all we needed to hear of the honey badger's preference for gnawing on the gentleman's area. With our legs crossed and hands thrust protectively into our groins, we scanned the dusty path around the edges of the watering hole for this terror in an ill-fitting badger suit. The elephants were still there, about ten of them standing around, drinking noisily and farting occasionally to uproarious applause from the crew. The crew kept quiet now, though: the honey badger had swaggered into sight. And it was magnificent.

At a foot tall and about three feet long, you might think 'magnificent' is not the best word to describe it. Yes, it was overshadowed by the willowy grass stems waving by the side of the red-dust path. Yes, it could look, from some angles, like a small, yellowish dog with no tail and quite a cute face. But, nevertheless, it is the right word: magnificent. It strolled up to the edge of the watering hole oozing enough attitude to fell a block of New York ganglanders. If it had been wearing jeans, the waistband would have grazed the floor. This was one creature that was absolutely not scared of anything. Had an entire pride of lions jumped on to the path in front of it, I don't doubt that it would have slowed to a halt, spat on the ground and invited them to make the first move or find another watering hole. It hip-swung past the elephants, not even bothering to look up at them. And the elephants watched its every move.

Our guide had told us of having sat by just such a watering hole and watched as a honey badger arrived and started having a go at a massive bull elephant – maybe it had spilled his pint or looked at his bird or something. Apparently unprovoked, the badger snarled at the elephant and ran at it, sinking its teeth into a massive grey leg. The elephant shook it off. And the badger ran back and did the same again. The elephant shook it off again and clobbered it with his trunk. It ran back again and sank its teeth back in. The elephant reached down, grabbed the badger and rolled it up in its trunk before it had time to turn round in its own skin. Then it threw it clear across the watering hole so that it landed in the bushes. The bushes shook, there was a lot of snarling, then silence and then the badger shot out of the water and bit the elephant on the leg again.

And I could believe this tale now, watching the honey badger walk among the elephants, rolling its compact shoulders and swinging its little head from side to side. It probably didn't even need to walk past the watering hole but just liked making elephants nervous for fun. I want to be a honey badger when I come back.

## Mending Oliver

As we neared the end of this epic trip, the miles and the terrain did start to take their toll on little Oliver. The fine dust would work its way into nooks and crannies, creating seemingly unsolvable problems. During a particularly arduous stretch of unmade dirt track through the Okavango Delta, his steering stopped working. The super-fine grade dust had worked its way into the steering rack and gummed it all up. The problem had begun manifesting itself earlier in the morning, but as the day wore on had worsened considerably. Towards the end of the day, our convoy had to make up time. We were behind schedule – having spent too long at the waterhole admiring the honey badger/comb-over combo – and needed to cover some distance before setting up camp. We would drive into the night. We buddied up to keep our spirits high. And I welcomed Jonathan Thursby into Oliver's cramped little cabin with joy and relief. Jonathan owns and runs the company that provides and operates most of the specialised mini-cameras we use to film cars, boats and whatever else we can throw at him and his team. To be quite honest, he doesn't really need to be out in the field, having more than enough to keep him busy at his desk running his company. But he can't resist an interesting trip and is always happy to sneak away from the office and leave his staff to keep things running while he gets his hands dirty with us lot doing something daft. I was glad to welcome him into my car for the night leg of the journey for two reasons; firstly, he is excellent company and we would pass the next few hours in amiable chat and laughter, secondly, he can fix pretty much anything and would, I knew, be handy if and when Oliver had a bit of a moment.

I had explained to Jonathan that, for reasons I had not at that point worked out, Oliver's steering was getting tough. He sussed the problem from the passenger's seat immediately, guessing correctly that the dust had been drawn into the steering rack as it turned from one side to another and had built up to the point where it was restricting movement through the rack itself.

'Gaiters are probably shagged. That'll let the dust in.'

He was right, they were. At a brief stop, I glanced underneath and saw in the light of my head torch that the rubber gaiters supposedly there to keep dust and grit out of the ends of the rack had dried out and disintegrated. No time to fix the problem now, though; the convoy was moving on through the night.

'Why don't you have a go? It's great fun driving on this loose stuff. You'll love it. Just watch the steering, though; not good.'

Jonathan's company has its roots in motor sport: he and his team developed the cameras used for many years and even today in the world rally championship. So he is no stranger to driving on loose surfaces at night. In fact, he's a pretty talented pedaller and I was more than happy to hand over the helm of my beloved Oliver to a guy who would almost certainly make a better job of driving him through the pitch-black African night than ever I would.

We set off with a gentle spin of Oliver's tiny little rear wheels in the soft dust. We floated over the surface, banked left and then hit a tree.

'Shit, there's no steering. None.'

He had gone to feed in the required degrees of turn through the steering wheel to avoid the tree and found it resolutely jammed at the straight ahead as firmly as if it had just hit full lock.

'Yep. Well, I did warn you. Been steering with the throttle and rear wheels for the last four hours.'

We dragged the car back off the tree, piled back in and set off again, laughing and wincing at every approaching tree.

And then the lights went out. In fact, it was me who switched them off on purpose. Oliver's alternator was failing; he couldn't generate enough power to charge the battery. If we ran with the lights on, they drained the battery quickly and, within five minutes or so, we would come to a complete halt and be forced to radio the convoy for a volunteer vehicle to drive over and give us a jump-start. Frankly, I couldn't stand the abuse any more. Jonathan agreed. So we flicked the lights off.

'Holy shit. That's a lot of dark.'

And it was. Very, very dark indeed. With typical resourcefulness, Jonathan produced a massive Maglite torch from his bag on the back seat. He shone it out through the windscreen. I could see ahead, just, and picked my way as fast as I dared along the unmade track. We both had head torches, too, so we flicked these on to add to our improvised headlighting.

We made it to that night's camp and began one of many all-night fixing sessions. Oliver was parked up on top of a tarpaulin spread out over the sand. This was to catch the nuts, bolts, screws and tools that would inevitably be dropped, mostly by me, as we performed whatever surgery we had agreed necessary. I had been worried that Oliver just wasn't producing enough power – a ridiculous concern really in a car that, when new, produced slightly less power than the average desk fan. But all the same, in a car making only forty-four horsepower every one of them tends to count. And I needed all I could get if I was to be able to carry on skimming Oliver over the top of the sand, dust and stony tracks we were running on. Ironically enough, in a car designed very much not for speed, it was speed that had turned out to be the answer to making it across the 'Spine of Africa' for Oliver. Where the other heavyweight, powerful cars would dig in and sink into the surface, forcing James and Jeremy to apply more and more power just to drive the wheels through the grabbing, broken surface, Oliver could happily skip across the top, not sinking in at all. At least he could if I kept my boot down. When we were moving, we weighed next to nothing and barely left tracks even through sand. Slow down and Oliver's lack of power became immediately obvious; he could hardly turn his wheels at all if they sank more than an inch or two into the sand and stones.

And this evening, in our improvised jungle workshop, as well as giving him back some steering I wanted to see if I could squeeze just a tiny bit more out of his skinny little engine. We took off and stripped the carburettor, laying out the barrel, float and jets on the tarpaulin floor and blowing out the accumulated sludge of dust and fuel with a tin of compressed air nicked from the film crew's lens cleaning kit. As one of us squirted the air into the nooks and crannies of the clogged-up carb, the other would cough loudly to mask the giveaway noise from the crew gathered round the campfire in a clearing thirty feet behind us. Though this subterfuge wasn't really necessary as the generator powering our overhead lights grumbled away through the night.

Working with us was Noah, a bush mechanic. A local guy, he could mend anything with anything. It is not unheard of for a bush mechanic to resort to using wood to mend broken suspension parts on a car stranded out in the bush. But then, break down out here and you don't sit by the side of the motorway waiting for an orange van to arrive. You fix it with whatever you can find or you cower in the car waiting for lions to arrive. Noah produced a compact toolkit, folded it out on the edge of the green tarpaulin, slid underneath Oliver's jacked-up front end and busied himself stripping the steering rack of its accumulated dust. Clearly not the first time he had carried out such an operation, he wrenched the wheel from lock to lock, persuading it to travel further each time before diving under the car to beat the hell out of the rack itself with the wooden handle of a wire brush, knocking the dust away.

Meanwhile, Jonathan and I reassembled the freshly cleaned carb and mounted it back up on top of the intake manifold. By now, the crew had retired to their tents to sleep. We had an early start ahead of us and the night driving had tired everyone, even those with headlights on their vehicles. Noah, happy that he had given me back at least enough steering to avoid the trees, said goodnight and padded off through the bush silently to his tent. Jonathan and I had nearly finished, too. For the sake of the sleeping crew, we cut the generator now and worked by the light of our head torches. He busied himself packing away the tools, I listened to the muted clunks and rattles as he slotted away the spanners and screwdrivers one by one to avoid making too much racket. Leaning in under the bonnet, I fastened down the last of the bolts at the base of the carburettor and mounted the air filter back on top. Leaning in further, I slotted a screwdriver in and fastened the jubilee clip securing the filter pan to the mouth of the carb. Jonathan had finished packing up the tools and now sat at the rear of Oliver, sucking up the last of a tin of beer in contented silence. I held the tip of the screwdriver between fingers and thumb as I turned it. It was tight. We would see in the morning if our work had given Oliver more power. I retracted the screwdriver and stood up slowly, stretching my arms behind me and looking up at the stars overhead in the perfect sky. And somewhere in the bush, close by and off to our left, a lion growled and rumbled. Another responded. It wasn't a bird, a frog, a hyena or a hippo. It absolutely and categorically was a lion. They were known to frequent the area we were camping in. Suddenly, out here on the edge of our camp, separated from our guides with their jungle knowledge and, more importantly, their massive hunting rifles, we felt very alone.

'I think we've done enough now.'

'Yup, me too.'

'G'night.'

## Bringing Oliver Home

### Diary of an Intrepid African Traveller and his Faithful Sherpa, Oliver

*We made it across the salt flats. I knew we would. And we made it into the Okavango Delta.*

*Technical situation:*

*Oliver is starting to feel the strain. Thursby stuck him in a tree and I think I might have cracked his sump on a rock — Oliver's that is, not Thursby's. He hasn't got a sump. Mind you, he is from Norfolk so maybe . . .*

*The steering rack is shot to bits, his headlights can't be used, the ignition switch disintegrated into the barrel and I now start him by hotwiring him every time. The boot won't open, one of the headlamp surrounds fell off when he hit a tree, Jeremy put a socking great dent in the back when he rammed us on a wooden bridge and the brakes now work on only one wheel. Cool. We're going well. I think we might make it. Still not seen a crocodile.*

The carb strip-down had not released a tornado of power. Another night, another temporary workshop with generator growling away in a clump of trees and tarpaulin spread out over thick, tussocky grass and I had another go at giving Oliver some extra grunt. If it wasn't that he was getting too much dust, maybe he was just not getting enough air. I whipped the air filter box off and opened it up to have a look. It was an old-fashioned type where the air on the way to the mouth of the carburettor must pass through an oil-soaked metal mesh contained in a cage surrounding the top of the carb in a circle. It was crap. Absolutely full of shite and gunk and this, I was sure, was the explanation for Oliver's lack of oomph. I cut off the metal cage with a grinder, borrowed a circular paper air filter off Noah and glued it in place with silicone sealer – also borrowed off Noah. The lid of the air box wouldn't clip back on over the new filter – it was too tall – so I glued that on with more silicone sealer and fixed it in place with a couple of tie-wraps – borrowed from Noah. Thinking that perhaps it was choking itself in the swirling dust storm under the bonnet, I even fashioned a makeshift snorkel out of a length of vacuum-cleaner pipe – borrowed from Noah – one end taped over the air intake, the other passed through the hole in the bulkhead where the heater would have been, had it been fitted, and lodged in the comparatively dust-free cabin. If the air in there was good enough for me to breathe, then it was good enough for Oliver.

And it worked. After what had turned into a pretty lengthy session in the jungle garage, I awoke feeling less than entirely fresh, but, all the same, sprinted out of the campsite and down to the cars, desperate to see if the effort had been worth it. I tapped the ignition wires together and Oliver fired up. Suddenly, he had a roar. This was not the result of some late-night supercharging effort, but was because the open end of the new snorkel in the cabin sucked in the air with, well, a roar. It sounded good. And Oliver was very happy with it, too – we belted off and he had a definite spring in his step. We covered more miles that day across broad, dusty tracks pitted by holes and craters deep enough to hide

YOU DON'T NEED A LAND ROVER IN SURREY

a lion in. And Oliver charged like a lightweight rhino. And then I drove him into a river. I had been trying to find a better river crossing route than the one proposed by James and Jeremy. We weren't messing about, it was a river we had to cross, to continue on our way through the Okavango Delta. And, as obstacles go, a river is fair enough on an off-road driving challenge such as the one we had undertaken. But the point they had chosen to make the crossing was, quite clearly, crap. I have been a keen off-roader for many years and, aside from all the obvious connotations regarding beards, talking in an adenoidally challenged way and murdering people for fun, I felt that this had prepared me rather better for challenges such as this one than a life spent mincing around in wine bars quaffing something crisp and white and moaning about taxis. So I went my own way. Our team was split.

I waved them goodbye, commended their souls to God, or whatever awaited them when they drowned, and went in search of a better crossing. I didn't take any special kit with me for this mission, just experience and the keen eyes of a seasoned veteran of many a thousand muddy treks across plains, through rivers and over hills. Most of those adventures have been limited to Gloucestershire, admittedly, and usually confined to the rather pleasant, leafy lanes surrounding the civilised Eastnor Castle estate near my home. But, nevertheless, I knew better than the other two and I was damned if I was going to risk ruining Oliver in crossing an African river at a point where it was clear to anyone with an ounce of off-roading knowledge that he would sink and be drowned.

They made it across. They sank up to their axles, Jeremy crashed into James's lumbering Merc, their doorless cabins took in water but they emerged on the other side, damp and triumphant. As I drove the muddy margins of the river, I didn't know this yet. Finally, after trawling the banks in search of that special spot, that sweet place where the slope of the bank is just right on both sides and the water itself, through subtle gradations of colour and surface ripples, betrays itself to be shallow and steady, I found it. And I even found a path. It ran down to the river, tyre marks were clear in the shallow layer of mud. So it had already been used. I looked across the broad expanse of brown water and there, emerging from the other side, was my exit path. This, then, was perfect. It lacked only a sign saying 'ford' and another picturing some ducks to complete a scene from a vintage postcard where a trusty old Austin Fartbanger splashes merrily through the water, scattering waterfowl and spreading little rainbows with its skinny tyres. I would drive through, barely getting Oliver's wheels damp, pop up the slope on the other side and meet the others; or go back to pick them up if they had sunk into the river at their ill-chosen crossing point.

And my route did indeed go very well. The broad path was sturdy under Oliver's tyres. I drove in the tried and tested manner of off-roaders crossing rivers: enough power to make decent headway – no point overtaxing the engine in the mud – and enough speed to push a little tiny bow wave ahead of the wheels if it grew a bit deeper in the middle. Which it did. A lot deeper. Then the path sort of stopped and turned into a shelf. Which we dropped off. And I experienced the novel though terrifying sensation of setting sail across a river in the middle of the Okavango Delta in a 1960s shopping car called Oliver. His front wheels gave up their grip on the ground with a gentle bob and he settled down on to the surface of the water as his rear wheels gave a final little push to the edge of the shelf. We were floating. And then we were sinking. Water gushed in through Oliver's dashboard, quickly filling the cabin until it came over my knees and began its slow, cold climb up my stomach.

I loved Oliver. I knew that. But I didn't fancy dying with him that day. I pushed the door open and hurled myself out into the water. My feet never brushed the bottom. With his load lightened, Oliver floated serenely alongside me now and we swam together for a while as my head whirled with the horror of what I had done. The film crew were to hand, of course. But they were temporarily incapacitated by an outbreak of hysteria that had, inexplicably, stolen the power of coherent speech, or even movement, from all of them. Instead, they variously lay or rolled around on the bank making hooting noises while I swam alongside my yellow Opel Kadett. With the hollow feeling known only to those forced to abandon a friend at sea, I swam back to the bank and clambered up the muddy shoreline. I stood and dripped, my mouth half open, no words coming to my stunned mind. I looked around, back to the river. Oliver floated freely. And alone.

We did get him out. Of course we did. A rope was tied to the back of a hefty safari truck and I swam back out into the river to fix it to Oliver. As I approached him, just his white roof and tall windows visible above the brown water, I felt pangs of guilt the like of which I had never experienced. I had killed him. And it was my own vanity and pride that had done it. Naturally, the crew had relayed news of Jeremy and James's successful crossing to me as I stood, dripping on the river bank. They had also pointed out that there are rivers in Africa, probably including this one, where little tiny fish like to swim up your todger and ruin it from the inside. I didn't care about the dreaded African todger-fish. I slid back into the water, kicked out and reached Oliver to tie the rope around his bumper where he bobbed, nose down. The door was still open, though pushed half closed again by the weight of the river. I climbed into the cabin and lowered myself chin deep in the water to sit in the driver's seat as we hauled him out. Back on the bank, when I opened the door again a rush of river water flowed out on to the ground and it symbolised, for me, the rush of guilt that flowed after me as I climbed out and stood next to Oliver's stricken form. The crew, for once, knew when to be quiet and they hung their heads as I searched for words. And then someone found them for me.

'Fuck me. Look at that.' The shout had shattered the forlorn silence and I snapped my head up to see why. As one, our gaze swung round to follow the soundman's arm, pointing shakily back along the river.

'Crocodile. There, on the bank. It's bloody massive.'

And it was. At least seventy feet long to my eyes. And, more to the point, no more than a hundred yards along the river from where I had been splashing and thrashing with Oliver. The croc looked capable of taking me and the car into its jaws in one go. Another silence descended. This was Africa, after all.

I figured he was dead. And so did everyone else. Thursby and his right-hand man, Gary, thought differently. With their encouragement, I set to and we stripped the carb once more, dried out the plugs and high-tension wires, turned the engine over by hand with the plugs out to clear any water that had made its way in there – none had – and disconnected, sprayed with WD40 and reconnected every one of the electrical points in the ignition circuit. There wasn't much to do. Oliver was a simple car. There were only about three wires lurking in there, and one of those was for the interior light. That I could live without. My makeshift air breather had probably helped, too, reducing the chance of the engine sucking in a lungful of water, trying to compress the uncompressible water in its cylinders and blowing itself to bits as a result. Having drained, dried and cleaned everything we could, long after the others had left to set up the camp and make dinner, we got him going again and I cruised into the new camp with Oliver purring away as if nothing had ever happened. I tried to act nonchalant but, typically, failed.

*Diary of an Intrepid African Traveller and his Faithful Sherpa,
Oliver*

*Stuck Ollie in a river yesterday. Thought I'd killed him but, no, we got
him going. We saw a massive crocodile on the bank of the river. Right
next to where I was splashing around with Oliver. I pretended not to be
scared. Got to see one, though. Nearly a bit too closely.*

*We're going to make it to the border, though. We are. Should be there by
tomorrow night. If we do make it, I am going to ship Oliver home to the
UK. He's got me this far, I'm not going to walk away and abandon him.
He's coming home with me.*

We made it. All three cars and their drivers drew up at the border
between Botswana and Namibia, dusty, battered and dented, having
driven 1000 kilometres across some of the roughest terrain Africa
could throw at us. We had no four-wheel-drive and no fire-
breathing engines. We had proved our point about school-run
4x4s.

And, yes, I took Oliver home. He's here now.

# Chapter 5

# AN ODD WEEK PART 1

## On Purpose. Inventing the Amphibious Car

*How Hard Can It Be?*

It was to turn out to be a very odd couple of weeks. First I would sail across the English Channel in a van. And a week later I would drive a boat down the B4213 to my mate's house to park outside his upstairs window in flood-stricken Gloucestershire. But right now, I was trying to find a car park just off the A2 where I would meet up with the guys to compare the results of our various attempts at making a *Top Gear* amphibious vehicle.

This was something we had, in fact, attempted before. Sometime early in the previous year, loafing around in the production office, someone or other had mentioned amphibious cars and wondered aloud why no one seems to have cracked what would, in an era of satellite mobile phones, keyhole surgery and lasers, seem like a pretty trifling business. It had become the subject of some typically well-informed debate in the office.

'I mean, what is it? Just a waterproof car, no big deal. Why do they always make such a hash of it?'

'If kids' toys can float in the bath, then a real car can float in water, surely.'

'And it would be great, wouldn't it, to have a car that you could drive on the water. Think of the leisure stuff you could do. We should all have them; it's ridiculous that we don't.'

'I think it's a conspiracy, they're trying to keep us down by . . .'

'Oh, fuck off. It's not a conspiracy, it's the car-makers, they want to sell us sports cars cos there's more profit in them and . . .'

'See, a conspiracy. It's the government . . .'

We knocked the idea around for a bit and cooked up a plan. We at *Top Gear* would solve this problem and prove to the world that amphibious cars were a simple but wonderful concept that we, the consumers, were being denied because of a complex web of conspiracy and deceit involving car-makers, the government, Ken Livingstone and speed cameras. All it needed was some proper thinking to make amphibious cars a commercial reality and bring to us all the life-enhancing benefits of being able to drive your car on the roads and, well, on the water as well. How hard could it be?

As it turned out, very. The three of us decided on the type of amphibious car we each felt the world needed, agreed on a budget – tiny – and drew up plans. Our ideas were, predictably, very different. Jeremy had gone for power. As the basis for his design he chose an elderly Toyota Hi-Lux pickup truck on the grounds that we had recently proved them indestructible by trying, and failing, to destroy one. One of the key issues with amphibious vehicles is devising a system to allow the vehicle's engine to switch over from driving the wheels on land to powering it through the water when it turns into a boat. All manner of things have been tried: diverting the power using driveshafts and levers so that the engine can power a screw at the back of the car, simpler systems necessitating getting out of the car before it enters the water to fit the propeller on to the end of the crankshaft – or you can do what Jeremy did and simply bolt a bloody great outboard motor to the back of his pickup.

I decided that if the intention was for these to be the ultimate recreational vehicles, then something combining the qualities of a road vehicle, a boat and a house might be just the thing. It could not only be driven on land and water, it could provide accommodation on land and water, too. The perfect holiday vehicle, in fact. I got hold of an ancient VW camper van and had it made watertight and buoyant. We devised a simple system for powering it in the water by fitting a propeller to the end of the crankshaft on a shaft of metal extended off the back of the flywheel. James went for a different approach: he converted a Triumph Herald convertible into a yacht by fitting it with a mast and a small rudder. Unfortunately, he omitted to fit it with a keel or to equip himself with any sort of knowledge of the finer or even broader points of sailing.

In the event, he drove his car into the reservoir we had been challenged to cross and bobbed about aimlessly for an hour or two while I drove in, tore the propeller off on the ramp, sank immediately and transferred across to Jeremy's pickup which was, annoyingly, performing faultlessly. Performing faultlessly, that is, until its one major flaw, the driver, turned too sharply towards the ramps on the other side and tipped it over. It managed a complete roll in the water, coming to rest on its back with its wheels sticking out of the oggin. We scrambled out as it rolled, I grabbed hold of a wheel as it passed and tried to use it to haul myself out of the freezing water and on to the underside of the car. The wheel, perhaps not surprisingly, rotated and so I was forced to scamper up the side of it in a way that Jeremy and the crew were happy to point out reminded them very much of, well, of a hamster. Not much dignity available on the underside of a floating Toyota, as it turns out.

But we had learned from this experience and we had got a glimmer from it of a future with real possibility. We believed in our schemes, we believed our plans for amphibious vehicles would work and could, in subtle but fundamental ways, contribute to a better life for everyone. And also, we were buggered if were going to give up and be beaten by the idea. And so we agreed to revisit it, to prove once and for all that amphibious vehicles really aren't that hard to make.

And so we met up in a car park with our masterpieces still in road-going mode, laughed at each other's efforts and drove to Dover from where we had been challenged to drive across the English Channel to France. You may have seen it on the telly: before we got to Dover, all three vehicles had caught fire, thanks to the foam we had squirted into their every orifice in the name of finding better buoyancy. The flotation foam would, undoubtedly, provide increased buoyancy, but along with it, also increased flammability, clinging to hot exhaust manifolds and engine blocks and catching fire as readily as a match. As it smouldered, the burning foam released huge amounts of dense, black, choking smoke into the cab of my van. I took shallower and shallower breaths until I feared it might possibly be dangerous to carry on. At an earlier stop I had stolen a length of rubber pipe from the back of Jeremy's pickup, something to do with the bilge pumps he had ordered fitting, I guessed, and likely to create problems for him when he set off without it. However, quite apart from its delightful potential to cause Jeremy to drown simply by not being there, its presence in my VW van now was a further boon. As I cruised through the early evening twilight towards Dover, I stuck one end of the pipe out of the window, applied my lips to the other end and breathed through it the cool evening air of Kent, unsullied by the acrid smoke of burning flotation foam in my, hopefully, amphibious VW camper, and I figured that this had probably never been done before.

By dint of sheer determination and bloody-mindedness, we all three arrived in Dover at the giant slipway used, ordinarily, by the passenger hovercraft. A huge slab of sloping concrete streaked with green stains and garnished with clumps of heavy, dark seaweed, the slipway slides down into the steely waters of Dover Harbour.

We stood on the edge of the water, feet lapped by the sea, and looked out past the heavy harbour walls. The grey sky met the grey sea in the distance and somewhere beyond that lay France. And in between, we all three imagined, were hundred-foot waves, out-of-control oil tankers, jagged, hungry rocks and sea monsters with dull eyes and curved teeth. It was too late in the day to try right now, so we made everything ready for the following day's adventures and all headed off to bed, agreeing on the way that a dawn start would be best.

## Why Do These Things Always Have to Start Early?

By mid-morning we were sort of getting there. Not getting there as in getting to France, but getting there as in getting ready to leave. I mean, we couldn't have set off to sea in a hurry if a klaxon had gone off warning us of invaders, but we were within an hour or so of being ready. More or less. There's a lot to do before departing on such a trip. Sadly, though, we couldn't find enough things to do to be able to justify putting off the entire voyage for another day. We had mooched about the town buying provisions. We stocked up on corned beef, bread and cheese for our boat trip like three giant castaways from *Swallows and Amazons*. We had to stop James buying enough ginger beer to give the coastguards reason to reclassify his Triumph Herald as a tanker.

With *Swallows and Amazons* provisions bought and stowed, we could delay no longer. All three vehicles approached the edge of the sea with, I'll be honest, some timidity. But, brave sea dogs that we are, at the given signal we headed out to sea. James, having made arrangements this time for a removable keel, got it stuck in the slot as he tried to drop it into the water and was left, once again, with no means of controlling his craft. So he set off into the harbour wall. Where he stayed. Jeremy's pickup drove in before me, he fired up the outboard and he set off, striking what he probably imagined to be a nautical pose, and headed for France.

As a veteran now in dealing with amphibious Volkswagen Dormobiles, I can say with confidence that such vehicles are at their most nervous and capricious at the very moment they make the magical transition from land-living animal to creature of the water. It's a delicate, mystical moment in which two worlds meet and a transformation must happen to cross the divide from one to another. What I'm saying is, the bit where you first drive into the water always scares the crap out of me. And now I had to do it again. Only this time I was driving into the sea and out there, beyond the harbour walls, lay open water that stretched over the horizon and was full of unimaginable terrors. And I was about to drive into those waters in an old van with gingham curtains at the windows and a kitchenette with a camping stove in it. I looked around and took some strange comfort from the fact that I would be doing it while my mate James rammed an old Triumph repeatedly into the base of the harbour walls in his efforts to regain control of his madly flailing sails and my other mate sat proudly in the load bed of a twenty-year-old Japanese pickup truck with a huge outboard fixed to the back of it and thought he looked like James Bond.

The worst thing about driving into the sea in an amphibious van is that to do it you have to be in the cab, at the wheel. In order to make the VW camper van watertight, we had to weld up the doors and seal all remaining gaps. And that meant the only way out of the van I was about to drive into the water was through the back door. In the event then, that something went wrong, and it always does, I would have barely seconds to flee the flooding cab, clamber over the driver and passenger seats, run to the back of the van, climb up on to the engine cover, shove open the rather elegant louvred wooden doors we had fitted to form a nautical-style hatch, climb out and bob to the surface like a cork. Gripping the wheel and flexing my left leg as it held the clutch pedal down firmly, I looked around and fixed once more in my mind the exact location of the doors at the back. I wondered if I would still be able to find them if the van drove straight to the bottom of the sea and turned over on its way down. I looked down at the life jacket I had been issued with and wondered if it was one of those self-inflating ones that blow up as soon as they hit water. What if it inflated before I could get out and I couldn't fit through the hatch as a result?

'Oh, bugger this.' I stamped on the throttle, lifted the clutch and pointed the van at France, splashing into the English Channel in what I hoped, but very much doubted, would look to the waiting cameras like a brave and flamboyant entry reminiscent of a lifeboat dropping down the slipway and diving willingly into the waiting sea. It didn't float. At first. They never do. Water rose up past the flat-fronted bonnet and climbed up the windscreen as I pushed a bow wave. I looked out through the side windows, too, at a cross-section of the surrounding sea water inching up towards the roof line. Then I felt the van lift as the front wheels cleared the ramp and floated free. I had hit the water with enough momentum for the van to carry on pushing out to sea and it bobbed as the rear wheels floated up from the ramp and settled into a level, contented float with the waves lapping at the sides of the van's improvised hull. The propeller was already turning and I felt its gentle shove as it bit into the water. Right, time to get the hell out of the cab and take a look up top.

I leaped clear of the driving seat, having taken the precaution of deliberately not fastening my seat belt prior to entering the sea. How I would have loved to take that one up with a safety campaigner. I passed quickly through the cabin, taking just a second to admire the view of the harbour walls through the neatly curtained windows as I lifted a leg to clamber on to the box at the back that housed the gamely chugging diesel engine. On my knees now, with one hand I steadied myself on the floor against the tipping, rocking motion of the van and, with the other, reached forwards and pushed open the rather natty louvred hatch. And, perhaps for the first time ever in the combined history of humans, the sea and VW camper vans, I stood on the rear deck of a VW camper van and took stock of the sea conditions as I sailed towards France. And I believed in it: I really believed that we were about to get something right on *Top Gear*, that my van was about to sail to France, where it would climb elegantly from the sea and prove to the waiting world that the amphibious leisure vehicle was not only within reach of this technological age, but was here now, a reality.

And then the steering jammed over to the left so that I could only go round in tight, anti-clockwise circles, Jeremy rammed James into the harbour wall while, he claimed, trying to rescue him, a massive ferry came in from the Channel and had to man-oeuvre around my now frantically spinning VW camper van and James's Triumph yacht finally sank in the harbour. We tried again the following day, James and I sharing the trip together in my VW. Jeremy headed for France as before, his pickup once again performing well. My van looked good for a brief while, then it took water into the engine, causing it to hydro-lock and tear itself to pieces, and the entire craft rolled on to its side, filled with water and sank. Jeremy collected us from the sea. Oddly enough, as James and I bobbed around in the Channel, necks chafing lightly against our inflated life jackets, surrounded by floating detritus left behind by our now sinking motor home, there was little need to say much to each other; we had done this sort of thing before. The only real bugger was when James managed to find the flask of tea bobbing by, but then dropped the bloody cup before we had managed even a mouthful.

You may have seen the rest on the telly. Jeremy picked us up in his truck and gloated pretty solidly for an hour or so – and, frankly, who could blame him? His craft was working and both James's and mine were now the basis of new man-made coral reefs just off

Dover. And then we all three settled in for the trip, each finding a spot in the cramped load bed of the truck among the flotation barrels, drums of fuel and bags of provisions.

The journey went on . . .

### Diary of a Brave and Salty Sea Dog

*We're on the way to France. My van sank just outside Dover and so did James's car. We're stuck now on Jeremy's pickup. Been at sea for hours now and no signs of seasickness – I'd hate a repeat of the Norway incident when I puked on telly. But I still say that was because I was hungover and not because I'm a seasick wimp.*

*All the sandwiches have been ruined in the spray, one of them floated free of the carrier bag it was stored in and got jammed in the collection nozzle of the bilge pump. We found it only when the load bed had begun filling with water. And it was me who eventually found the problem. I got hold of the nozzle that feeds the bilge pump and pulled from it the soggy ham sandwich that had blocked it and stopped it clearing the water from our improvised hull. The other two were very pleased that I had fixed it and I decided not to tell them that the reason we had only the one pump operating in the first place was that I had stolen the pipe from the other to use as a breathing tube in my smoke-filled camper van on the way to Dover. Sometimes, in a survival situation, you have to share the right information at the right time – and this wasn't the right time.*

And on . . .

*It's actually quite boring now. Jeremy's hogging all the driving and James keeps calling things by their nautical names. It doesn't look like we're going to be shipwrecked and I don't imagine we'll have to do any navigating by sextant, which is just as well because we haven't got one and, even if we did, James would hog it and get everything wrong.*

We weren't eaten by sea monsters, we didn't get run over by an oil tanker and we didn't catch anything with our fishing rods – even with twenty Marlboro as bait. It takes a long time, sailing across the Channel three-up in a pickup truck. The sea flattened and grew calmer the closer we got to the midpoint. Some miles out, we were buzzed by the local coastguard who were, we guessed, surprised to see three men in a Toyota, fishing. They flew over in a bright red plane, said 'hello and good luck' on the radio, or something to that effect, and buzzed off. We crossed the busiest part of what is, I think someone said, the busiest shipping lane in the world and came very close to some very, very large ships in the process. It was a navigational feat, to stay out of the way of these huge, lumbering beasts in our tiny, not entirely sharp-handling craft – something akin to three mice in a roller skate trying to cross the dance floor at a pissed-up elephants' disco. But we did it and, when we opened our eyes again, were safely at the other side just a few miles from the French coast.

Things got bumpier the closer we got to France. The single bilge pump, now cleared of ham sandwich, was doing its best to keep us afloat, but much of the English Channel was now sloshing about in the bottom of our pickup boat and we were floating ever deeper in the sea. James crawled 'for'ard' – as he insisted on calling it – to see if he could find the cause of our amphibious vehicle wanting to return to 'truck' mode at a more than slightly inconvenient time. He didn't identify a cause, but he did report back that the cab was filling rapidly, with water gushing in through the air vents and now covering the base of the seats. We tried to make plans for abating the flow – we couldn't come up with any and decided simply to hope that we wouldn't sink before we hit France.

The coast of France is not particularly impressive to look at – at least not the bit that lay in front of us now just beyond the grey slabs of English Channel that were becoming increasingly streaked with white foam. Topographically that bit of the French coast lacks the impact, glamour and romance of, say, the White Cliffs of Dover, but, nevertheless, the dull plains of France lay in front of us as temptingly as the most Red White and Blue of Cliffs and we each prayed quietly that we would make it. And we did, sort of. We still had some semblance of steering available now and we used what little we had to manoeuvre our unlikely craft towards what appeared to be a small slipway of sorts, extending out of the sea by a small, rocky patch of beach. It was a busy bit of beach, covered almost entirely with French people enjoying a rare splash of sunshine. They lay around in T-shirts and shorts, read newspapers, discussed things and generally did French stuff. They were not, I suspect, expecting to see three damp Englishmen chug up to their beach in what looked, even from a distance, to be a floating pickup truck.

## The Shipwreck – in a Pickup Truck

There was evident surprise on the beach, even to our straining eyes, as we grew closer. We could see from the scratching of French heads, the shrugging of French shoulders and the shading of eyes better to see our approach that we were causing a bit of a stir. And so was the sea – causing a bit of a stir. In fact, it was getting beyond being choppy and could justifiably be referred to as rough by the time we drew within a hundred yards or so of land. And at this moment, it occurred to the three of us that we had not, at any point, planned this bit. We had designed our craft, planned our launch, made sure we had sufficient provisions and flares and life jackets, but had at no point even discussed where and how we would tackle the business of getting out of the sea and on to France. And this was, if we were to prove our vehicle's amphibious success, one of the most critical stages in the entire operation.

Our discussions were at this point cut short. At least, they were for me. An especially large wave hit the side of the truck and pitched me straight over the edge. I fell towards the sea and landed, to my surprise and immediate discomfort, with a considerable thump on the base of my spine. I had hit the concrete slipway just a foot or so beneath the retreating sea as the tide drew back and made ready to hurl itself once more at our vessel. I barely had time to formulate thoughts to the effect of what a piece of luck it was that I had landed on hard – very hard in fact – ground rather than plunged into shark-infested waters before I turned my head to see the pickup truck, and its two remaining sailors, pitching towards me in a manner that suggested I was very much about to be killed. I didn't want to die under a poorly made amphibious pickup truck piloted by the world's two most irritating men and so I squirmed and semi-swam my way out of its path. Splashing, gasping and struggling my way ashore, I turned my head again to watch as the truck rocked and bucked away from land once more, taken wher-ever the, clearly French, waves willed.

I didn't have time fully to take in the surprise and consternation registering on the faces of the gathering crowd of French observers around me: I was too busy shouting instructions at James and Jeremy as they rode their boat/truck along the wave-lashed fringes of the beach. They appeared, to my mind at least, to be sharing an amphibious bucking bronco now, with no control over where they went and how high they were bucked. Nevertheless, I issued loud instructions concerning where they had best head for, when they should make a determined drive for the beach, how best to avoid the many jagged rocks snarling at them from just beneath the waves and when they should hold back and when they should hold on. They responded by shouting back at me, probably to confirm receipt of my instructions. Though it was difficult to catch their wind-torn words, I did catch scraps of them across the sea. 'You useless —ing cowardly little —', may have featured at one point; 'thanks for your help, you turncoat bastard . . . you're no more a

—ing sailor than you are a driver, you hopeless little —.' Difficult to be sure. It all looked rather impressive from the beach, though, very manly and daring, and I found myself gripped by a momentary twinge of jealousy as I waddled around in my life jacket and waterproofs wondering how I might better facilitate their smooth and safe landing. At least I was the first get to France – I made a note to point this out to the other two, though at a better time.

The steady rhythm of the advancing tide was, surge by surge, having the effect of slowly bringing the guys in to shore. The question was whether they would be deposited gently on to the smoothly sloping concrete slipway, from which they could make a dignified landing in front of the assembled masses, or be smashed to bits on the many rocks to either side of the narrow opening on to the slipway and be horribly killed in front of that same assembled mass. No steering was available to the two sailors by now, the outboard motor having long ago been incapacitated by the repeated grinding of the vehicle to which it was attached against the bottom of the sea. It fell, it would seem, to me, as the lone sailor on dry land, to do something about their predicament. I looked about me and tried to think. The noise of the sea, the crash of the waves and the surge of the ever-growing crowd made this a bit tricky. But I could appreciate the need for haste at such a time and did my best to turn up the wick a bit. I needed some means of securing the pickup, some way to ensure it was brought to shore here, where I stood, on the concrete slipway's welcoming slope.

And then I remembered. In one of those sudden flash, do-or-die moments, I recalled the coil of rope that James had made fast – and that's how he referred to it, 'made fast' rather than 'tied on' – to the front of the pickup. It had ended up, I saw instantly, draped back over on to the bonnet, a single length of blue nylon rope. It was exactly what was needed. The film crew had by now arrived at the scene and were running about the place pointing cameras at our attempts to replicate the scene from James Bond

when his Lotus Esprit calmly drives out of the sea, impresses the
locals and helps him get off with Ursula Andress in that fur bikini –
or whatever happened. Either way, our efforts were not looking
too close to it right now. The film crew had a Range Rover – they
always do – and I needed it. Get the rope from the pickup attached
to the Rangie and, bingo, we would have ourselves a heroic rescue.

'Lads, this is a bit serious now. Those are bastard big waves and
they could be killed if that thing goes over.'

There was a brief, almost wistful pause as a few of us looked out
to the madly lurching pickup and its two remaining crew members.
No one had to say anything. As one, we accepted that common
decency demanded that we try to do something, and so we did.

We got the Range Rover backed down the slipway to within
thirty feet or so of the water's edge. With a second length of rope
made fast – oh, God, now I was sounding like James – to the back
of the Rangie, we could splice it – steady, Hammond, getting
carried away with this nautical stuff – to the length already attached
to the pickup and then simply drive the Range Rover up the slope
and tow them out gently on to the slipway. I tried my best to
communicate the plan to James and Jeremy. The truck was now
pitching too wildly, the wind tearing at us too strongly, for us to
be able to understand each other well. Added to that, they were,
perhaps, becoming more aware by the second of the perilous nature
of their predicament and, as a result, beginning to feel somewhat
pressured.

Nevertheless, I managed, by a series of frankly brilliant mimes
and gestures, to communicate to them that we needed them to
throw us the end of the rope attached to the bumper of their truck.
It would not be easy. I could see the rope, lying draped over the
bonnet at the base of the windscreen. To get it would require
clambering over the roof and reaching down the slippery slope of
the windscreen to retrieve the frayed end from where it lay caught
up in the windscreen wipers. And this would have to be done on

a truck that was pitching and rolling on a sea wild enough to daunt Captain Ahab himself. And, from the look of things, James was about to try it. It's always an enjoyable spectacle, watching a less than athletic man attempt something demanding physical resilience, strength and balance. James acquitted himself remarkably well. Despite being cocooned in a bulky life jacket and a blue waterproof coat huge enough to protect a tall ship from the elements, he wriggled himself over the roof of the truck and extended an arm forwards, down the windscreen and towards the end of the rope. The truck pitched and I feared he would be thrown from it to die in the sea beneath it. He held on, somehow finding the grip in his trailing left hand to fix himself to the wildly slanting roof by holding on to some part of the metal structure fixed behind it to support Jeremy's improvised wheel position. Jeremy himself stood guard behind James; he, too, had to keep a mighty grip on the sides of the load bed to avoid being thrown into the sea.

And before I could register the strength it must have required to keep himself clamped, whelk-like, to the smooth and slippery surface of the truck, James had the end of the rope in his hand and was slithering back towards the load bed. He stood next to Jeremy and made ready to throw it. I splashed forwards into the sea to be ready to catch it. He coiled it carefully. Very carefully. He may, in fact, have stopped to measure the lengths to ensure consistency of looping.

'Throw the bloody rope, May. Before you both drown out there, you twat.' Some member of the crew, probably Iain May who, as a keen and experienced sailor, had spent the last two days stamping about the place in a set of waterproofs as commanding as anything sported by Admiral Lord Nelson looking down his nautical nose in disgust at the lot of us, was getting frustrated by the growing tension. Or it might have been an equally frustrated French bystander. And, goodness knows, we had enough of those by now.

A crowd worthy of a decent-sized football match had congregated around the end of the slipway and were all staring avidly out to sea, their attention fixed on the madly rolling truck and the two figures clinging to it. As we watched, James steadied himself immediately behind the cab of the truck and made ready to throw a length of rope coiled, with impressive precision and regularity, in his right hand. He heaved backwards and his arm described an arc. The end of the rope, clearly frayed even at this distance, left his open hand and stretched out towards us. I dashed forwards to catch it, splashing into the foaming sea and bracing my legs against its steady pull and push as I waded in past my knees. I made sure of my footing in an instant and looked up to see the end of the rope snaking towards me. I extended my arm, stretching my fingers in the mist of sea spray, waiting to feel the soggy grip of the rope biting into my waiting palm. I held it and drew my arm protectively back towards my chest. I looked back towards the truck and watched as the other end of the rope, which was not, as it turned out, attached to the front of the truck, splashed down into the waiting sea. I hauled the rope in, watching with sinking heart and rising bile as the free end of it tugged and jerked towards me through the waves. It would be as much use in saving my friends from peril at sea as a packet of crisps.

'May, you fucking hopeless goon.'

A chorus of baying abuse sprang up behind me as the crew realised what had happened and, quite unfairly, placed the blame for the unattached rescue rope on the shoulders of the very man whose life had been put in immediate peril by its lack of a fixing point. In fact, as I coiled the wet lengths of rope over my arm and watched it shed the weight of sea water back into the waiting waves from its dull blue twists, I wondered if it had, in fact, been me who had untied the rope at some point earlier in our voyage. I remembered untying it from the towing eye immediately underneath the front bumper at some point earlier the previous day.

And I remembered thinking to myself that it was probably quite important to reattach it at some point before we left. And I didn't remember reattaching it. This, though, was not, I decided, the right time to share this information with my fellow survivors. It was the right time, in fact, to focus on ensuring they could still be counted as my fellow survivors of this voyage and not remembered as part of the tragic cost.

'It's okay,' I shouted and ran further into the sea, towards the truck. 'I can tie it back on.'

A crazy plan worthy of a bad dinosaur movie had formed itself in my head, as they do. The truck now seemed to be confining the majority of its wave-bidden manoeuvres to the immediate shoreline, where the water barely ran to three or four feet deep. I would simply wade up to it, reattach the rope to the bumper, retreat and allow the waiting Range Rover to haul them out to safety. It would be a) a doddle, and b) a proper bird-puller for me. It would certainly make up for being cast as the landlocked duffer while my two heroic colleagues paraded themselves up and down the coast in front of the crowd of now, I was quite sure, admiring French folk. Turning my back on the crowd, I waded in until the waves pulled at my thighs. The truck bounced around barely ten feet away. I edged closer. It was five feet from me now and I extended my hands towards it as I advanced.

And then it was barely two feet from me. The waves shoved and barged at me as the truck, obeying their every whim, drew even closer until I realised it was about to crush and kill me. I dashed back, my sudden movement thwarted by the weight of water around me. The truck dipped suddenly and was jerked backwards by another wave. I moved as if to follow it, the rope held out in my extended right arm, and then thought better of it. This was like being lowered into the holding cage at a rodeo and invited to tie a rope through the nose ring of a mad bull. It could only possibly result in my grisly death. Bird-puller maybe, but I would be dead. Discretion being the better part of valour and all that, I ran away as best I could through the dense and swirling sea water.

'Tell you what, I'll throw you the rope and you tie it on.'

I made sure I held an end of the blue line and hurled the other at the truck. Needless to say, it dropped some twenty feet short of the target and lay limply on the rolling swell.

'Bollocks. They're going to die,' I muttered grimly and hauled the rope back in for another attempt.

It took many, but we did it. The rope eventually flapped wetly on to the truck, within the grasp of James and Jeremy, who made it fast. The other end was, by then, already fixed to a second, longer rope tied on to the back of the Range Rover. The strain was taken up, the rope pulled taut and twisted and, sure enough, the pickup drew closer and closer to the slipway, settling visibly as the wheels made contact with the concrete and isolated it from the sea's whims. We pulled it further and it rose from the waves like some dreadful mistake from a monster movie. The crow cheered. Well, some of them did. It wasn't, perhaps, the rapturous welcome we had looked forward to had we managed to pull off the whole James Bond out of the sea in his Lotus thing, but, all the same, the general air was one of approval that the show was over, if nothing else. We slapped one another's backs, thanked everyone, and the three of us clambered into the Range Rover together. There were dry clothes and shoes waiting inside it and a ticket each in the glove box for the train back to England.

'Thought we were gonna die there.'

'Me too.'

'Thought I had.'

'Right, where's that train then?'

# Chapter 6

# AN ODD WEEK PART 2

## Very Much Not on Purpose.
## The Flood

*One Week Later . . .*

The B4213 connects Ledbury with Cheltenham. It's a busy little road and one I use often. My mate Zog Zeigler lives just off it, in a handsome old riverside house where it crosses the River Severn on a low, stone bridge. And today I was going to see him; always a good thing.

'Bollocks.' I had caught the prop on a gravestone.

Perched in the bows of a wooden Romanian punt he usually kept in the grounds of his beautifully dilapidated watermill for ornamental purposes, my mate Johnny Vizor smiled back at me, told me not to worry about it and turned back to survey the slowly moving branches overhead as we passed along the B4213 and floated over the graveyard of St Michael and All Angels Church. It was a calm, really quite lovely day. The sky shone blue through the hypnotic leaves above. And everything around us was six or seven feet underwater and irrevocably ruined.

'If I snag it again and we tear a bloody great chunk off the prop, we'll be stuck.'

Johnny told me not to worry, again, and flashed one of his beaming, beatific, happy smiles. It's the sort of smile that would disarm Darth Vader.

'Okay, okay. I believe you. It'll be all right.' I had put down my light sabre and was happy to chat.

'Wish I knew which way his house was from here, though.' I looked out past the churchyard and across an entirely new sea, fringed with strange clumps of bushes that were the tops of trees peeking out of the water and dotted with awkward, rectangular islands with sloped, tiled sides gathering to regular peaks.

'Everything looks completely different. I don't know if I'll even recognise it when we get there.'

The little outboard motor chugged away obediently behind me, measuring the seconds with its metronomic tock-tock and sending low vibrations up through the handle I gripped in my left hand. The flood water rippled past the dark wooden flanks of the little boat. Otherwise it was quiet; there was no car noise from the B4213, because it was underwater now. We both shifted our positions and the narrow, blunt-ended boat rocked tremulously on the flat, brown waters. The bloated River Severn was now four miles wide at this point. Somewhere ahead, lost in the swirling mass, was Zog's house. We had stayed in contact all day as the waters forced him to retreat upstairs, abandoning the landline and preserving carefully his mobile phone's battery. Finally, as he and his wife, Jill, sheltered in the upstairs rooms of his house without power or communication and the dark waters pooled up the stairs, we reached a point at which even Zog, stoic and the brave gentleman to the last, had betrayed a little of his misery and worry in his tone of voice. And it was sufficient for me to pull out whatever stops were necessary, borrow a boat and get off my backside to mount a rescue mission to collect Zog and Jill and transport them to safety until the floods abated.

They had been fast in coming, these waters. You will have read about them in the papers last year. You may have been caught up in them yourself. Living near the Severn valley, the floods of 2007 dominated the thoughts and conversations of us and our friends for months and affected everyone we know. Typically, I was away when they arrived, the floods. Working in London, I had heard on the radio that things were getting a bit damp in Tewkesbury and, to be perfectly honest, was looking forward to driving around in my old Land Rover and surveying some of the excitement when I got home.

And so, I set off for the long drive back to Gloucestershire with a light heart. Uppermost in my mind, in front of floods, famine or pestilence, was the fact that we would be celebrating my youngest daughter Willow's birthday the following day and I was, for once, going to be there. In actual fact, her birthday had already been and gone. It fell on the Wednesday of that week; today was Friday. But I had been away on some long-booked event or other. As it was only Willow's fourth birthday, she didn't yet have mobile phone, PDA or personal assistant and was unaware of the precise date of her anniversary – she just knew it was coming up. So Mindy and I told a small white lie. We told her that her birthday was on the Saturday and I made a promise, one of those solemn, daddy promises that can't be broken, that I would be there.

'What, with my presents?'

'Yep. I'll be there, baby. I promise.'

'And a cake?'

'Yep. And a cake.'

'Will we play games?'

'Yes, we'll play games.'

'What games?'

'We'll decide that later. But I will be there. I promise.'

'I want a donkey.'

'Yes, all right. And I'll be there, too.'

'And a sheep. I love sheeps.'

## Dead Crows

It was not shaping up to be a good trip. The journey from London to our remote corner of Gloucestershire is not a short one anyway, but it is one particularly blighted by changeable traffic. The trip home can take anything from two to four hours. I was hoping for a quick one. It was just after lunchtime, and I wanted to get some distance out of London and along the M4 before the usual Friday afternoon rush started and every office in London and Wiltshire disgorged its workers to leap in cars and clog the motorways.

'Bloody-buggering-bastard-hell.'

I swore out loud as we slowed once more to a halt on the M4 and punched the steering wheel when I saw the queue extending out of sight over a crest in the motorway ahead.

'Shite.' I looked skywards and then slumped forwards, head in hands. Alongside me, in a dark VW, another driver had just clocked the bloke off *Top Gear* in his grey Porsche 911 and must have been wondering if I was having a heated discussion with someone on a hands-free mobile phone or going mad and shouting to myself. I looked across to see him grin and wave, mouthing 'Top Gear' and sticking his thumbs up. I smiled back and turned to stare ahead at the queue. This was a bad one. Even by the standards of the M4 – which is an appallingly run, constantly broken ribbon of crap – this journey was getting sticky.

The dismal constrictions of roadworks where no one does anything but put up signs and then line up cones to keep their signs safe from traffic, had worked their usual magic on the flow. We had bunched up, slowed, speeded up, slowed again and narrowly missed a multi-car pile-up when some numpty driving a lorry load of bog roll just an inch off the bumper of a Nissan Micra piloted by that bloke with the bad skin out of the Daleks had decided to demonstrate the astonishing potency of his airbrakes and caught out the driver of a van full of decorating supplies following behind who was considering masturbating over the newspaper picture of a twenty-year-old model from Billericay he held spread out on his lap to catch crumbs from his Ginster's meat pasty.

And now, for no apparent reason, we were slowing again. Only this time it felt different. The radio had been warning of jams, the traffic reports threatening to take longer than the programmes they were supposed to punctuate. The news was dominated with stories of floods rising, roads being blocked by water and landslides and of schools being closed down. Gradually it was seeping into the warm, leather-lined cocoon of my Porsche that things were actually getting a bit nasty out there. And I was still a long way from home.

Ten hours later, I arrived in Cheltenham. I had switched back, changed routes, taken cut-throughs and navigated my way round countless shallow but impassable floods. I had got, at one point, within fourteen miles of home according to the Sat Nav. But there had been nowhere to stop and gather my thoughts and the road ended with police 'Stop' signs and barriers. Cars littered every verge – gravel, slim branches, rags and rubbish were draped across sections of road where flood waters had swept through. Crawling around a corner of the main bypass around Gloucester, I glanced down from the side window, my eye drawn to dark lumps lying flatly on the shining, wet tarmac. As I drew up and passed them, I saw that they were birds, hundreds of them, lying dead on the road. And occasionally a larger, different coloured lump appeared: cats. Dozens of them. Also dead.

It was dark now, nearly ten o'clock in the evening, and people were congregating by cars ramped up on to traffic islands or half buried in hedges. Cars queued on every road, making way in tiny jerks for police cars and vans to pass, sirens blaring on their way to yet another emergency in yet another flood-stricken house. Overhead, the still stormy sky erupted occasionally with the beating blades of coastguard and RAF helicopters swooping to attend to remote farmhouses and villages in the surrounding country. Their lights flashed along the roads from above and added to the unearthly sense of panic and strangeness. This, clearly, was an emergency on a big scale.

The radio was now given over entirely to reporting on the floods. Lists of schools offering accommodation to flood victims were read out. Interviews were held with people whose homes had been ruined and possessions taken away by fast-moving waters. And already there were reports of people looting, vandalising and stealing. People had stockpiled water from local supermarkets in anticipation of the mains supply being cut off. But some had pushed their way to the front of the queues of anxious residents and bought up every bottle of water they could find, scurrying back to their cars with crates and crates of them, leaving young mothers and families with nothing. If society ever really came down to the sort of dog-eat-dog existence that these mindless thugs like to think they already live, their lack of principles and social awareness would help them flourish for a few days and then they would die off through their own inadequacies, inabilities, lack of imagination and fundamental lack of actual physical and mental toughness.

But right now I was facing a decision and so switched off the radio and took a few deep breaths. I was stranded in a solid mass of unmoving traffic on the outskirts of Cheltenham. A few miles ahead, the M5 passed under the dual carriageway on which I seemed to have ground, finally, to a permanent halt. The motorway, too, was clearly blocked. Trucks, heavy vehicles and obvious motorway traffic lined the verges all the way back into town. Every hotel car park was full to overflowing, lights shining out of every window. People were settling down in their cars for the night. The central reservation was full of parked cars, some with newspapers and coats pressed up against the windows to allow a little privacy and comfort for the sleeping occupants. We had not moved for an hour or so now. I had been on the road for more than twelve. The mobile phone network was working to full capacity and beyond, making it difficult to get through and let Mindy know how I was doing.

There was a gap in the parked cars on the central reservation to my right. Glad of the movement, I steered right and clambered over the kerbs, the Porsche's low nose collecting a painful scuff as I dropped off the other side and headed for the opening into the supermarket's car park opposite. I had spent the time formulating a plan. It wasn't a particularly clever one, but I knew it was achievable. I rang Mindy. And I got straight through, for the first time in hours.

'You're going to run home, aren't you?'

'Yup. I'm not just going to sit here in the bloody car, am I?'

'Yes. But be careful. Please.' Mindy had known all along, through every conversation over the past twelve hours that, if it came to it, I would get home even without the car. She knows me well enough to know that I would, secretly, welcome the opportunity.

'You're enjoying this, aren't you?'

'Mindy, there are people whose homes are ruined and they've lost everything and . . .'

'Yes, and that's terrible, I feel sorry for them, too. But you're enjoying your bit, the chance to run home and do heroic stuff.'

I took a sharp breath, about to defend myself.

'Yes, all right,' I laughed with the release as I confessed it, 'yes, I am enjoying it. I like an emergency, you know I do.'

'Well, just be careful.'

'Yes, I will. Look, I've got my running kit in the car, I was bringing it home to go in the wash, and I've got a waterproof jacket and other stuff that'll be useful. I'll enjoy it, you're right. It's what . . .' I looked down at the Porsche's Sat Nav screen for the millionth time to check the distance after I had put in our home address, '. . . nineteen miles. God, I can run that and if it gets tricky I'll walk. Kids do that sort of distance in the Lake District and think nothing of it. I've walked thirty miles a day for ten days on the trot before now.' I was getting boastful and Mindy could sense me building momentum with one of my standard rants.

'You'd better save your phone battery, darling. I want you to be able to call in as you make your way back.'

'Don't worry, Mindy, I'll phone every hour or so and let you know if I'm up to my neck.'


## How Deep Is Too Deep?

I switched off my phone and turned the keys off in the ignition. The Porsche was parked now in a perfectly ordinary slot of the Sainsbury's car park on the outskirts of Cheltenham. All around were other cars, similarly parked, with people bedding down in them for the night to see if the morning would bring clear roads and a chance to get home. Perhaps they had been aiming for the M5 up ahead; maybe they lived tens or even hundreds of miles away. I tried to imagine what it would be like to be trapped in a strange town, knowing you stood no chance of finding a hotel room for the night.

I slipped out of the car, hit the key fob button to open the boot lid at the front and walked round to check out my kit. I had running trousers – lightweight, best suited to gym work; running shoes – old, but still going; wellies, a fleece, a shower-proof running jacket and a baseball cap with Scania written across it. Figuring that modesty was not going to be an issue in a car park full of people sleeping in their cars, I opted to get changed outside the confines of the car. The ground was wet and, at first, I was worried about getting my running outfit damp. And then I remembered where I was going. I had given the journey some thought over the past hour. Nineteen miles is a reasonable walk or a stiff run. I chose not to take the wellies. These would give me no choice but to walk the entire way. And I wanted to run. I wanted to get back as quickly as I could. And running would be a way of staying warm. I would take the running shoes. You can run and walk in trainers, but you can only walk in wellies.

There was little point, I figured, in trying to keep the water out. I didn't have heavy-duty waterproofs with me and my lightweight running gear would barely stand up to a shower let alone the cloudbursts that were still hitting us at intervals. Leaning on the wing of the Porsche, I pulled off my jeans and threw them into the boot between the front wheels. From the pile of kit I had laid out on top of the roof, I dragged the black running trousers and hauled them on, taking care now to stand on the empty kitbag to at least avoid starting this trip with wet feet even if I stood not a chance of finishing it in a similar state. I stripped off my black socks and pulled on a pair of white, running ones. I slipped my feet into my trainers, taking care over the laces – these feet would be busy for the next few hours and I wanted to give them every chance I could. I swapped my shirt for an old T-shirt with a picture of a motorcycle on it and pulled the grey fleece on over that.

The lightweight running jacket matched the trousers, black with a narrow white stripe down the sides. Ordinarily, running around London or in the country at home, I feel slightly self-conscious in it, as though I have made too much effort to coordinate my running kit. Today, though, surveying the crammed car park around me and wincing as another ambulance wailed slowly by on what few corners of clear verge it could find to navigate, I figured no one would care. I dragged it on over the fleece and it settled itself into place with the swooshes and hisses of a very man-made fibre.

I had no torch. I'm not really the type of chap to travel with an emergency kit at all times in the glove box. And even if I were, I'm certainly not the type of chap to regularly check the emergency batteries in the emergency torch in his emergency kit just in case of an unforeseen emergency. I bloody wished I was. But I knew the route well enough and hoped I could find the way. It was mostly along narrow, country lanes with no street lighting. Once clear of Cheltenham's fringes and over the M5, I would be out in the countryside navigating by whatever light the moon could shed from behind the shifting, swirling layers of cloud that had led to this problem in the first place.

Standing by the open driver's door of the car, I suddenly wondered if it would be okay. I'm not exactly gung-ho about having nice things; this car represented a hell of an outlay to me and I was and am very fond of it. I didn't like to think of it being washed away on a muddy tide of flood waters sweeping the Sainsbury's car park like Noah's flood. And then, looking around at the dozens of cars around me with their occupants huddling together to pass the miserable night, stranded many miles from home, I realised there were bigger and better reasons to hope the floods got no worse than concern for the abandoned German supercar of a telly presenter. It would take its chances along with the rest of them. And it was insured, so sod it.

I didn't want to leave stuff in it that I might need, though. I wanted my wallet and notebook. And I had to carry the car keys somewhere, and the bottle of water I had found in the footwell — it seemed ironic to be concerned about having anything to drink on the long trot home, but I guessed that the brown and sludgy waters of the floods were a long way from gaining mineral water status and I would be burning energy and fluids fast, running in the cold night air. I grabbed my tan-coloured canvas shoulder bag from the back seat. It rattled and jangled as I swung it forwards and dropped it on to the driver's seat in front of me. I would need to empty it first; no point lugging loads of stuff I didn't need for the best part of twenty miles through God knows what. I rifled through it.

A packet of nicotine chewing gum, three old diaries, four biros — mostly stolen from hotels — a waterproof map of London, another strip of nicotine gum, a blister pack of headache tablets, a tube of stuff for obscuring zits, a copy of *Motorcycle News*, an empty passport cover, a child's plastic earring and a receipt for petrol and a burger – these were things I could run home without. I piled them on to the floor in front of the passenger's seat and covered them up with my rejected jeans, more out of a sense of shame over the mess than out of concerns for security. I placed back into the shoulder bag my wallet, keys to my flat in London, my small Moleskine note-book, the bottle of water and my iPod Nano with earphones wrapped around it – this last, I reasoned, would be especially useful on a late-night trudge through floods.

And then there was no more to be done. So I rang Mindy. The lines were busy again and it took several attempts to get through.

'Right then, darling, I'm off.'

'What's it like there?'

I looked around at the full car park; beyond it the road was jammed with abandoned cars and lorries. Another pair of ambu-lances were trying to work their way through, blue flashing lights reflected back up from sodden side roads. A police helicopter flew overhead. Room lights blazed in every window of every building. A baby cried in one of the parked cars nearby.

'It's like a scene from a disaster movie. Never seen anything like it.' I stood up and twisted my torso left and right as I spoke on the phone, stretching my muscles out ready for the run.

'Well, take care. Don't do anything daft. If it gets too deep, turn back.'

'Yeah yeah. Look, it's going to be great. I can't wait to get moving again. I'll only be a few hours anyway. And then we'll have a bottle of wine. Don't worry about me, please. I'm looking forward to it, really, I am.'

'All right. Well, call me as soon as you can.'

'Every hour. But, look, don't be daft and try and stay up all night. Just go to bed and get some sleep. I'll need you to be awake and running a hot bath when I get in. Actually, I'll call in only when I need to. I'll leave the phone on meantime, but if you get the chance to kip, then kip. Please. I'll call you when I'm round the corner.'

We finished off our chat and I hung up, dropping the mobile into my canvas bag. I slipped both arms through the bag's long neckstrap so that it hung down at my back like a misshapen rucksack. It was raining gently now and very dark. I checked my watch: 2.20 a.m. So much for that bottle of wine when I got home. I reckoned I could average a mile every ten minutes comfortably over that sort of distance, which would have me arriving home at about 5.30 a.m. But, then, I didn't know what the roads and lanes would be like. I could get stuck in floods or find them blocked by fallen trees and debris. And, if I was honest, I had never really run that sort of distance – certainly not in the middle of the night after a busy week at work. Walking averages out at 3–4 miles an hour. That would mean I wouldn't get home until nearer 8.00 a.m. Willow would wake up on her birthday and find me not there after all. Not an acceptable option.

I had stretched my calf muscles while I thought things through, leaning forwards into a plunging stretch with my hands flat against the sides of the Porsche's roof and my leading knee nuzzling up to its plump, grey flank. I gave myself shin splints the year before when I overtrained for the London Marathon. As a result, I couldn't do the Marathon or even run for weeks on end. It's not an especially impressive sounding complaint, shin splints – it certainly struggles for status in pub boasts alongside, say, shark attack or karate injury – but it hurts like a bastard and the only way to cure them is to stop running. Which, when you run primarily to keep sane and balanced as well as healthy, is a problem. They cleared up eventually, but I remain paranoid about them returning and still stretch my calf muscles out obsessively before so much as trotting through the

living room to the fridge for a beer. It was cold now, and I had
to get moving to warm up.

I left the car park and skirted around ranks of cars to the street.
I ran the first few miles tentatively, not knowing what to expect. I
trotted the pavements and walkways to the very edges of the city
and headed off on the main road out of town. Still under the bright
glare of the street lamps here, I could easily pick a path along the
verges, managing to stay off the roads. No vehicles were moving,
but it was packed solid with parked cars, lorries, vans and coaches.
Those people not sleeping milled about between them, chatting
in low voices, sharing snacks and doing that Blitz thing. Some
zones resembled a subdued street party, until the drone of another
helicopter interrupted festivities or blue flashing lights pulsed
nearby. A few folk waved as I passed through, probably wondering
where I was going and why I was running. A few looked past me
as I approached, checking, perhaps, that I was not dashing ahead
of a wildly pursuing tidal wave leaving Cheltenham.

A fine but persistent rain fell, strengthening sometimes to a
denser sheet. The neon street lamps reflected crazily off the broad,
deep puddles. After a while, the traffic thinned; only a few cars
were parked now, on their own or in small groups, as if gathering
together for comfort. And then, at the bridge where the A4019
out of Cheltenham passes over the M5, it died out completely at
a police line. This, clearly, was where traffic had been stopped and
was the reason for the logjam now some three miles behind me in
Cheltenham. Yellow warning tape stretched across between the
bridge railings and looped down, almost touching the surface of
the gathered water. It got deeper here. I splashed ankle deep on
the crown of the carriageway, staying off the edges and the central
reservation where it glimmered menacingly under the street lamps
and looked like it could swallow me up entirely.

Occasionally, the flood at the verges would meet up in the
middle and I had no choice but to run straight through, wading

up to my knees in places. I wondered how I would manage when I left the street lighting behind and headed out on the narrow, winding country lanes that led home. I had calculated that I had four or five miles until I left the major roads. And then it would be very, very dark. Pathfinding would become guesswork and a test of memory over a route I had travelled many times before, but always in a car or on a motorcycle. Nearly always in daylight. And never underwater. I paced my breathing, set a steady, easy rhythm, tightened the shoulder strap of the canvas bag to stop it slapping against my lower back with every step and ploughed on. It was best not to think about how I would tackle the next stretch and just focus on the one I was on.

## All in Black

I hit the traffic lights where the A38 crossed, usually a busy T-junction thronging with traffic opposite the petrol station and the pub. But not tonight. Even so, despite it being as deserted as some post-apocalyptic movie set, I looked left and right as I crested the top of the slope up to the A4019 before swinging to the right. This took me further away from Cheltenham's glow now and I got my first taste of what it would be like running with no lights at all. Bastard dark, was my summation. But the road here was still broad, stretching across four lanes in places and lined further on with lights. The crown stood proud of the water much of the time and I could splash along only ankle deep in the tough bits, staying well clear of the murky, swirling pools gathering at road drains and dips. Still not a car passed. I guessed that this stretch had been effectively marooned when they closed the road into it from town. And I guessed, too, that further flooding on other roads had closed down other routes into it. All the same, there were still a few cars abandoned here and there. Presumably those who had found themselves caught between two floods and unable to escape. I peered through steamed-up car windows like a damp and badly dressed dogger. I didn't know what I would do if I found some poor elderly man or woman cramped up in a corner and obviously in trouble. But I had a fresh mobile phone battery and a bottle of water, at least.

And then there was no one and nothing. Not a car and not a building. I made my way along the normally fast and busy A38 to the junction where I would turn left on to the B4213. This was it, the point where the street lights and what little comfort that running through the middle of a night blighted by catastrophic floods on a major rather than a minor road could afford would end. The junction is furnished with traffic lights, though they seem hardly necessary given the scale of the road at this point. It's not an impressive and important piece of civil engineering. Just a small and insignificant road peeling off from a large and busy one to God knows where, unless you are driving home along it – as I would ordinarily be. I peeled off across three lanes and set my head down as I plodded on to the opening stretches of the road home. Very quickly, quicker than I had hoped, the residual glow from the street lights along the A38 died away. Within yards I was running almost blind along a lane I knew to be only a car and a half wide. Either side of it, I knew, too, from past trips, were deep ditches fringed by hedges and trees giving way to cultivated fields. The water in the fields would be deep. I knew this from seeing how it had gathered here in previous, far less dramatic floods. Whether it would have broached the ditches and hedges and flooded across the road, I didn't yet know. And wouldn't until the moment I splashed into such floods. If they were waiting there.

They weren't. At least, I didn't disappear up to my waist. My trainers slapped wetly on to the road. I waited for the tug of deeper water. I focused my vision, trying to peer through the darkness to make out and steer by the high verges and trees I knew to be lining the route. Occasionally, I glanced down at the road itself, trying to determine if a darker patch approaching was an uncrossable stretch of water or a faint moon shadow from a tree stretching across from a gate opening into a waterlogged field. And I was loving it. This was a guilty pleasure. I felt bad about it, but couldn't help myself; as helicopters churned overhead, making their way to ruined farmhouses and distressed villagers whose lives had temporarily collapsed into the water, I was enjoying a good run towards a home that was, last time I called, not underwater. I would be there for my daughter's birthday. The returning hero was actually in the process of returning and I enjoyed the role.

I increased my pace a fraction, pushing deeper and breathing steadily. I glanced at my watch; the illuminated dial told me it was 3.15 a.m. I tried to work out the earliest time at which this pace might allow me to arrive at the front door. And the calculation became too painful. And then I remembered my iPod. Without stopping, I reached round into my shoulder bag and pulled out my Nano, taking care not to drop it or its accompanying tangle of earphones into the water, which was now ankle deep. This must mean I was nearing the dip at the bottom of this stretch of road and I saw, in my imagination, the tight left-hand bend approaching. There would be a gate ahead. It led into large fields and they would, I knew, be badly flooded, too. Another helicopter thrashed the sky to my left. It sounded like a large one. From the flashing searchlight and slow progress it was making as it circled low, I assumed it was searching for some poor, lost soul. I hoped they would be found. And I hoped, too, that I wouldn't end up as yet another case radioed in to the overstretched crews working shift after shift tonight, tomorrow and for who knows how long to come. I could imagine the call . . .

'He did what?'

'Tried to run home.'

'Where from, exactly?'

'Sainsbury's car park in Cheltenham.'

'Where to?'

'His home just outside Ledbury.'

'Jesus, that's nearly, what . . .'

'. . . twenty miles, just under.'

'Christ, is he an athlete?'

'No, telly presenter.'

'The twat. All right, well, we'll see if we can find him. Tell his wife we're on the case but don't get her hopes up too high, not tonight. What was he wearing?'

'All black.'

'For fuck's sake.'

It was best not to imagine the call. I jammed the earphones in and grappled with my iPod. It's always on shuffle, so I hit play, set the volume so that I could hear it over my loudly slapping feet but still be aware if a helicopter was about to land on me, locked it to avoid accidental track-skipping as I ran, slipped it into the front pocket of my jacket and ran on.

## My iPod Is Haunted

A long straight shaded by trees, a sequence of gentle left and right turns flanked by dense hedges. A high bank to my left and another, smaller road opening up to the right: this was the picture I ran through, but it was sourced almost entirely from my imagination and memory – I could see little or nothing. Fast-moving holes in the ragged and wind-torn clouds scudding across the moon afforded me glimpses of the terrain around me; allowed me to get a fix on a remembered gate, a particular old oak leaning on a corner or a turn in the road. From these, I could piece together a full enough picture to let me maintain a steady jog without fear of plunging over an unexpected cliff edge. And I ran on. And on.

All iPods are haunted. At least, mine is. It has a particular knack of taking in the surroundings and the context in which it is being used at a given time and selecting, from the thousands of tracks lodged on it, only those that fit especially well with the moment. These are not always the obvious, literal musical interpretations of what's going on. It doesn't, if I'm lying on a lounger bed by the sea, chuck on endless versions of 'Hot, Hot, Hot' and 'Summertime'. It doesn't wait until I get up to walk across the sand to the bar and play 'Walking on Sunshine'. It is nothing like the editor who chooses the tracks used to illustrate local TV news reports; the man or woman – though I suspect it is, in every single case, a man – who insists on digging out any old piece of crap to play as long as the words feature something to do with the story: '. . . and so very soon, OAPs will be able to take advantage of this piece of local legislation and travel by train, to anywhere in our wonderful country for free'. Cue The Beatles and 'Ticket to Ride'. 'Sadly, all of them died in the blaze at this orphanage three hundred years ago.' Cue The Bangles and 'Eternal Flame'.

My iPod, though, is a paragon of taste, versatility, creativity and diplomacy, and this despite the immense piles of assorted shit with which I load it up. This is the machine I am praising, not my musical choices. I make no claims for my own taste; it is awful. I listen to a huge range of stuff, all of which, with its disparate roots, themes and tones, has only one thing in common: I like it. Motorhead jostles for space with Albinoni, B.B. King and The Blind Boys of Alabama. I make a point of never saying that it is my musical taste that is important here – it's not, it's my iPod, it's haunted. It's got taste, not me. I know people who, armed with one of those devices that connects your iPod to the car stereo via the radio, will spend hours on a long journey trying to persuade you that the music they have chosen to load on to their iPod is the best in the world and demonstrates that they, and they alone, hold the key to the meaning of music and have an empathy with the human condition, the nature of the soul and the process and universal significance of artistic creation that might just, given the chance, save the world.

And you have to sit there in the face of an avalanche of shouted, whimpered, dreary, frothy, lightweight, overly complicated, unmusical or downright poncey bullshit while nodding your head and agreeing that, 'yes, they really had it back then', and, 'no, they can't do it now', and, 'yes, this is the best selection I've ever heard', and, 'yes, music says a lot about us, you must be great', and, 'I wish I had taste, too'. 'Now kill me please, just drive into a fucking motorway bridge and end this torture. Look, I've found a lighter, here, let me set fire to my ears. ANYTHING – JUST STOP PLAYING AWFUL MUSIC AND LOOKING AT ME EXPECTANTLY AS THOUGH I'M GOING TO HAVE AN ORGASM WITH THE SHEER MUSICAL JOY OF IT AND CONVERT TO WHATEVER WEIRD RELI- GION IT IS THAT YOU THINK YOU COULD FOUND WITH THIS POINTLESS FREAK SHOW ASSORT- MENT BOX FULL OF MUSICAL DOG TURDS.' I get quite angry about music. It's important to me.

Needless to say, my iPod's ghosts deejayed for me perfectly as I ran through the night, throwing out tune after tune to keep me going, give me the chance to settle into a rhythm, to break out from the monotony and pump it for a bit or trot on and soak up the atmosphere of a truly strange night. Seventies rock, heavy metal from the eighties, 1920s blues recordings, hip-hop, gospel, raw folk and pure P-funk that had me grinding my hips as I ran. My haunted iPod chose the perfect motivational tracks to drive me on when my legs ached and my mind shrank from the darkest, spookiest corners in the road, set up the perfect steady-rolling beats to help me cover the miles and, along the darkest stretches draped with overhanging branches, floated in haunting melodies played on saws and old euphoniums by Tom Waits and his circus of strange friends just to make sure I didn't forget that I was lucky to be doing something wonderful, weird and memorable.

On one such stretch, I stopped. The moon was breaking through the clouds more steadily now and managing to cast watery, dappled tree shadows across the black and shining road. I halted on the verge, trainers squelching into soft mud and flood-borne silt and bent to stretch my quickly cooling calf muscles, rested my hands on my shins and breathed deeply. Straightening, I yanked the earphones out of my ears, rolled the wire around my hand, reached into the pocket of my thin, damp running jacket and turned the unit off before stuffing the lot into my improvised backpack. I would run without music for a bit now; I wanted to enjoy the sounds and the silence of the night. It was 4.25 a.m. I reckoned I had covered nine or ten miles. Nine or ten still to go. Halfway. I breathed deeply again and felt a soft mist of rain drift across my path.

I had stopped in front of a medium-sized house that stood directly on the side of the road. I knew it well from passing it in the car as I rushed to and from Cheltenham. But I had never looked at it. Not really looked. The moonlight washed over the red-tiled roof, softening the colour of the tiles and taking away their warmth. They looked blue. The house stands sideways on to the road and, at the mid-point of the longest wall, projecting up from the eaves and making a triangular peak running perpendicular to the longer, larger peak of the roof itself, is a small dormer window. No more than a foot from top to bottom and ten inches across, it most likely gives on to an equally small eaved bedroom with sloping walls gathering towards the roof above simple, plain furniture and a single bed covered by a hand-stitched patchwork quilt of a thousand warm colours. Or it might be a teenager's bedroom full of posters of Pamela Anderson and boxes of socks and trainers.

Whatever, it is someone's refuge from the world, someone's

haven. It is part of someone's home. A family, a retired couple, a lone bachelor – whoever lived there, this was their final resort, the cave in which they slept. And I wondered if they had been threatened there by the floods. I guessed that the fields behind the house would be full of water, the edge of the lake inching closer to the house. Perhaps the householders had stood in the windows and watched its advance. As it prowled closer, inch by inch, maybe they had suddenly, as one, rushed into action and moved their most precious possessions upstairs for safety. And then returned to the windows to watch this irresistible force, this unstoppable thing, nature, advance on them and decide their future.

Not yet fully aware of the extent of the flooding, but well aware from the radio reports I had heard before setting off on my run, of the impact it was having already, I wondered how many people had faced it. How many people had retreated to the safety of their home, their refuge from the world of work, school, colleagues, commercial pressure, street violence and shopping centres and found that, even there, they were not safe. How many people had peeked out from behind the door of their cave and waited to be attacked in their own home by something as indifferent to their wants, needs and fears as gravity.

My home still lay ten miles away. I rolled my head on my neck, settled the canvas strap of my bag across my shoulders, checked the zip of my jacket, raised up on to my toes briefly, dropped back down and set off at a gentle but determined lope. I wanted to ring Mindy, but I would need to ring her early enough anyway as I got closer to home. I would need a hot bath ready when I got back and Mindy had agreed to run it for me. No point waking her now, only to wake her again in a couple of hours. I needed to make some distance.

More bends in the road, gentler ones here. A pub, on the left, standing behind a car park of loose, large-grained yellow stones. Big pub sign on a mound of grass. Wooden post. Usually a lot of cars here, parked up on the verge. None to see tonight, too dark. Hedges high along here now, sure of that. Another house off to the right, no lights on, all asleep. Lucky sods. A long, straight run now, probably a mile, with deep dips and crests. Great fun in the car, goes light over the tops and stands up on its relaxed springs before crouching down and compressing them in the dips. Not such a dynamic experience running, takes longer. Head down, time breathing with paces. Soaked to the skin. Neckstrap chafing across neck and shoulders. Swing the bag off without stopping, pull damp jacket off, feel rush of cold air against wet fleece, swing bag back across behind, looping strap across shoulders, tie jacket across small of back, knotting the sleeves at the front, forms a pad to stop bag hitting kidneys with every step. Better. Settle, run. Run.

And I ran. I passed over the river where Zog lives. I would be here again, very soon. The waters would get deeper and the road vanish altogether. But I didn't know that yet and I stuck to the rhythm of the run. As the sky began to hint that day was coming, I cleared Staunton, the last village before home, and pushed on. A handful of miles to go now. It was 5.30. My dreams of setting a decent marathon time evaporating with every minute. But I would be home in time for Willow's birthday – she would be happy to see her daddy, even if he was a crap athlete. There were a few cars now. Parked on verges or in lay-bys among piles of gravel and broken tree branches. The floods had not yet hit this area hard, but they had cut off access and stranded cars full of people. As the morning grew light, it hung grey and damp as an old tea towel. I plodded past the Rose and Crown and on to the final straight leading up to the M50. Cross this and I would turn three corners before limping up the lane leading to our drive. I knew that this lane might be badly flooded. Mindy had reported it passable, but a foot or so underwater by late last night. She had offered to collect me from the main road in her Land Rover if it was bad. It was kind, but the fact is a human being can cross water deeper than even a Landie can wade. And I would complete the journey alone and unaided. I was bloody determined on that one.

As the road rose up towards the bridge across the M50, it got busier again. Nothing moved but clearly the motorway had been shut down in the evening and hundreds of lorries, cars, vans and coaches, were stranded on the road leading to and from the junction. Many must have been stranded trying to get on to the M50 and, as I got closer and saw the motorway transformed into a broad river, I understood that many would simply have been washed off it and forced to shelter on higher ground. They were parked on the road now, not stuck in hedges. They were lined up in two facing streams as if the flow of traffic had simply been frozen in time, instantaneously. The damp tea-towel morning grew gently in intensity and provoked a few sleepers to wake and climb from their vehicles. Stretching, yawning, staring around, they looked like they had slept for a very, very long time. I passed between the ranks of vehicles, smiling sympathetically, nodding and giving people space. There were not many, maybe ten, maybe twenty souls were stirring in total, out of a queue of perhaps two or three hundred vehicles. It was like the day after a particularly lengthy student party. Or the day after the Triffids had struck.

'What's it like?' a lone figure, male, mid-thirties in shirt and suit trousers, emerged from a blue saloon and rubbed his eyes, looking nervously around and settling on me. I was annoyed. For no good reason.

'What's what like?' Knowing full well what he meant, I probed anyway.

'Well,' he looked at me as he might an idiot who had asked him what day it was. 'The flood. What's it like? How is it?'

'Well, I can tell you every inch of it between here and Cheltenham. And it's . . . wet.'

He looked mildly deflated, his puffy face registering a residue of the fear he must have felt the night before when he gave up his journey and slept in the car.

'Where you trying to get to anyway?' I wanted to know.

'Gloucester. I live there.'

'Well, that's only eight miles or so away.'

'Couldn't get any further.' He waved an arm at the ranks of parked vehicles frozen in their stationary tableau of a busy road.

'You could have left the car behind and . . . why didn't you ring your wife, ask her to run a bath and set off on foot. You can cover eight miles walking in a couple of hours, even in your office shoes. Why didn't you just, oh never mind. Look, hope it's all okay when you get back.' I set off towards home and shouted back over my shoulder at the pudgy figure standing next to his impotent car on a motorway bridge over a new river. 'Good luck.'

Have we really become that hopeless? If our cars stop, do we just stand there and hit them with a stick until they work, hoping that whatever is chasing us doesn't catch us up in the meantime? I love cars, really I do. But I can as happily sling one in a ditch and carry on home on foot to see my family as I can abandon a broken microwave in favour of a campfire, given the chance.

It was light now. Light, but not bright. A watery, diffused and consistent light that seeped through the branches overhead and showed the tired, muddy remnants of the previous night's excitement for what they were: miserable. The colours in the trees flanking the lane in front of our house were pale and muted, as though the pigment had been washed away with the steady passing of the water running off from the Welsh hills miles away. Only their branches stood out, their intricate tracery black against the pale sky. The lane was flooded, as Mindy had predicted. But it ran no more than thigh deep and I waded through, anxious to complete the journey to my front door and family. The colours, the flood, the stranded man staring blankly at the idea of running or walking home – nothing mattered, not to me. I was home and Willow would wake up and ask her daddy for a sheep or a donkey. All was well in our little world.


## A Mouse Has Eaten My Boat

Zog would have come over to see Willow on her birthday but the lane running up to his riverside house was already flooded and impassable by car. He and Jill were stuck at home until the waters receded.

'Mate, what are you going to do?'

'We'll be fine. It'll abate. Until then, we've got food and everything we need.'

He wasn't going to let me or anyone else worry about him. Zog's little spot alongside the River Severn may be beautiful, but it can have a habit of suddenly becoming *in* rather than *by* the water. This was a big flood, a very big one. In smaller deluges, the more regular floods of winter every year, the house looked after itself. Underfloor sumps and pumps contained and controlled the water, firing it straight back out again. For the river to encroach on Zog and Jill's house a little bit was not unheard of; it had never happened in the time they had lived there, but the previous owners had fitted enough kit to make sure that, should a couple of inches of the River Severn decide to set up.home in their house, it would be dealt with easily.

'We've got machines to take care of it, mate. Not a worry. The pumps are all working, everything's fine'

But this was the worst flood in hundreds of years and would get a lot worse yet.

As Saturday rolled into Sunday, I grew more worried about Zog and Jill. The TV news was full of images of people being airlifted from the roofs of their flooded houses. And something in Zog's voice, something about the way he said they were okay and comfortable and not worried, told me that they very much were worried. They were reduced to sitting upstairs in pitch blackness all night as the water lapped and splashed around their house, invading desk and kitchen drawers, investigating long-forgotten places and permeating every corner of the place where they felt safest in the world.

'Bugger this Mindy, I'm getting them out. We can't just sit here and, and, what, hope the helicopters have got time to pick up Zog and Jill? They're fit, healthy adults whose kids are grown and away from home. When will they get looked after? It'll be women and children first, and rightly so, and Zogs and Jills last. Bugger this. Where are your Land Rover keys?'

My Land Rover is a truly magnificent thing: 4.6-litre hand-built V8, four-inch suspension lift, custom-built rollcage, winch, massive stereo – the works. But it has a petrol engine and these are famously useless if they get wet. Mindy's Land Rover is a diesel. It is also bright yellow and permanently filled with horse-riding hats, half-eaten biscuits, children's toys, sacks of dog food, lollipop sticks, coats, scarves, hats and pots of make-up. And she'll get rid of me before she gets rid of it.

'Oh, so Mindy's car comes to the rescue again, hey?'

She laughed and gloated after me as I ran for the car, keys, complete with ridiculous key fob in the shape of a pair of green wellies, jangling in my right hand.

'You see, Lollipop to the rescue again.' She and the girls called it Lollipop because, because, well, just because they are who they all are.

'See that, girls. Daddy's off to rescue Soggy Zoggy in Lollipop.'

I left the squeals and laughter behind as I leaped in the car – unlocked, as always – stuck the keys in the slot and fired it up. The diesel engine clattered into life and I knew I would be returning soon with Zog, Jill and whatever wine we could rescue from their always impressive selection for a damn good evening of making ourselves all feel better.

'Mindy, there's no way. No way at all. I've just rung Zog and told him, no way can I get through. No, not even in Lollipop. The road is just a river, you can see just the very tops of the road signs sticking out. It's weird. Must be five or six feet deep. And Zog's lower than this, his house is down off the road.'

I craned around to see where I knew his house to be, lost now in the water. And I realised that I was not where I thought I was. I had driven as far as I could, before pulling over and walking up to the edge of the water where it spanned the road in front. I had assumed that the house now to my left was the one marking the turning point into Zog's lane. And now I realised that house was still a couple of miles ahead of me. A couple of miles entirely covered by water.

'Christ, the river must be four miles wide. Maybe more. We can't leave them there. Not an option. We have to get them out of that. I'm on my way back. Get me a boat. Doesn't matter what it costs, we can worry about that after. He'd do the same for me, I know he would.' And he would.

Bit of a tall order, that last one, though. Boats were, as we very quickly learned, in rather short supply. I took over the search for a craft as soon as I got home. Ironically enough, though perhaps not surprisingly, most of the local boating stores were based in and around the very areas most affected by the floods. This wasn't the result of some astonishing prescience on the part of local store-keepers but was simply because those towns based along the county's rivers were the ones where people were most likely to want to buy a small boat and, inevitably, the places most likely to be devastated by a flood such as the one still unfolding and worsening now. I rang shops specialising in small boats, chandlery, fishing and 'leisure craft' – whatever they are. No one answered. Some were in Tewkesbury or parts of Gloucester I soon realised to be flooded and I imagined a lonely answerphone in a now underwater store room flashing and dimming in the water.

'This is impossible. We'll not find one to buy. Who do we know with a boat?'

It turned out, no one. But Mindy had a friend who she claimed knew everyone in the area and could find anything at any time.

'Well, get me a boat.'

And she did. Through a friend of her friend's friend, she traced someone who had a small inflatable boat, wasn't using it right now and was willing to lend it to me. I scribbled the directions down, leaped back in the Land Rover and tore over to his house where I picked up a small, blue and white deflated inflatable boat, an equally small outboard motor to fit it, a foot pump to inflate it and, in case things got dire, a pair of plastic oars.

I dashed home, took the boat out and surveyed it on the yard outside our house. Green mildew clustered in its corners as I unrolled it. Patches of differently faded and stained rubber suggested it had already been repaired more than once. The owner had warned me that the mice in the stable where he kept it did sometimes like a nibble at it. But we could find no evidence of them having snacked on his craft since its last outing and I felt confident. I rammed the hose of the foot pump into the inlet nozzle and pumped. I hadn't called Zog yet. I wanted to check things were all ready and working before I set off. Then I would call him.

The first half of the boat was inflated. It stood and quivered in the yard, a yellowing tube of rubber about four feet long. A wooden backboard – I don't know the nautical name for it, but it almost certainly has one other than 'backboard' – hung suspended now from one end by the inflated tube. The other side would not rise up and level the board off until I had inflated the opposing tube. This was the board on to which I would attach the rusty little outboard. I decided to switch the pump over to the other side and finish inflating the boat, travel there with it tied to the roof of the Land Rover and fit the motor when I got to the water. I pumped. And pumped. And it didn't work. Feeding the rubber through my hand inch by inch, I found the problem: a mouse or mice had eaten away a disc of rubber the size of my thumb. The air being forced in through the nozzle flopped straight back out again, barely having the energy to disturb the frayed edges of the hole.

I did some energetic and creative swearing, yelled for Mindy and we sat down and thought, really thought. A bicycle repair kit wouldn't do it. And I didn't have one anyway. Someone we knew must have a boat. They did. We hadn't thought of it immediately because the boat concerned was more an ornamental than a strictly practical craft. It belonged to Johnny Vizor. He had founded a business discovering and importing antique garden furniture and equipment and selling it, mostly through high-end, glamorous London shops. We had already bought quite a few bits and pieces from him. And he himself lived his life surrounded by examples of precisely the sort of age-worn, time-served, work-proven things so in demand from his high-class clientele. And among those things with which he happily surrounded himself, we knew, he had a boat. It was a small wooden rowing boat, no more than six feet long and three feet wide. He had brought it in from Eastern Europe and was very proud of it. He had kept it on the water outside his mill house before he moved about six months earlier. The mill house was probably badly hit by the flood, but he lived elsewhere now and, hopefully, was high and dry with his boat ready for action.

He was. One phone call and Johnny volunteered the boat and himself for the mission. A dash in the Land Rover to pick it up from where it now lay, in his storage warehouse, and we were off. Johnny was typically upbeat. We both knew that this mission was only necessitated by Zog's horrible misfortune. But the mission itself was inherently fun. Get boat, drive as far as we could, put boat in water, attach the outboard motor that came with the non-inflating inflatable and sail to Zog's house to fish him out. Despite the circumstances, we were upbeat. As would Zog have been had the situation been reversed.

## Ivan's Engine

At the water's edge we were far from alone. A small crowd had gathered alongside the newly formed lake. It was immense, a huge plain of water encompassing entire villages up and down the River Severn. We were still two or three miles from Zog's house and would get no closer to it by car. Even by Lollipop. We shouldered through the lightly scattered crowd with the boat and lowered it into the water. It floated. It would: it was wooden and didn't need to be inflated with a foot pump. I had taken the precaution of pulling on a wetsuit and so I waded in with it and attached the tiny outboard to the back with the simple clamps supplied. It was a cool but pleasant day. The sun broke through the light covering of clouds from time to time. It could have been a boating lake. But it wasn't, it was the village of Tirley. I shoved the boat back until it ground out on the road and Johnny climbed in. I hauled myself over the gunwale and flopped into the back. The engine was reluctant to start, but it finally sputtered into action like a sheep waking up and settled down into an uneven grumble.

'Here we go then. That way.' Johnny took up position at the front, I took the helm. The crowd cheered with good-natured friendliness. Some of them knew Zog and Jill; they too lived near the river but had escaped flooding and were naturally concerned for their neighbours. The appearance of that bloke on the telly with a wooden boat and a competent-looking mate provided both hope and instant entertainment at an otherwise gloomy time.

I twisted the throttle and the tiny propeller whirred its best and pushed us gently out into the lake. A Give Way sign stuck out of the water a couple of hundred yards ahead, only the top of the signboard itself visible, side on to us, just above the water. It marked the point at which we would swing left up a side road before turning right to cross the churchyard and drift across the fields leading up to Zog's lane. There was little point in sticking to the roads. We could go anywhere we wanted now. It was strangely exhilarating.

As we chugged up to the junction, we encountered strong side currents. The River Severn still drove through this lake and brought with it considerable power, boosted by the run-off from the mountains that had caused the flood in the first place. It pushed us back over towards the sign, away from where we wanted to go. I moved the outboard from side to side, trying to steady our drift and keep us heading the right way. I twisted the throttle to maximum. We started to make some headway against the current, which was insistent and visible as broiling trails through the brown, muddy water. A substantial wire fence lay twisted and broken in the water to our left, destroyed presumably by a passing piece of floating wreckage. I worried that we might snag the boat in it and get stuck. I didn't fancy getting out in this current and trying to untangle it. And then the engine cut out. There was no warning, no lengthy illness followed by a welcome release. It just upped and died. And it left us pretty deeply in the shit.

'Oars!' we yelled, simultaneously grabbing a short-handled wooden oar each and paddling against the current while the boat, now without even the subtle nudge of the outboard to keep it going in the right direction, drifted backwards. The crowd had caught the sudden silence brought about by the little outboard's demise. This was getting more entertaining by the second.

'Johnny, if we go through that fence back there and out into those fields,' I waved my oar back towards what had once been hedged farm fields but was now a huge and unbounded lake the size of the Atlantic, 'we'll be utterly screwed.'

'It'll be fine. Paddle for the shore.' Johnny is an unflappable kind of guy.

We paddled, the crowd ooh-ed and ahh-ed, the boat completed a 360-degree spin, and another, and another, and we inched slowly back towards the shore and the cars. No one hummed the theme tune from *Hawaii Five-O.*

Once back, we agreed that the motor was knackered and that it was unwise to try and complete the mission, paddling all the way to Zog and Jill's house, through heaven knew what other similar trials and then back again with four people on board without the motor to drive us. And then Ivan appeared. He stood at the edge of the water and smiled at us with amiable recognition. Ivan is Zog's next-door neighbour and one of those people you suspect will still be here even when the entire planet has been reduced to rubble by nuclear war, plagues and robot rebellion. He's not a survivalist or anything weird, but he is a survivor. Just born to it, I guess. Fortyish, slight, with a smart, jet-black moustache and gentle brown eyes, he exudes the sort of solidity, reliability and practicality that nations were founded upon. He fixes things for a living. Anything. He can work as a blacksmith, a metal founder, a carpenter, a farmer, a mechanic, technician, fisherman, vintage motorcycle restorer – he can do pretty much anything. None of us knows quite how he accumulated all these skills. He just did. If he were a musician, we would have said he had met someone at the crossroads and cut some sort of deal. But he was here now, having been flooded out of his own house and would, I knew with absolute certainty be able to fix our borrowed outboard with nothing more than a hair comb and chewing gum and send us back on our way.

He did better than that. He gave us another motor. And not any motor.

'Oh, I can help with that.' He walked off to his car, and came back with a bundle of old cloths. And he unwrapped the exact same engine, only in better condition. I knew it was in better condition, because it was Ivan's and every cog, every connection, every shaft and every bearing would have been dismantled, honed, greased and replaced. Before breakfast.

'Been pottering about in my own boat after the floods hit. Had to get out to the shops and then transfer us all out of the house when it finally went under. So, here it is.'

He handed me the engine.

'Bloody hell, Ivan. Thanks, mate. We'll get it back to you whenever all this,' I waved at the encroaching flood with my elbow, careful not to drop the precious motor, 'is over. How're you? How's your house?'

'Oh, we're fine. We'll be okay. Here, give me the other motor and I'll service it so you can give it back working.' Some people are just better than me. Ivan is one of them.

We fixed the new motor on to what Ivan called the transom and headed back out into the newly formed Tirley Lake.

'This is more like it, much better.' Johnny laughed at my enthusiasm for the new engine. We were still unlikely to be troubling the surface of the water to produce a bow wave, but we were moving smoothly and the engine just sounded better. Stronger. Reliable. Ivan-ised.

And Zog and Jill huddled in their upstairs bedroom in the dark, while thick, black pools of water advanced up the stairs. I rang them. We had been sparing with the calls because he had no way of recharging his mobile when it died and, if we couldn't get to them, they might just need it later when the helicopter came.

'Mate, had a bit of trouble with stuff. But we're on the way now. With you in minutes. Be ready for the arrival of our magnificent craft.' I looked along the length of our wooden boat and hoped there would be room for us all.

'Hammond, what have you done? We would have been fine. And where the hell did you find a boat. Ivan?'

'Nope, but we did run into him. Tell you later. Johnny Vizor provided the boat. She's a beauty. Get your stuff ready. No furniture though, bit small.'

We crossed the graveyard, the propeller clonking off the top of gravestones. I wondered if we would have to cruise through piles of ancient bones, floating on the surface like the aftermath of some time warp submarine sinking. We didn't. After the churchyard, we broached the field boundaries, pulling the top branches of trees aside to ease our passage and passing into the fields beyond, now just another stretch of the lake. As the sun shone weakly past the now fluffy, soft clouds, it could genuinely have been fun. The water was muddy and thick with debris, but the lake we were crossing was fringed with greenery from the tree tops. The church spire, the only part of the building that now protruded above the water, made a magnificent landmark. I doubted if anyone would be congregating there for some time.

## No One Commented on the Wine

We found the house. It wasn't easy. Roads look very different when they're underwater. And the house that I had visited so many times before looked different, too. The lower storey was gone completely, the upper-storey windows resting a foot or two above the surface like square portholes. And I suddenly remembered my last visit and felt bad. I had nipped round to Zog's for coffee and a gossip on the pretext of picking up or dropping off some piece of kit or other. There had been a lot of rain and we had been joking on the phone about the dangers of flooding when you live so close to a river. I had arrived at their doorstep in my Land Rover wearing a snorkel and diving mask, 'just in case'. Zog pissed himself, called me a cheeky young twat and made the coffee. And now I felt like I might just have been tempting fate. I hoped Zog wouldn't remember it when I finally saw him again in a few minutes.

We bumped the boat up to the top of the front door, I slipped out and swam in while Johnny held his boat in place by gripping the top of the porch roof. Inside, all was ruined. In the darkness, sofas and armchairs floated upside down, their delicate, turned legs sticking proud of the water and glinting in the light of the torch I held in my mouth. Zog and Jill have, or had, a fine collection of antique furniture dating back through their families for generations. It didn't look like any of it would be salvageable. In the kitchen, the brand-new Smeg fridge floated on its side, its contents long since disgorged into the mayhem around it. I found the stairs and slowly hauled myself out of the water.

They were in amazingly good spirits considering what they had sat and watched happen to their home and their possessions. People often are, I guess. Gripping black dustbin bags full of a few clothes and whatever else they could save, they made their way down and swam into the living room. We couldn't get back into the boat; it floated barely a foot below the top of the doorway and there was no way to throw yourself back in without braining yourself on the doorframe. If we pushed it out, we would be trying the same manoeuvre in the confines of the porch roof, which would be worse. We needed something to stand on under the water so that we could climb over the gunwale and flop into the boat. Despite the devastation, I looked guiltily at Zog as I grabbed a dining chair floating past.

'I need to use this as a step. It'll probably get damaged, mate.'

'It's fucked. Let's get in the boat.'

I shoved the chair down under the water, feeling it knock against the stone floor and settle. Jill, then Zog, climbed in, slithering through the gap under the doorway like cavers. Johnny let go of the roof, I pushed the boat out and swam after it. Jill asked me to lock the door. 'Looters,' she said. And, without hesitation, we all agreed that, yes, we must lock it. It didn't matter that the house was probably ruined and everything in it almost certainly so. Jill was about to leave her home for an as yet unknown period of time. When you go out, you lock the door. It's what you do every day when you leave your home. I tried to heave it shut and couldn't. Diving down into the black water, I kicked at the bottom corner, shifting some of the accumulated sludge and silt and, finally, it shut slowly.

We made the trip back in a strange state. They were happy to be out in the sunlight. We were all happy to be enjoying a boat trip together. It was, in an odd way, fun as we floated back across the fields, fixing our bearings by the top half of the church spire and carefully manhandling our way through the greenery as we passed over trees. And above us all floated the knowledge of what had happened to Zog, Jill and a great many other people that weekend. He told me later that the hardest part hadn't been the loss of the antiques or the paintings. He had sat in his bedroom, chin on the window sill, and watched as the firewood he had carefully gathered, trimmed and piled through the summer, floated past, liberated from the barn by the house, and disappeared up the now four-mile-wide river. This simple assault, nature taking from him what nature had given him, as a human being, to survive the onslaught of another winter, was what cut the deepest and left him feeling most frustrated and helpless in the face of forces too big to resist. We got thoroughly and properly pissed that evening, the lot of us, on cheap and awful wine from my kitchen. And no one commented on the wine.

# Chapter 7
# NEVER MEET YOUR HEROES
## Evel Knievel

Evel Knievel died on 30 November 2007. He was old, he had broken nearly every bone in his body at least once, he had pulmonary fibrosis, was on a full-time oxygen supply and had suffered at least one stroke. And still I was surprised to hear that he had died. And so were a lot of people all over the world. Because Evel Knievel was a legend. He was invincible. He was, well, he was Evel Knievel. He soared across the sky, star-spangled cape flowing behind him, motorcycle glinting in the sunlight, heading for the perilous ramp far below him, back on the ground where we mere mortals waited with bated breath. Something would go wrong on the landing, because it always did; he spun out of control, rolled, flipped, was chased across the arena floor by the out-of-control bike now turned into a charging bull, smashed into the hoardings and then got up, took the applause and limped out supported by his friends. That's what Evel Knievel did. None of that involved dying. If he was the kind of bloke to do dying, he would have done it decades ago. And even though I had only just come back from spending two weeks with him to make a documentary about his life and had seen first hand how old and fragile he was, had held his skinny arms to help his wasted, birdlike frame in and out of cars, I still couldn't believe that this tough, grisly old hero had finally given up the ghost. He left a unique gap in the world and I, among millions of others, shall miss him.

I had not been expecting to make a documentary about Evel Knievel. It came, rather like Evel himself, out of the blue. I got the call in a pub. I pretended to be working. When the phone rang, I hit the button to accept the call, waved my free hand to excuse myself from the friends grouped round the table and shouldered my way past the crowd to stand outside in the night where I could better hear the voice on the other end.

'Sorry about that. Busy, er, meeting.'

'That's okay. Can you hear me now?'

'Yup, perfectly thanks.' I pulled a tricky lump of salt and vinegar crisp residue from my teeth with my tongue and looked up at the sign hanging over the pub doorway. There were pastel-coloured stars hand-painted against a deep blue background. Something featured at the bottom of the picture, possibly a fish. Or a tree. I looked back down at the street. It had been raining earlier in the evening – warm, gentle rain that left broad, shallow puddles in the road for the street lights and car lights to reflect and play in. I could smell late-night food. I may have been slightly drunk. Another car prowled slowly by, wheels drawing neon trails through the puddles. I snapped to it. The voice on the other end was talking. At me, I supposed.

'Good. So, hi, Richard, my name's Ben and here's the thing. Evel Knievel has granted us permission to spend a week filming with him at his hometown in Montana. He's very ill and this will probably be the last documentary made with him.'

I stood up straight, arching my back and frowning with the effort of listening more and more closely. The voice on the phone was talking to me about Evel Knievel. I liked Evel Knievel. Had a model of him as a kid. Dad bought it for me one Christmas.

'He's agreed to be interviewed and to sit and be filmed talking us through the archive of footage and photos of his career. It's for the BBC and they want to broadcast it sometime near Christmas. Are you interested in making it with us?'

'Er, well,' it was all I could do not to climb into the telephone and pop out on the other end to grab hold of this bloke's leg and never let go until he had promised to let me make his telly programme about my childhood hero. 'It's, er, got something to it, yes.'

'So you're interested?'

'Christ, yes.'

## I Did Some Thinking – Never a Good Thing

First things first; we needed a plan. I met with Ben, who turned out to be engagingly bonkers with an impressive track record of making intelligent, compelling documentaries. We talked things through, I got excited and bounced around, shouting about how I had spent my childhood emulating Evel's jumps on my bicycle and once broke a pane in our French windows with my Evel Knievel wind-up motorbike. Ben, with a mop of unruly hair and an ever-present grin but the air of an intellectual in a world of TV buffoons, spoke of the cultural significance of Evel, of how he was pretty much at the forefront of the kind of merchandising and commercial exploitation of celebrities that we take for granted today, and sprang into being at a time when the world needed a real-life hero with an almost superhuman invincibility tempered by very human fragility – Ben's cleverer than me. But we both agreed that this was a hell of a chance to make a great film and we had better not cock it up.

I went away and did some thinking – never a good thing. In the meantime, Nigel Simpkiss agreed to direct it. Nigel is one of the key directors on, among many other things, *Top Gear*. He has down the years turned out some of *Top Gear*'s very best films as well as fleets of commercials and pop videos. He had directed our polar expedition and I couldn't have been happier that he was prepared to get involved with this project. The two of us held a meeting in the tiny sitting room of my London flat. To make it feel more like a meeting and less like just another get-together with a mate round my gaff where we end up talking about music and arguing over who uses the iPod speakers, I had set us up at the glass-topped dining table. And turned the telly off. We sat opposite each other.

'Listen, Nigel,' I was determined to bring my own input to this project, to take a key role in shaping it from the outset. 'I think what we have here is a chance to make the most authoritative, informative and insightful documentary ever made about the life of a global icon and one who came into being at a critical and fascinating time on the worldwide scene.'

I had, I'll admit, rehearsed this bit ready for our production meeting. Nigel watched me carefully, his deep-set eyes not flickering as he took in my every word. I went on with my pre-prepared presentation.

'He has granted us unheard-of access to him, his archive and his associates.'

I leaned towards Nigel and tried my best to load my words with significance and sincerity. 'Nigel, we must take advantage of this opportunity. What I want to do is produce the definitive Evel Knievel documentary. The one that people will refer to and that will stand as the, well, er, as the definitive, er, one.'

Nigel, typically calm and quiet, leaned forwards and rested his elbows on the table. He drew a breath. And his eyes sparkled mischievously. He likes to upset the apple cart, Nigel – it's a director thing. He smiled. That's quite a frightening thing.

'Yes.'

He arched his hands in front of his face and rested his fingertips together.

'But I'd rather set out to make the worst Evel Knievel documentary ever. It would just be, well, more fun.'

We weren't, it appeared, singing from exactly the same hymn sheet. Or even in the same church.

'Erm, okay.'

And we talked. And he explained that he didn't want us to saddle ourselves with being pompous and grave. He wanted us to be honest, to show a bit of the documentary-making process on the TV screen once it was finished and to keep it human and, therefore, more meaningful. He was, annoyingly, right. Of course. Ben Joiner, another *Top Gear* regular and one of the best cameramen in the business, would shoot it. We would use a local sound recordist based in the States and a second cameraman sourced locally, too.

Our filming was scheduled to fit around a unique festival held annually in Evel's hometown of Butte, Montana. Called, with typically far-reaching US imagination, Evel Knievel Days, it amounted to a week of celebrations in honour of one of the town's most outstanding sons, Evel Knievel. Organised largely by Evel's own son, Robbie, it draws people from all over the world to the dusty town of Butte to gather and watch people jump over things on motorcycles – generally with a greater and more reliable degree of success than the man in whose honour the festival was held – eat hot dogs and burgers, live in motor homes, dress spectacularly badly and drink with moderate to vigorous enthusiasm. Evel no longer lived in Butte; his failing health and dwindling finances had forced him to retreat to Florida, where the lower altitude suited his ailing lungs and he could, I guessed, more easily lose himself among the fleets of similarly impecunious and wheezy octogenarians seeking sun and comfort by the sea. I hated to think of the great star-spangled legend reduced to shuffling about the boardwalks moaning about the heat. So I didn't. I looked forward instead to spending time with him at the festival and, according to the agreement we formulated with him, sitting down together and sifting through the extensive archive of photos and footage of his life in stunts. He travelled to Evel Knievel Days every year, meeting his legions of international fans and even leading the motorcycle parade around the outskirts of the town. Hundreds of bikers took part in this and it was agreed that I, too, should throw a leg over my hog and ride out with the boys behind Evel Knievel.

## Except It Was Burgundy

Another flight, another airline meal, another ten hours spent trying not to get busted for admiring the stewardess, another queue at passport control, another airport, another cheap hotel. Another first day on a shoot. I sat astride a Harley-Davidson in a lay-by, waiting for the signal over the walkie-talkie resting on the fuel tank to tell me that everyone was set up, the cameras were rolling and I could ride up for my first meeting with Evel Knievel. And this really was my first meeting with him. We had been kept apart in all the pre-meetings and discussions, giving us a better chance of capturing the genuine first encounter rather than some attempt at re-enacting it afterwards. It's a cringe-making, agonising moment on telly when two people who have clearly already met and spoken at length have their pretend first meeting on camera and shake hands and say their hellos with all the conviction of stereo salesmen.

I had been told that Evel would be sitting in a large SUV in the car park of the Butte Shooting Club where they had already filmed him shooting clays. They wouldn't tell me which car he would be in or where exactly it would be parked – all in the name of 'keeping it real'. I was pretty nervous. This wasn't some bloke who thought he was great. This wasn't someone emulating Evel Knievel. This was the man himself, the legend. And me – a bloke from Birmingham who grew up playing with his Evel Knievel wind-up bike, who grazed his knees trying to jump his bicycle over six toy double-decker buses and who went to sleep every night staring at his Evel Knievel wallpaper – about to meet him and spend a week interviewing him. How the hell did that happen?

I checked again over the radio.

'Nope, not ready yet. Buzz you when we are.' Nigel's voice was typically calm, but I knew he was under pressure. He was making sure we didn't cock up the very first shots of the documentary. A car hissed by on the hot road, disappearing into the heat haze between the hills leading out of town. We were in the rolling, dry countryside around Butte. This was the dusty, hard-assed mining town he had grown up in. A young bloke, facing a future that held only a tough job down the mines, a few nights of paid-for passion with one of the town's legendary legions of prostitutes, a marriage troubled with poverty and too many raggedy kids and an early death from a selection of the lung diseases available to Butte's miners; somehow, he had elevated himself from that humble and, perhaps, hopeless start to become an international legend, a multi-millionaire and a hero to millions. He had created and become Evel Knievel.

I checked again that I had the measure of the bike on which I would ride into shot and meet Evel. It was a rented Harley-Davidson Road King. A good bike in many ways. Long, low, stable and pretty cool. Except this one was burgundy. A colour that only exists in America where it is used for Harley-Davidsons, draylon recliner chairs, nylon trousers, plastic belts and motel curtains. Nowhere else in the world will you find the same dismal, light-sapping and hopelessly unsexy shade. The spectrum can only handle it in the States. And the broad, fat curves of my rented Harley were the deepest of burgundy littered with scraps of thin, cheap chrome. The exhausts were the standard, factory-fitted ones dictated by American legislation and they strangled the archetypal Harley bellow and rumble to a soft, faintly effeminate chuffing cough. It may as well have carried a ten-foot neon sign on the back screaming 'Rented bike. This guy's only pretending.' Worse still, I had been unable to bring my own crash helmet thanks to the luggage limitations on the flight. And the one that came with the bike matched it. It was a burgundy bike helmet, as large and round as a space hopper with an equally proportioned shiny black peak and press studs at the back to attach the strap of the goggles they forgot to include with it. As a result, my eyes had collected a huge number of small, black flies that lay now in my lower eyelid like a dense, black snowdrift.

Another car went by and I hid my face behind my hand. I felt stupid on my rented burgundy bike. Staring closely at the low-cut leather glove I had selected for the trip, I tried to convince myself that my arrival would be up to scratch for Evel. Obviously, I would rather come screaming down a ramp with the bike's tail on fire, jump the crew van and slam down in front of the legend himself before ripping off my bike helmet, flashing a white-toothed smile, flicking my floppy, heroic hair out of my eyes and saying, 'Hi, Richard Hammond', and Evel saying, 'Yes, I know, it's great to meet you, Richard, I'm an admirer of your work.' Well, if you're going to fantasise about meeting a childhood hero, make it a good meeting at least. Sadly, though, I would have to settle for rolling into a car park on a rented bike, wearing a matching, massive burgundy bike helmet and a pair of too new Harley biking boots that looked suspiciously like something worn in special-interest clubs and usually teamed with a pair of leather chaps and nothing else.

'Okay, Hammond. We're ready.'

'Righto. On my way.'

I stuffed the walkie-talkie into the front of my leather jacket, thumbed the bike's start button, checked for traffic, clunked it into first, eased out the clutch and stalled. A small, municipal-looking truck rumbled past and a large bird squawked softly overhead. The

grass along the verge of the lay-by was tall and brown. It rustled in
the draught following the truck. The shimmering air smelled of
hot metal and petrol.

'Bollocks.'

I leaned forwards, lifted my left leg back up on to the footboard
to snick the gear lever up into neutral and I restarted the engine. I
twisted in the saddle to check for traffic. The walkie-talkie fell out
of my jacket, rattled across the fuel tank and fell to the ground.

'Shit.'

A plane droned slowly overhead. I was hot and getting hotter.

I couldn't reach the radio from where I sat, not without risking
dropping the bike. I flicked the side stand down, levered myself
out of the saddle and stooped to pick up the walkie-talkie.

'With you in about ten seconds.' I tried to sound calm and
unflustered and pocketed the radio properly this time before climbing back on board the burgundy Harley.

## Am I Driving?

It was less than a mile to the gun club. As promised, I came to a
large but crudely painted sign pointing to a dusty track leading off
to the right. Along the track, a group of low-lying, single-storey
brick buildings slumped in the heat, surrounded by a few, thin
trees. Behind, the hills of Montana grew and painted themselves
across the horizon. There were a lot of cars in the car park. I knew
that I would be able to tell which one Evel Knievel was waiting in
because there would be a film crew next to it. But first, I needed
to make sure I didn't let the bike slip on the loose, dusty, gravel
track. Falling off right now would, I decided, be too embarrassing
to cope with, even for me, and would require me to find a way of
being killed in what would, by necessity, only be a very, very slow-
speed accident. I came to the conclusion that, in the event the bike

went over just as I was approaching Evel Knievel under the cruel gaze of a TV camera, I would try to fall in such a fashion that my head and hands were shielded from view and would then, before anyone could get to me, strangle myself.

I didn't fall off and I rounded the corner of the largest of the buildings. The crew were gathered near an enormous SUV parked under a few straggly trees. Nigel looked up expectantly, smiled at me, nodded towards the car and then flicked his gaze back down to the monitor he held cradled in his hands. This would show him a feed direct from Ben Joiner's camera. Ben Devlin, the man who had originally phoned me, stood back from the crew. He had done his work in bringing us all this far. Now it was up to the crew and me, under Nigel's supervision, to make his idea, his concept, into a film. Cameraman Ben stood off to Nigel's right, his eye clamped to the eyepiece, the body of the big black camera resting on his shoulder. A tall, athletic bloke, he moved smoothly a couple of feet to bring the camera round on to me. On the back of the camera perched the tiny antenna that sent a signal to Nigel's monitor via an infra-red link. Behind Ben, shackled to his camera by the umbilical cable between them, the local soundman, Jeff, hunched over the mixer strapped to his chest and held the mic boom ready. He would be disappointed by the bike's choked warble, I was sure. Jeff wore a peaked cap under his headphones, a holiday T-shirt, a pair of ill-advised soccer shorts and sandals teamed with white running socks. Fortyish and irrepressibly enthusiastic, I had liked him immediately when we met the previous evening in our motel. He reminded me of Chevy Chase. Our second cameraman, Ian, stood off to the other side. Young and unnecessarily handsome, with a host of film-trip anecdotes from past adventures, he, too, had proven himself to be excellent company in our meeting of the previous evening. Now, though, we were all working together for the first time.

'You got me, Jeff?' I dipped my head to speak, barely having to raise my voice over the bike's soft burble to check that the radio mic Jeff had clipped to my T-shirt was working. Jeff looked up, grinned, nodded and mouthed 'gotcha', raising his right hand from the range of mixer knobs on top of the unit to give me the thumbs up. His other hand held the boom pole braced into his side, like a Roman spear-carrier at ease. Ian, his eye fixed to the camera's white eyepiece pad, prowled in the background, waiting to pick up the wide shots of the bike pulling up next to the car to be cut in later with the tighter, close-up footage Ben would record of my actual meeting with Evel. He would have to be able to cut the rest of the crew out of frame if his shots were to be of any use. And it was precisely this sort of coordination and instinctive choreography that would either happen magically now in our first shake-down together as a team, or never happen at all and we would all fall over each other's cables.

I drew up to the car. It was huge. And out of it, from the driver's window, a head appeared. And it was him. The head was small, the features drawn and thin, but I recognised immediately the hawkish brow, the severe expression, the deep-set eyes and sharp nose of Evel Knievel. I pulled up, not even thinking now about manhandling the bike. Adrenalin had kicked in, at last, and I flicked out the side stand, propped the bike up, hopped off, pulled off my gloves and helmet and walked up to Evel.

I had been warned, many times, that he could be difficult, that he had a fiery temper and didn't suffer fools gladly.

'Hi, Evel.'

'Hello, Richard, nice to meet you. You're a long way from home. We've got some work to do, buddy. I'd like to show you Butte, Montana – if you're ready to go, I'm ready to go.'

'Am I driving?'

'You can if you want to.'

'I will.'

ABOVE Botswana, the view from Khubu island over the saltpans of the dried-out lake. Oliver is parked just to the left of the ancient baobab tree.

RIGHT Camper chat, none of it remotely broadcastable.

The cult of Evel Knievel.

"He Proved a Man Could Fly"
Robert Craig "Evel" Knievel
(October 17, 1938 – November 30, 2007)

ABOVE We photographed his gravestone. Sadly, a few months later he needed it.

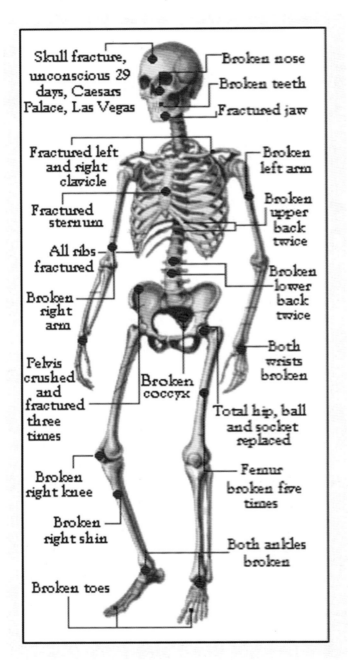

Skull fracture, unconscious 29 days, Caesars Palace, Las Vegas

Broken nose

Broken teeth

Fractured jaw

Fractured left and right clavicle

Broken left arm

Broken upper back twice

Fractured sternum

All ribs fractured

Broken lower back twice

Broken right arm

Both wrists broken

Pelvis crushed and fractured three times

Broken coccyx

Total hip, ball and socket replaced

Broken right knee

Femur broken five times

Broken right shin

Both ankles broken

Broken toes

Evel Knievel's injuries. He was nothing if not thorough.

Wembley Stadium, May 1975. Evel trying his hand at 13 London buses. It all went horribly wrong and he was carried off with a broken pelvis. This wasn't meant to happen, but it usually did.

RNAL LIFE

**MAIN PICTURE** Gene Sullivan, Evel's one-time bodyguard, performing a jump to the glory of God and to illustrate the necessary leap of faith in mankind's struggle with the forces of evil.
**LEFT** Hell's Angels from the Ventura chapter discussed their view of Evel. They didn't let me join but they did offer a tattoo.
**RIGHT** Gene blesses the faithful.

TOP I didn't expect to meet a hero in a golf buggy. But it was worth it.
ABOVE His next words were… 'Now get outta here.'

I moved closer to the car, feet trailing through the Montana dust. He wasn't an ogre. He didn't attack me on sight. He didn't take one look at me, refuse to have anything more to do with the film and roar off. But there was a sense of tension and impatience crackling around him. As though, at any minute, he might just decide that he wanted to do something else. With a bunch of other people.

## Pork Sandwiches

We drove a full circuit of Butte. There's a dignity to the place. It is rundown, there are ranks of cheaply built stores selling garden furniture and cut-price clothes. There are hopeless street corners with broad, uneven pavements and broken-down walls. But there are parts of it where the streets are broad and flanked with huge, once elegant buildings. It's not a place that would ever have rivalled Edinburgh for grandeur, but the peaks and troughs of the mining town's fortunes are written across it in bricks and mortar. At the turn of the century and at various times before and after, it was of considerable significance globally. With the advent of electricity, Butte's mines worked to meet a large portion of the world's demand for copper to use in making wire. Or, if you believed Evel as he acted as tour guide, pointing a sinewy, trembling finger at buildings and features, Butte's mines supplied all the copper needed by the world.

He turned out to be a fine exponent of the great American boast, the kind of boast told by visiting salesmen on horse-drawn carriages who would address the townsfolk on the incredible healing powers of their bottles of tonics and potions. There was nothing sinister or malevolent about Evel's boasts for Butte; they were the enthusiastic outpourings of a man who loved his home-town, despite all its faults. And some of his claims were true: Butte really did have what was reputed to be the oldest brothel in the States, it really did rival some of the biggest cities in the world for importance and stature. And it really was known widely as the 'richest hill on earth'. But it had long since faded from such prominence. The move from pit mining to open-cast marked the beginning of the end and it went into decline from the 1950s. The acid levels in the water, the haunting, rusty pitheads and mine-ravaged landscape are all that remain now of the boom-times past. But the town has an indomitable feel; it's a tough place and so are its people. Evel, in standing up for it now and telling of its past glories, was perhaps showing just how deep that toughness ran.

We drove the broad streets and we cruised the smaller, narrower roads around them. In these places, we saw how the tough times for Bute had affected its people. Many of the houses here were little more than huts; single-storey dwellings barely amounting to more than a single room. Some were ruined, dusty and empty. Some were lived in, the occupants' cars, trucks and rubbish scattered around them. And some were proudly maintained and groomed; crisp, white gates standing between fresh-painted picket fencing. We were in, I guessed, what amounted to Butte's suburban sprawl – these low buildings dotted among the hills and hollows carved out of the landscape by the industry that had given rise to the place.

'Evel?

He looked across from the passenger seat, his small, grey-blue eyes giving away nothing of what he was thinking but sparkling all the same. We had stopped at a sandwich bar that, according to Evel, made the best pork sandwiches in, naturally, 'the whole damn world'. And now, driving through Butte's version of suburbia, the air inside the car thick with the greasy aroma from the pork sandwiches we were eating, our feet rattling and rustling in the wrappers and empty Coke cans littering the footwells as we looked out at the places where people gathered and played and lived out their lives, I thought this touch of normality might help me to understand a bit more about Evel's life.

'Evel, so this is where you grew up?'

'Yeah. Right round these very streets.'

He listed names of families, he showed us where he lived, the house where he grew up.

'Did you use to cycle round these streets on a bike then? As a kid?'

'Yeah, course I did.'

'Did you do stunts?'

'I could wheelie better'n any kid in town. Any.'

'But, Evel. When I was a kid, when we were all kids' – I waved an arm round at the crew in the car with us; they had leaped in before we set off and now Nigel, Ben Devlin, cameraman Ben Joiner, Ian and Jeff huddled in the second and third row of seats behind us – 'all of us, we rode round on our bikes pretending to be Evel Knievel. We made jumps out of bits of wood and bricks, we tried to do wheelies. We pretended to be you. Who did you pretend to be?'

'Joe Chitwood. He used to do auto stunts around when I was a kid.'

The thought of Evel Knievel, not as the old man now slumped in a corner of a car bigger than the house he grew up in, but as the young Bobby Knievel, knees pumping as he cycled round the streets we now drove, silenced us all for a bit. Evel, either sensing the mood and feeling the need to fill the awkward moment with happy reminiscence, or just getting bored, broke the silence.

'Our bikes were everything – we lived and breathed 'em.'

'Us, too.' And I remembered the ragtag bunch of kids I grew up with in suburban Shirley on the outskirts of Birmingham. 'We used to tape a piece of cardboard to the chain stay,' I looked straight ahead as I spoke now, feeling more comfortable sharing a car with this old, sick but vital and still powerful man.

'Yeah, me too.'

I couldn't believe that he could have done the same, here, separated by thousands of miles and several decades. He went on.

'. . . it caught in the spokes and made a noise like a real bike. It went clack-clack-clack in the spokes and sounded like an engine.' He held his wiry arms in front of him, gripping imaginary handlebars and hunching his shoulders. He grinned when he finished talking and his eyes darted about the car, seeking and finding recognition and agreement.

I felt goose bumps rise on my arms at the thought that he too had indulged in the childish fantasies of speed, danger and power that had taken me and my mates and a million others through their youth. He was human, then, this living legend. And the atmosphere relaxed. We all chipped in, recalling the best types of cereal packet to use for your bike's cardboard motor and how it would get worn down in just a couple of laps of the block. After another hour or so, we drove back to the Butte Shooting Club where Evel's minders were waiting to take him away in the huge SUV. Our first encounter was over. We had met, we had talked, Evel had shown me around his hometown and Nigel was happy that we had caught it all for the film.

## They Don't Do Drive-in Movies in Birmingham

That evening we had arranged with Evel to rendezvous at a local drive-in movie theatre. The owner of the Silver Bow Drive-in had agreed to screen archive footage of Evel's first major jump at the Caesar's Palace Fountains in Las Vegas. The plan was to sit with Evel in his massive SUV, watch the footage together and talk. And film the conversation, obviously. We hoped that, when confronted with the film, Evel might drop his guard and feel able to open up, to share his thoughts of the experience, what it meant to him personally, how it felt. He is, was, the consummate showman — that's how he made a living. And having watched previous interviews with him, we knew that there was always a danger he might slip into the sort of brash showman talk he could do so well but which, really, was no more than automatic pilot. We wanted something more from him. We wanted to find out about the man himself. I was crapping myself. What if he hated the idea? Or punched me? He punched an interviewer once, years ago. I read about it. Thinking about it now while supping on a post-mix Cola out of a paper cup as I waited for the crew in the car park of their motel, I decided that being hit by Evel Knievel would actually be pretty cool. Dammit, if he hit me I would ride the punch, stand back up, shake him by the hand and thank him. It would have been an honour. I'd ask him to sign the bruise.

We got there early, sensing that Evel wasn't a man who liked to be kept waiting. I'd never been to a drive-in before — they weren't big in Birmingham — and was looking forward to the experience, while still feeling nervous about another meeting with Evel. Parking the bike up on the dusty forecourt of the drive-in, I climbed off and walked over to the waiting crew van to sort out what we would do and how. The footage we were going to see was not just of Evel's first big stunt, but also included his first big crash. He had landed badly at Caesar's Palace and the accident had made him worldwide news. I wanted to talk to him about how much he owed this accident for putting his name on the map when, until that point, he had been just another struggling daredevil plying his trade round the country fairs of his home state. The parallels with my own recent experience were obvious and uncomfortable, but this was a programme about Evel Knievel, not Richard Hammond, and I was sure as hell not going to raise the subject of my pathetic effort in the company of a man who knew how to crash properly and with style.

I paced the tiny wooden projection hut sipping lukewarm coffee and tried to think like Paxman getting ready for a heavy-hitting interview. I didn't feel like Paxman. He exudes a confidence and a grasp of the facts that enables him able to corner, cajole and bully his subjects into giving him what he wants. He is smart and dignified and clever. I am not. I was wearing a T-shirt with a picture of a motorbike on it. And I had already got rather badly sunburned. I caught my reflection in the glass frame of an old film poster hanging on one bare wall of the hut. My sunburned face glowed beetroot-red in the half-light of the projection room. Looking closer into the reflection, I saw that the sunburn formed a patch down the middle of my face that corresponded with the opening in the giant burgundy crash helmet I had rented with the bike. No, not Paxman, then. I tried to remember all I could from the extensive Evel Knievel research I had conducted on the aeroplane from Heathrow. The projectionist, a thin, bearded man well past retirement age who did the job, I am sure, for love, clattered about the place, shinning up a ladder to the projectors above to thread film and check lenses ready for Evel's arrival.

And he arrived, typically, in some style. A red and white 1950s Cadillac convertible, driven, I would later discover, by an old friend of Evel's, rolled into the dusty arena and I saw the now familiar sharp-featured face glowing pale in the spotlights. With the oxygen tubes glinting beneath his nose and his whisps of white hair describing a sharp peak, Evel looked in turns sinister and fragile. The enormous SUV followed him in and parked next to the Caddy, disgorging three helpers who ran round to Evel's car to help him out and to follow him with the wheeled oxygen trolley. The crew were at the back of the projection hut throwing stones at a Coke tin. We gathered ourselves together, checked the mic, checked the cameras and headed into action and, for the second time, I found myself greeting a childhood hero and feeling not altogether comfortable in addressing someone as 'Evel'.

We sat together in the SUV and watched the film. And Evel did speak personally and honestly. And he did open up about the pain and the doubt. He volunteered, before I had even asked him, that the crash at Caesar's Palace was what put him on the map. We spoke about breaking bones, about accepting risk, about being a daredevil. We were talking gently, in convivial and contented tones. I thought I had it all in the bag. And then, suddenly, Evel said that he'd had enough – he was exhausted. We stopped the tapes. I ran round to Evel's side of the car to help him out. He would travel back in the Caddy, of course. And as I held his arm, I felt the bone of his elbow through his shirt, I felt the loose, thin muscles lining his skinny arms and I felt the lightness of him as he leaned on me to lower a leg from the car and on to the bare ground. As he bent low and lifted a shaking hand to adjust the oxygen tubes in his nose, I looked down at the sparse hair across the top of his head and realised that this one-time hero, this invincible man who had been speaking to me moments ago about the stunts he had performed for the amazement of a global audience and the private struggles he had endured to come through the resulting injuries, was locked in the biggest battle of his life. This was not a glorious, glamorous battle; the world was not watching this one, but he was fighting it, nonetheless, with the same dogged toughness and strange dignity as he had every other battle. And so my hero was real, a genuine tough guy.

## And You Got Your, er, . . .

He attracted people nearly as colourful as himself, Evel Knievel. That is to say, in his wake there was a constant trail of characters seemingly every bit as bonkers as the man they were there to help, accompany, harass for money or just plain worship. And I kept meeting them. Standing on a railroad crossing, talking to the

camera about Butte and the festival, I was obliged to stop by the
arrival of a thin, stooped man in a blue-striped business shirt who
walked into shot and stood in front of me. I said hello, he spun
round and hit me with a smile wider than a piano. In his mid-
fifties, with thin hair scraped across a domed head and eyes squinted
shut to make room for his mouth, he spoke with the caricature
American-Jewish twang of a cartoon character. He was, it turned
out, a representative of a toy company. His company had, he
punched out in staccato bursts of enthusiasm, secured the rights to
manufacture the original – the original, mind – Evel Knievel wind-
up motorcycle toy. And the man exploded into a sales routine
straight from the back of a snake doctor's trailer.

'So, you've got your full Evel Knievel set. Boxed.' He held up
his hands to frame the size of the doubtless vividly coloured carton
that would accommodate the piece of memorabilia he wanted to
sell to the world via my bemused camera crew, who were still
rolling. They looked over their cameras and mixing units with
puzzled and delighted expressions. I smiled and rolled my eyes at
the now effervescent salesman to let them know that, yes, keep
going. This could be gold.

'Inside the box, you've got your Evel Knievel doll, you've got
your Evel Knievel helmet. Your Evel Knievel cape.' His fast-
moving hands mimed and framed every object as he listed them.
His watch was big and cheap and hung limply off a thin, brown
wrist. I caught the distant, tinny blare of the PA speakers building
up for yet another 'crayzee' stunt for the milling masses gathering
around the fringes of Butte for Evel Knievel Days. Later in the
week, a young daredevil called Trigger Gumm had announced his
intention to try to set a record at the festival. He hadn't been
specific about what the record was, but had said he could well be
killed breaking it. I wondered if Trigger would ever have a boxed-
set child's toy replica made of him. And I focused back on the
salesman in front of me, seizing his chance to pitch to the world

from the railroad intersection just by the Butte diner on the outskirts of town.

'Then there's the Evel Knievel ramps, a take-off ramp and a landing ramp. You've got your Evel Knievel flags, your Evel Knievel banners, your, er . . .' his patter was faltering, the metronomic beat of features he listed was slowing. A light sweat filmed his expansive, sun-wrinkled brow.

'And your, er, you've got your,' his wild eyes narrowed further with the effort of recalling the missing item. He looked like a python trying to pass a badly digested gazelle. We waited, breath held, cameras buzzing quietly. 'The, you've got, the . . .' It grew uncomfortable under the heavy Montana sun. I savoured the moment and hoped a train didn't clatter down the tracks towards us and spoil the tension. The PA speakers squawked softly in the distance. A big out-of-town truck slowed at a junction with hissing airbrakes and a soft metallic clunk as the trailer rested up against the hitch plate.

And then he got it.

'The bike, you've got your Evel Knievel bike!'

Ben Devlin, standing to the side of the camera but just in my field of view, hopped from one leg to another and fought to contain himself. Ben Joiner, on camera, sniggered, unable to control it. He looked across at Jeff. They shared the joke. Significant bit to forget, the bike. We thanked the man and laughed ourselves stupid once he was safely back in his car across the tracks.

Later that day I rode out to a trailer park to meet with Gene Sullivan, Evel's one-time bodyguard. A giant of a man with a gentle disposition but the body of a rhino, Gene now travels the country performing motorcycle jumps to the glory of God. He sets up his ramps in church car parks and dresses in red and white leathers, a crucifix and a flowing cape to perform allegorical jumps through fire to illustrate mankind's struggle with the forces of evil, the necessary leap of faith into the unknown to escape eternal hellfire and the welcome relief of God's landing ramp on the other side as a just reward for our unerring faith.

His huge trailer rig was set up on the outskirts of Butte as he was there to perform a Jump for Jesus in the course of Evel Knievel Days. I would make sure we would be at the jump to film it, but I wanted to meet Gene first and talk about his time with Evel back in the heyday of his daredevil career. We stood by a plastic picnic table outside his motor home and talked for the cameras. He spoke gently and with a ready smile. My burgundy Harley glinted embarrassingly in the shade under the nearby trees and traffic rolled past on the broad main road back into Butte.

This was the first time Gene had taken part in Evel Knievel Days. Throughout the seventies he had been there with Evel at every jump. He had held back the crowds, fought off rioting Hell's Angels, protected Evel from crazed fans and picked up his employer's shattered body after the inevitable crash that always followed the showmanship and glamour. Gene, too, had enjoyed his fair share of the superstar lifestyle that accompanied Evel's travelling circus back in those days. He wouldn't be drawn on specifics, but living and working with an international superstar through the seventies in an endless road show that attracted as many girls and party animals as the hardest of rock bands, he must have seen his fair share of the rock and roll life. And sometime towards the end of the seventies, he turned his back on all of it. He and Evel fell out. He wouldn't elaborate on exactly what caused the split, but Gene left Evel and turned to God. And since that day, his ministry has toured the country with his ramps and his sermons, performing Jumps for Jesus, and he hasn't spoken to Evel since.

We wrapped up the interview and agreed to meet again at the out-of-town church car park where Gene would be performing his Jump for Jesus later that week. I did not know it, but I would be seeing Gene again much sooner. And it would be unexpected.

## Evel Is in the Building

Too often, far too often, the accusation is levelled at TV types that it's all made up and put on for the sake of ratings. Well, yes, a lot of it is. But where do you draw the line? Those people don't just gather together and happen to set out to see who is the best at ballroom dancing by sheer coincidence just as a TV crew is passing. It's all organised and put together on purpose. It's a TV show. Someone has to book the studio, put the cameras in the right places and make sure everyone's got tulips in their dressing rooms. Where it gets tricky, of course, is in the world of documentary making. And here, the intense pressure to make sure everything is real and genuine is justified. And it makes those special moments, when they happen spontaneously, naturally and – God forgive me, I'm about to use a buzz word – 'organically', all the more enjoyable. Today would be such a day.

   We had arranged to meet Evel once again to watch footage from his career. A local cinema, this time an indoor, multiplex set-up, had agreed to screen the film of Evel's attempt to jump over thirteen buses at Wembley Stadium in 1975. This was Evel's chance to break Europe and to make himself into a genuine global name. World domination lay at his feet. He crashed, of course. As he landed, there seemed to be no suspension at the bike's back end. This has since been rumoured to be the result of a missing suspension part that Evel knew full well was not there. And yet he took off from the ramp anyway and sailed across the stadium towards certain injury and probable death to avoid losing face in front of the millions of European punters he had spent weeks wooing in advance of his first big European jump. He had come a long way from Butte and wasn't going to miss the chance to make his name and his legend even bigger just because of some missing bolt. There was little enough science put into his stunts anyway. Nobody with a laptop scampered about the place measuring distances, checking tolerances and calculating launch angles and trajectories. Evel and his henchmen took a look at the buses, the fountain, the canyon or whatever else he was planning to try and jump, stuck a finger in the air and pretty much guessed how high, how far and how fast he would have to be going to do it. And 99 per cent of the time they were right. Or thereabouts. And so for Evel to set off on a bike he knew to have a problem was not so crazy. At least, not so crazy compared with everything else he did.

At Wembley that day, as he landed the suspension failed under the impact and the back wheel collapsed. Evel was catapulted up and forwards off the bike. He hit the ground and rolled towards the hoardings at the side of the arena, the bike in hot and surprisingly accurate pursuit. He broke his pelvis. I watched the footage on my laptop in my room that morning, getting ready to talk to him about it. And I saw how, as the Wembley announcers told the crowd to stay in their seats and keep away from the injured man, Evel lifted his head and spoke to the friends and colleagues around him as they made ready to drag him out and to hospital. The camera moves closer and you can see the pain creased across his face. And he tells them that he wants to walk out.

'I walked in,' he says through gritted teeth, 'I wanna walk out.' And he does, held on either side, legs trailing and stumbling as his feet are dragged. He is supported by his helpers, yes, but he walks. He walks out. It was a stupid thing to do; he risked making worse the injuries he had already received in the pursuit of doing something stupid to start with. But I found it a strangely moving piece of film to watch and I looked forward to talking with him about it.

And he would be at the cinema soon. I rolled up first, cruising the burgundy Harley through the empty car park and pulling up alongside the plain, brick wall at the back of the cinema building. The spot was marked for me, I knew where to be. The door I had been told to look for was plain, anonymous and blue. But it had an Evel Knievel poster pinned to it and running up to it was a strip of red carpet, borrowed, I guessed, from the nearby carpet store in the same out-of-town shopping complex. Standing on either side of the door were Stars and Stripes flags, the flagpole of each supported in a traffic cone. A blue velvet rope looped its way back from the flags, flanking the red carpet, supported by wooden posts. I kicked the bike stand down and dismounted, pulling off helmet and gloves as I did so. As I'd pulled up, I had seen a man I very much wanted to meet. And I walked towards him now.

He stood by the flags, his plastic, lace-up shoes standing out black and polished against the red carpet. Short and thin, his black hair was slicked back and oiled, his moustache thick, black and clinging to a lip so sweaty it might slip off at any moment. The man's eyes were deep-set, brown and very close together. And they looked confused. He wore a vivid Stars and Stripes waistcoat underneath a black suit jacket too large for his rangy frame. His chin jutted forwards underneath a narrow, tense mouth. He was shouting into a hand-held walkie-talkie.

'He will be here soon. He will be here. Get yourselves ready. Stand by.'

He was very, very excited. I learned that he was the cinema manager. And Evel Knievel was his hero. This, then, was a state visit and a day that had loomed huge and gilt-edged on the calendar pinned to a peeling wall of his suspicious, close-smelling office for months. We shook hands. We spoke about Evel Knievel. The man was honoured, *honoured*, that Evel should come visit him and his team in their cinema. They were proud to have a son of their town go on to such great achievements and worldwide fame. He himself had tried to live his life in a way that Evel would understand. He liked to think that Evel would approve of what he had done and how he had done it. The flags in their traffic cones lifted limply and dropped; the morning was still and heavy with heat. The car park stretched away, empty and quiet. The air shimmered above its smooth, black surface. Beyond, through the heat haze, the low-lying, primary-coloured shops and stores welcomed buyers of cut-price furniture, electrical goods, shoes and carpet.

The tension around our particular patch of red carpet intensified and I decided to slope off and sit inside, the better to get myself ready for another encounter with Evel. Ben Devlin would arrive with Nigel soon and I had to talk it through with them. I wanted to get the questioning, the tone right when we watched the film of his Wembley crash and his struggle to walk out of the arena. Half an hour later, I felt the atmosphere crackle with excitement as Evel's huge SUV pulled up at the end of the red carpet. I peered around the doorframe from inside the cinema and watched his face as he took in the arrival they had planned for him and I studied him for traces of resentment, of irritation or of enjoyment or pride. And I saw nothing. He dealt with it as a diplomat. The cinema manager, his moustache visibly quivering with the thrill of it, lifted his walkie-talkie and barked into it,

'He's here. Evel is here. Be ready. Be ready everyone. He's here.'

A second vehicle arrived and disgorged an array of helpers. As one of them made sure Evel's oxygen bottle was freed from the SUV and set on to its wheels on the red carpet, I watched as another stood back from the scene and yet dominated it. The character did this partly by dint of his size – he was huge. I saw arms the thickness of Evel's waist and a dense neck giving way seamlessly to a solid, heavily engineered jaw. But something else allowed this figure in the background to dominate the scene. It was his manner, the self-assurance, the confidence. He might not be fussing around Evel, checking his oxygen tubes and asking if he felt okay, but he was there to look after him and would do so at all costs, whatever happened. It was Gene. The Jump for Jesus guy. Evel's bodyguard of thirty years ago, the man who had protected him from rioting Hell's Angels, who had fought, drunk and partied his way across the States with him in the seventies only to fall out and never speak with him again, had rejoined him.

He stood back from the rush and the fuss at the door of the SUV. He watched with calm, placid eyes as Evel walked gingerly up the carpet. His arms were folded in front of him. I would hate to be the one to give him cause to unfold them in a hurry. I would later discover that the previous evening they had spoken over the phone for the first time since the seventies and Gene had asked to come and look after Evel today. I wanted to know why, to ask what this reunion meant to each of them. But I watched now as Gene held Evel's elbow and walked the last few strides to the door with him and I knew that this wasn't the time. Throughout this session with Evel, as we watched the films and talked through his experiences, Gene sat a few seats behind. He never spoke, never joined in. But I saw him watching, could see small expressions cross his broad face as Evel recounted the glory days of the early seventies. It was strangely moving, to sit in a dimmed cinema with these two old warhorses reunited. To not talk about it and leave it as a private matter made it all the more special.

## Riding with the Angels

Tomorrow was the day when Evel would lead the annual, celebratory ride around Butte. And me and my burgundy Harley would be rolling among the hundreds of bikes from all over the world. In the meantime, though, I had another ride ahead of me. This was to an altogether darker and less wholesome event. And I was looking forward to it intensely. In researching the story, we had found that Evel appeared to have something of a problem with the Hell's Angels. At his height, Evel blamed them for pretty much everything in the world. He would regularly harangue his audience, made up as it was largely of families, on the dangers of drugs and idleness and he figured the 'Angels' were key pushers of drugs and arch-practitioners of the sort of feckless idleness that the Evel legend could not abide. He fought with them, too. Well, he didn't do much of the actual fighting, but there were rumbles in which Evel's minders, including the mighty Gene, tackled very big, very angry men in Hell's Angels' get-up in the circus and carnival around some of Evel's stunts. Evel always claimed that the Hell's Angels hated him. I wanted to know why.

We had arranged a meeting. George Christie, head of the Ventura chapter of the Hell's Angels and the deputy head of the entire movement, would see me and the crew and talk about Evel Knievel. He was travelling through the area, though not directly to Butte, and had kindly agreed to meet us at a motel some fifty miles or so out of town. I say 'kindly', because that's the sort of thing you find yourself saying a lot when you are dealing with the Hell's Angels: 'Oh, really, that's sooooo kind. Thank you, thank you, thank you. Yes, we'll be there. No, we won't be late. Yes, we'll be quick. Thank you, thank you, thank you.' It all gets a bit, well, a bit creepy really. They may be seen by some as cartoon characters on big black bikes with Viking horns on their crash helmets, but they are also a very large, very organised group who still enjoy a pretty fearsome reputation. I'm even doing it now: 'enjoy a pretty fearsome reputation' – any moment I shall praise them for being a smashing bunch of chaps and really damned good eggs all round and then look over my shoulder, just in case.

Everything was set. We would drive out to the motel, record an interview with George and then get out of his way. Naturally, I decided to take the bike. I was not about to turn up to meet with a top-grade Hell's Angel in a van. I would ride there and he would see immediately that I was a kindred spirit, a fellow lone wanderer of the world with an appetite for life and a stomach for chaos. It being a rented, burgundy bike and everything, though, he might not welcome me into the 'Angels' with open, tattooed arms. But at least he would know I was one of them. As it were.

This was my first opportunity of the trip to enjoy a cruise on genuine American roads on my genuine American motorcycle. I slung an extra sweater in the leather panniers at the back of the bike, just in case it got a bit chilly later in the evening, and reassured the team that, yes, I would rather ride than drive and, yes, I would follow their tail lights all the way and cruise there quite safely. Directors tend to get a bit jumpy around me these days when they have to call upon me to do anything in which I might conceivably get hurt. Obviously, this stems from the experience of the poor soul who had to stand there and watch his presenter go flying past him upside down in a jet car at 300 mph and resign himself to a very great deal of paperwork over the next few weeks.

Unfortunately, the experience of that director – Scott was his name – has engendered in other directors around me a rather cautious approach to anything they feel might remotely be classed as a 'stunt'. Walking down stairs for instance, using a pair of scissors, opening a jar of jam – these are the kinds of activities which, when appearing on a television script with my name next to them, cause some directors to reach for a hi-visibility vest, the number of the local air ambulance service, an extensive medicare kit and a good lawyer just in case. It's quite annoying. We were to travel just fifty miles or so on broad, American roads with no bends in them – they were American, after all – conduct a brief interview and then ride home. I have been riding bikes for twenty-five years. It was a lovely evening. The bike was rented and working perfectly. I reassured Nigel that even I couldn't mess this one up. Nigel, being Nigel and made of sterner stuff than most directors, accepted this readily. Ben Devlin, taking his lead from Nigel, agreed that it was daft to worry about a little motorcycle ride through the mountains and we set off.

All the cheesy, clichéd stuff that people say about motorcycling is true: it really is a kind of freedom that you just don't get in a car.

You really are closer to nature, you can smell it and feel it closer to you. It is just you and your bike against the world. Some of the really bad stuff is true too: it is dangerous on a bike, people in cars and lorries don't look out for you and you spend a lot of your time screaming. If you fall off, there's a good chance you'll be badly hurt or killed. So there are very good and very bad points to biking. But what they tend not to warn you about is the more mundane, less exciting stuff. Like the inconvenience of stopping for a pee when you're wearing full leathers, the short range between fuel stops thanks to the small petrol tank on most bikes, the difficulties of enjoying a road-trip snack on the move and the fact that you can't have the radio on to while away the miles when it gets boring. It's also quite difficult actually to enjoy that motorcycling 'freedom', because your head is encased in a big fibreglass box with a visor full of dead flies on the front of it. So the warm Montana breeze was not going to be rushing through my hair at any time as I set off behind the crew van for my meeting with a Hell's Angels boss.

My helmet wasn't a 'full-face' one with a chin guard and a visor, though; it was open at the front so at least I would feel that warm Montana breeze on my face. And I did. It made me smile as we swooped along the roads out of Butte towards the mountains. And then I felt the cold Montana rain on my face. Which really stings. If you're travelling at the US legal limit of 50 mph, it means that, relative to you, the raindrops are also doing 50 mph. Which is like being hit in the face with marbles. My sunglasses protected my eyes, though, and the rain soon dried up as we twisted and curved our way up through the mountains and then out over the plains beyond.

There were wide fields of crops here, fringed by trees and bushes. And they were full of flies. They are fascinating creatures, flies of different types, with many amazing abilities and features. Primary among these features at that point for me, though, was the fact that they were harder than raindrops and so hurt more when fired into your bare face at 50 mph. I improvised a face mask using a black neck scarf with skulls on it that I had bought from a street market earlier in the day. At least my eyes were safe behind sunglasses. And then it got dark. For me, of course, it got darker earlier than it did for the rest of our team. They probably wondered why I flicked on the bike's extra running lights and slowed my pace behind them just as the sun smouldered gently along the shoulders of the soft hills to create what was, I have no doubt, a beautiful twilight scene. For me, though, eyes sheltering from the blinding onslaught of flies behind black sunglass lenses, it just became instantly dark, as though a light had been turned out.

I flagged the van down, propped the bike on its stand and leaned forwards in the saddle to pull the fly-smeared neck scarf off my mouth. Around me, black shapes loomed and spoke. I ripped the shades off.

'Er, anyone got any really pale sunglasses I can borrow?'

A couple of the guys had sussed the problem and ran back to the parked van to sift through their kit. I was hoping one of the team would be carrying shades with pale lenses, maybe even Reactolites.

'How the hell can they forget to put the bloody goggles in with the helmet?' I shouted at the remaining crew. 'I mean, don't these people ride bikes? For God's sake.' I climbed off the bike and kicked a stone and stamped about. I knew full well that it was my own stupid fault for forgetting to check they were there when I picked up the bike. And so did the crew. But no one said anything.

Ben Devlin ran back from the van. He had some shades. They were darker than mine. It was the same story all round.

'Look, I can't ride in these.' I held up my shades, their thick, black lenses sprouting a feathery coating of flies' wings across their surface. 'Got an idea, though. Let's go on, but really slowly. I need to find a farm or some sort of industrial place. Anything that might have a workshop.'

The sun had gone entirely now and we crawled on through the night as the road made its way further into the rolling countryside. The shades were in my pocket and with my eyes naked to the cold wind I seldom drifted over about ten miles an hour. Eventually I found a farm on an exposed bend where the road wound down the shallow valley between two hills. We pulled over in the yard and switched off, our extinguished headlights plunging us into the night-time darkness of the countryside.

A tall, thin man in his fifties came out to greet the strangers. He stood in front of us, lit by a single overhead lamp attached to the wall of his dark, narrow house. He had hollow cheeks and dark, sunken eyes. His brown, greasy hair was cut like a school child's with a simple, flat fringe in front and a sprout rising up from his crown at the back. His neck was skinny and distorted by a huge Adam's apple that bobbed above the open collar of his blue checked shirt. Shapeless denim jeans hung off his angular legs, terminating in heavy work boots. He was, in short, going to tempt us into the basement of his isolated homestead and turn us into handbags for his friends.

'Hello. Er, hi there,' I raised a hand and figured that sprinkling my conversation with local phrases might help break the ice. And I wondered which of us he would kill first. Would he make the others watch?

'Yeah, hi. We're in a spot of bother. Er, we're in trouble.' I thought, 'Too bloody right we are. We're about to be butchered by the madman of the mountains.' The crew shuffled about by the van. The evening was cool now, but I felt sweat prickle across my shoulders under my leather jacket. Maybe he preferred the biker look. Oh God . . .

'Thing is, er, I saw the workshop and the farm, er, and all,' I was still trying with my Americanisms as I swept an arm around the gravelled yard to take in the low-lying, industrial-looking building behind our murderer and the fields beyond, 'and I wondered, er, do you have any goggles? You know, work glasses? Eye protectors?' I mimed fixing a pair of large glasses in place in front of my pale and cold sweat-beaded face, just to make sure the language barrier had been successfully leaped over for this crucial part of the exchange.

'Sure. Hold on.' And he turned his narrow back, striding towards the folding doors to his workshop. I hadn't explained why I wanted the goggles. I wanted him at least to appreciate my cunning genius before he killed me and ate my liver. I shouted after his slumped shoulders:

'You see, I've got no riding goggles and I can't see through these in the dark.' I held up the fly-covered shades between finger and thumb, waving them at the now empty doorway to the workshop. I waited to hear the buzz of his chainsaw starting.

'These do ya?' He came back out, holding up a pair of clear plastic protective work glasses of the type used to stop sawdust flying into your eyes in a wood shop.

'Yes. Yes, they're perfect.' I wondered; had he done this before? Was it a standard event, then, peculiar little Englishmen turning up at night with their faces covered in dead flies asking to borrow a pair of goggles? He seemed so unperturbed, so calm.

He held them up to look at us through them.

'Hold on, though. Can't see a thing through these. All scratched. Get you somethin' better.' He turned again and went back inside. He was going to come charging through the door with a pitchfork this time and skewer us like a giant kebab. I knew it and looked across at the crew milling about by the van in the corner of the yard. He walked back out carrying another pair of goggles. These were bigger and still wrapped in plastic. I saw through the doorway behind him a workbench and a blue pillar drill on a stand. Wood shavings were scattered across the floor. A window was fixed in the blank wall to one side of the door, the privacy glass opaque and grey. Through it still I could make out the unmistakable shadow of a toilet roll sitting on the window sill. The lavatory, then. I caught something else curving from behind the open door – the front wheel of an exercise bike.

'These're better. See.' He held them out to me. They were perfect. Clear plastic lenses in a silicone frame, like a diving mask with striped elastic to hold them on.

'Wow. Thank you. Thank you so much. Here, let me pay you.'

I fumbled in my jeans pocket for a note.

'No, that will not be necessary. Take them. I got hundreds. Have a great trip.'

And he turned, waving a skinny arm to us behind him as he retreated into his dark house.

There was a lot to say between the crew and me, but we saved it all. They crammed into the van and I leaped on to the bike. The goggles fitted snugly under my crash helmet. I pulled on gloves, fired up the Harley and rolled out of the yard. With my eyes now protected behind my new lucky goggles, we could hit the gas. I enjoyed the ride. And I was very keen to meet George, the Hell's Angel waiting for us in some motel about forty miles down the track.

Above all else, a bike ride gives time to reflect. Even with a passenger on board, talking is tricky. It is possible to arrange some Bluetooth device to connect your telephone to your crash helmet, but I have studiously avoided this so far; the bike and the bog are the two places in the universe I don't wish to be bothered by my phone. So I rode on undisturbed and thought. I've worried in recent years that biking is becoming just too mainstream. There are too many self-satisfied, middle-aged, middle-management types turning up at their accountancy firm on the latest sports bike wearing smart, matching leathers and talking about track days and the Nürburgring circuit. In the next breath, they go on to chat about school fees and golf. You see them pulling up on their 'metal charger' outside the delicatessen to fill their designer rucksack full of anchovies and pitted olives. They care about the percentage of cocoa solids in their after-coffee chocolate. People in cars have started smiling appreciatively at them when they pass on country roads.

I started riding precisely because I didn't want to be mainstream. As a teenager I was drawn to it because it was still seen then as something done by outsiders, by loners. There was still a trace of dark glamour to it. It was done by rebels, not nice, cosy people with mortgages and reading glasses and pastel, sexless clothes. I didn't want elderly ladies to smile indulgently at me as I passed and nod in approval that, yes, I did indeed have the new 'S' version with the carbon-fibre front mudguard and comment that my leathers matched it a treat. I wanted people to be scared and upset when I rode into town. Though how I thought the appearance of a short, thin bloke with long straggly hair riding a yelping moped with a lot of smoke pouring out of its tiny exhaust pipe would ever scare anyone other than my parents, I don't quite recall. The point is, I wanted to be an outsider. As biking and a new breed of biker has been getting steadily more acceptable to the masses, it has occurred to me that the everyday, mainstream folk that real bikers want to step away from will soon include most motorcyclists. George Christie, as a representative of a very much older-school approach to biking, could certainly be considered an outsider. And I was looking forward to meeting him. I adjusted my massive, borrowed workshop goggles with my left hand and rolled the throttle on with my right before settling on to the rented burgundy Harley to tick off the last few miles to the motel. Hopefully there wouldn't be too many lights in the car park and George wouldn't see me until I'd pulled the bike over and whipped off the goggles and the huge, burgundy crash helmet.

The motel stood on a wide corner on a broad street lined with huge, dark trees that hung damply in deep shadows between a sparse file of street lights. It was a clutch of buildings set back from the road behind a car park flanked by wooden rails that looked better suited to having horses tied to them than being nuzzled up to by the metal snouts of the collection of hatchbacks and family sedans gathered there that evening. An ornate wooden sign hung over the entrance to the car park, supported by a wooden pole rooted in a raised flower bed made out of logs. Nothing was growing in it, but a single Coke can lay forlornly on its side next to the base of the signpost. The main building of the motel was two storeys high, with external covered walkways running around it on both floors. Some rooms showed orange lights and the pulsating colours of the TV, others stood dark. It wasn't late, but it was past suppertime.

We pulled in and Nigel dashed inside to see if our Hell's Angel had checked in. We discussed this before he went in and agreed that it was reasonable to assume that Hell's Angels did actually check in these days, rather than just arrive and stomp through reception with a headless chicken under their arm. I parked the bike between the grey crew van and a small people carrier. The car park lights glinted off my Harley's bulging burgundy flanks. It didn't look much like the sort of thing a Hell's Angel would ride. I glanced around, half hoping to see a fleet of black bikes lurking in the shadows like folded crows and half hoping not to.

A few cars away, leaning in the corner of the car park where the building made a return on itself to form an L shape, I saw them. Two bikes. One, a stripped-down, raw and angry looking chopper. My eyes scanned it as slowly and carefully as some nightclub king checking out his next target. Sharply angled black tank perched on a narrow frame that flowed into long forks and a dangerous, skinny wheel at the front. It rested low and contented on a fat tyre under a wide black fender at the back. The engine, surprisingly, was not a big Harley twin, but a Japanese four-cylinder lump with sharply slashed pipes ending barely inches from the outlets and four chromed air intakes straining greedily forwards from their carbs like the round, shiny beaks of four hungry, metal chicks in a nest. Now that, I felt sure, was a Hell's Angel chief's bike. Next to it, though, was something else.

The shadows collected and pooled in the corner, where the rails met. And then the shadows deepened. I saw among them brief glints of chrome and of bare metal. Where the fluorescent orange light fell, it flowed and curved in thin lines along black panels, giving away the shape of the bike only where it changed angles at intersections between panels and parts. I walked closer. It was like walking up to a werewolf in an alley. It was wide and low. I saw the flat, metallic rectangle of a number plate, so this was the back. I drew closer still, took in the fat back tyre under the glinting fender giving way to the saddle above it. Either side, black pannier boxes lay at cocked angles, leaning with the bike on its side stand. Ahead of the seat, the black tank squatted, broad and muscular, behind the chromed headstock and fork yokes. The bars stayed level and grew wide in the deepest shadows behind a jet-black fairing in the shape of bat wings sprouting either side of the steely chromed headlamps. I corrected myself. No, *this* was the bike of a Hell's Angel chief. Something about it said, 'Look, but you don't want to touch. Not ever.'

I drew as close as I dared now, hungry for detail. The clocks, speedo and rev counter lurked in deep, dark wells behind the fairing. A low screen stood above. The front fender was deep and black, hiding the front wheel almost round to the point where it kissed the tarmac. I looked back along the bike. Below the tank, before the glinting, meshed air intake, something else shone. I leaned closer and stared. A metal badge had been fixed in place. It was a single silver death's head with a roaring mouth and flowing hair. I decided that if everything else about the bike hadn't warned a potential thief that this one was not for the taking, then the badge would finally set the seal on it. The ten-year-old in my soul shivered, partly with fear and partly with delight. This was his bike, I knew it. And I was right.

George was coming. I ran back to the motel entrance where Ben Devlin was pacing.

'He here yet? Nigel been killed?' I hissed at Ben and stood next to him.

'Nope. He went up there.' He swung his eyes upwards and indicated the room directly overhead where a broad window glowed brightly into the night.

'Christ. Will he fly out through the window and over the edge now and land in the car park on his face?' We grinned at each other, enjoying the tension. No traffic passed on the broad road, but the air was light and moved under a gentle, soft breeze. A door clicked open and we both jumped.

'They're coming.'

'I know.' Ben smiled again; he was lapping up the cloak and dagger stuff, the late-night dash, the motel car park.

'That's them now.'

Nigel walked out of the door and strode into the car park where we stood.

'Hello, everyone. Right, this is George.' He waved his arm as a figure moved past him and towards us.

'George, this is Richard. Our presenter. Sorry, host.' Nigel had caught himself and corrected the British term 'presenter', which is meaningless to Americans, for the more familiar 'host'. Even Nigel was making an effort to be nice to this one. And he's not scared of anything or anyone.

George stepped forwards into the light from the single overhead lamp. I tried to take in as much as I could as quickly as possible. He was not tall, maybe not much taller than me. He was squat, though, solid. He looked to be well planted where he now stood in front of me. His face, older than I expected, fifty, maybe more. His hair, too, short and flecked with grey. He wore a leather jacket, heavily decorated. That would be his 'patch', the badge showing his allegiance, his area and, in George's case I guessed, his rank. He looked unshaven but there was an air of crisp smartness, of neatness almost, about him.

'Hi, George. I'm Richard. Really pleased to meet you.' I stepped forward and extended a hand. I didn't know what to do; was there an etiquette thing here? How does one greet a senior Hell's Angel? Bite a chicken's head off and spit it at his feet?

'Hi, Richard. Good to meet you. Good ride?'

'Yeah. Great.' I rolled my shoulders and rubbed my forearms in a manly way, glad I was wearing a leather jacket. I thought of telling him the story of borrowing the goggles, but decided not to.

'You? You get here okay?'

'Yeah, sure.' He sounded assured, confident and polite. It was like meeting the manager of a high-class hotel.

'So, George,' I swung into the standard meet-and-greet presenter chat about what we were going to do and how it would all work. Usually, this is to put an inexperienced interviewee at ease. I wasn't sure how to pitch it in George's case. Do they undergo media skills training in the Hell's Angels?

'Sooo, we're just going to record a bit of a chat, nothing too taxing, and then be on our way. No tricky questions, nothing difficult.'

'No problem. Whatever you want. I'm happy to do it.' He couldn't be more accommodating. For the second time that day I stood and waited for something to go horribly and dreadfully wrong – for someone to suddenly kill me.

'Where d'you wanna do it? Here?' he waved at the corner of the car park. Nigel stepped in.

'Actually, George, no. Can we go over there, by the steps to that building?'

'Sure. No problem.' George set off towards the end of the motel, to the building Nigel had indicated.

'Er, George, er,' Nigel spoke towards his retreating back now. I waited for George to turn and throw a knife at his face.

'George, we wanted to get the bikes in, if that's okay. Would that be okay?'

'Yeah, of course.' He shrugged. Another figure broke away from the shadows at the motel's door and moved down the steps from the covered veranda as George walked back. I saw dangerous biceps, a narrow tattoo, a black, capped T-shirt, sneakers and long black hair.

'This is my second, Crash.'

Crash was not one for chatting. He nodded and his dark eyes scanned us as he walked down the three or four steps from the motel. In his mid-twenties, with a brooding, thoughtful air and a faintly hurt expression, Crash passed us and walked over to the two bikes I had been studying in the opposite corner. He stood by them, gaze fixed on George like a Rottweiler on its master. I hoped never to have cause to find out exactly what Crash's job as a second entailed.

'Er, right then. So, er, well, let's get the bikes moved then, shall we?' I smiled and clapped my hands together like the irritating father in an American family movie. It wasn't the most appropriate gesture and it was met with a stony and, I felt, rather confused silence from Crash. George was happy enough, though, and duly walked over to his huge black Harley. Nigel and the crew gathered their kit together and started hauling the boxes and bags over to the steps of the building at the other end of the car park where we had decided the interview would take place. It was a miniature rendition of a stately, colonial mansion. Only it was based on something the size of a large garden shed. A tiled roof, supported on thin, fake alabaster columns, ran around it to form a veranda. The steps leading up to the front door were broad and shallow and should have been made of stone. They were wooden and the crew's footsteps echoed through the void beneath as they set up their shot. I heard them telling each other to shush and then start giggling as Jeff dropped a lighting stand and tripped on a box.

'Right then, George. I'll get my, er, my ride.' My bike was a few metres away from theirs, back towards the building they had left.

'Sure thing. You do that.' George reached his Harley and threw a booted leg over it, settling into the saddle like a heavy bird alighting on a familiar tree branch. I tried not to scamper towards my rented, burgundy Harley, tried to keep a bit of swagger in my walk, to measure my pace. But I was excited. I had an idea. George and Crash were clearly going to start their bikes to cover the couple of hundred yards to the interview. I would do the same. This was an opportunity I had never foreseen in my life. I reached the burgundy shame and hopped on. George and Crash fired up their engines and they settled down to idle, George's Harley coughing and growling with a surprisingly mellow grumble and Crash's chopper barking and snarling beside it. I hit the starter button and my strangled Harley whimpered into life. I looked across the car park to see the silhouettes of the crew as they finished their preparations. They had rigged up a couple of lights, the camera was on the tripod and the guys were milling around ready to go. Nigel and Ben Devlin stood behind the camera in earnest conversation, deciding what they wanted from this scene.

I had to get a move on if I was to achieve what I wanted to do here. I wound the throttle on, lifted my feet and moved towards Crash and George just as their heads went up and they, too, gunned their engines and pulled away. The three of us rode across the car park slowly, the two Harleys beating a bass rhythm to the staccato yelps and screams of Slash's chopper. In seconds we were there.

We passed the camera and pulled up at the bottom of the steps.

I couldn't help it. I tried to contain my excitement, but it just sort of got out.

'There you go. I've ridden with the Angels. You see that, guys? I've ridden with the Angels.'

I nodded my head slowly and deeply, dipping the bike on to its side stand as I did so and standing up off the saddle once it settled.

'Yeah. Rode with the Angels there. I did.' I saw smiles on their faces, but the crew didn't look up. Perhaps they felt I had overdone it. Crash, his bike pulled up discreetly a few yards away in the shadows beyond the TV lights, remained impassive and silent. George hauled his huge, heavy bike over on to its stand and stood up.

'Yup. You can tell all your friends back home.' And he smiled. He got it. He knew why I was excited. He understood the romance, the childish thrill some people get just from being around these guys. And I knew we would be fine.

## Have We Gotta Hold You Down?

'And, action,' Nigel gave the shout and looked up at me before retreating a pace back behind the camera. We sat on our bikes, George and me; it had seemed the appropriate set-up for an interview with a Hell's Angel. We were framed by the wooden steps to the tiny colonial shed and a single street light to one side threw a yellow glow across us. In front of us, behind the silhouetted camera with Ben hunched over it and Nigel standing attentively to one side, was a broad corner in the road. It stretched back into the dark, and led off up wide drives flanked by tall bushes and trees. To one side of us, Crash slumped on his Chopper. He never took his eyes off George.

'So, George, great to meet you.' I started the interview in chatty mode. It was like walking up to a grizzly bear with a microphone and asking what his favourite type of donut is.

'Great to meet you too, Richard. How're you feeling after your crash?'

'My what?' He had caught me off balance there.

'Your crash. Sounded nasty.'

'You know about that? How?'

'Our boys in London told us about it when they said you were coming over.'

'What?'

'Sent us a file of stuff on you . . .'

'What, the Hell's Angels in London told you I was coming?'

'You've gotta be informed.' And he smiled, eyes sparkling.

My head felt a bit swimmy. George was charming, intelligent, confident and articulate – good company, in short. But he had just reminded me that he was also a very senior figure in a worldwide organisation with its fingers in many different pies. He was having fun with me, of course, he knew how to play to a camera, how to enjoy himself without coming across as too intimidating or sinister. Before we finished, I asked him if I would be eligible to join the Hell's Angels. George gave a non-committal answer, so I told him that I was thinking of getting a tattoo. Would that help?

'Yeah, sure. We can do your tattoo for you. Have we gotta hold you down?'

I did ask him about Evel Knievel. And he told me that the Hell's Angels had no dislike for the man, no problem with him at all. Never had. He was a biker, clearly, and so was all right in their book. He had, for a while, blamed them for pretty much everything that was wrong in the world, but then Hell's Angels tend to have pretty thick skin and they can cope with that. We wrapped it up, shook hands all round and thanked George for his time and his patience. He introduced us to his wife, who travels with him. She, too, turned out to be charming and cultured. She was younger than George, well-spoken, fresh-faced and easy-going – quite the scrummy mummy in fact. Though I felt it best not to engage in any behaviour that could possibly ever be described as flirtatious. In any universe. As we spoke, I learned that George's list of friends is also a list of the most famous and influential names in Hollywood. Clearly the murky glamour of the Hell's Angels works its magic with particular effectiveness on Tinseltown. We laughed and joked until the crew announced that all was packed and we had to head off. I came away realising that I had uncovered the perfect dinner-party guests. It had been full of surprises, but the meeting had not disappointed, not by a long way. George had shown himself to be a well-rounded and fascinating man. He had enjoyed making me squirm and feel uncomfortable but had known when to stop and give sensible answers. We had laid to rest the idea that the Angels had a big problem with Evel Knievel. It seemed pretty clear from everything that George had said that they weren't really all that bothered about him either way. And, above all, George had kept alive for me the idea that there are still bikers out there who ride to get away from 'normal' life, to be outsiders, to be free. I know I could never, never in a million years, be one of them. But somehow it cheered me immensely on the ride back to Butte to know that they were somewhere out there, the real deal, riding their black bikes through the night and living apart from the rest of us folk with our normal, nine-to-five lives.

Months later, when the film was finished, I would be disappointed to discover that we had no choice but to drop George's interview out of the final edit. We had assembled so much footage with Evel and needed all of it to tell the story of the man who was, after all, the subject of the documentary, that we simply could not fit in what was, for the purposes of our film, a bit of a diversion. But I found a better way of recalling my meeting with the senior Hell's Angel. The memory of his bike had stayed with me. Its sinister form stalked my dreams for a bit. And so I visited my mates at Warr's Harley-Davidson in London and I commissioned them to build me one like it. We worked out what George's bike had been based on, got hold of one and set about ordering parts and having it customised and rebuilt until it, too, now lurks with a menacing air of potency and sinister presence. Of course, the rider is a bit of a let-down in the menacing department, no one has ever felt compelled to run for cover when I climb off it, but I adore it for being like something that has stepped briefly out of a comic book. Mindy rides a Harley, too, and we cruise the lanes as the smallest and least intimidating motorcycle gang the world has ever seen. Secretly, though, we know we're scary.

## Chilli Sauce

Evel didn't turn up for the celebratory ride around Butte. Every year he led the procession and thousands of bikers arrived from all over the world to follow the legend on a parade around his hometown. I turned up late on the burgundy Harley, but, by careful manoeuvring and a lot of apologetic British bluster, made my way to the front of the queue of bikes waiting behind a white pickup with Stars and Stripes painted on it and Evel Knievel emblazoned across it. This, I was told later, was the 'Evel Knievel pickup', obviously, and would carry the man himself as he was no longer able to ride a bike. There were thousands of us crammed between the shops, stores and hotels along a stretch of one of Butte's main streets. The riders varied from long-haired cowboys lounging on stretched-out choppers to chubby middle-aged couples wearing matching jackets and bumbags, riding pastel-coloured tourers with white-walled tyres, tiny American flags fluttering on the top box and stuffed toys tied on behind the fairing screen.

It was a carnival atmosphere, people talked and shouted backwards and forwards along the line of bikes. Someone shrieked but it was a girly, exuberant yell of recognition and happiness as someone they knew turned up to join in the fun. Kids milled around, wandering up and down the line to check out the bikes. Older kids, teenagers, dressed in the denims and leathers of twenty years ago, stood further back and checked out each other. Further up the street were fairground stalls and market traders selling T-shirts with Evel's name and picture on them, belts with huge buckles and ranks of model cars in yellow and red boxes that would be bought, broken and soon lost. I had wandered the stalls earlier and was talked into trying a locally made hot chilli sauce. The sturdy woman selling them had cornered me in her temporary, canvas-walled lair.

She stood in front of me in her sprayed-on denim jeans, her feet planted firmly apart like an angry referee, and spoke to me loudly in a strong, American voice both friendly and potent:

'You just gotta try it. Folks round Butte love their chilli sauce, and this,' she held the small bottle in her chubby hand, dark-red false nails clashing uncomfortably with the green label, 'is the best darned chilli sauce in the state.' I let her put a lentil-sized drop on to my finger and I stabbed it into my mouth quickly before I could change my mind. There was a pause, an all too brief moment of peace, and then it burned like hell. I feared it might burn straight through my tongue, hiss through the floor of my mouth and the soft flesh and gristle of my neck and land on the ground to sit and fizz on the stones. I tried not to show it, though. The white-bleached hair, tattoos and straining, tour T-shirt of the stallholder told me she wasn't a woman who would appreciate being around men who squeaked when they tried her famous hot chilli sauce. Further into the impromptu outdoor market I found two stalls selling a vast array of sinister lock knives and massive sheath knives with serrated blades etched with panthers and Ninja warriors to children. It was a carnival, then, but a carnival a very long way from home.

Evel had not yet arrived. We were all waiting for him. Once he got there, he would give a brief speech from the back of the truck and we would fire up the hogs and ride. I was desperately excited at the prospect of cruising the streets of Butte in a throng of several hundred bikes. Even on my rented burgundy monstrosity. But Evel still hadn't arrived. At the head of the line, just behind the Evel Knievel pickup, his son, Robbie, was in the middle of a crowd of tense looking people. Robbie knew about our documentary, we had already met and spoken, and I decided it would be best to slip over to him and check what was happening. I leaned the bike on to its stand, hopped off and wandered towards Robbie. We spoke. Evel wasn't coming. Robbie told me that his dad had taken a bad turn, maybe had a stroke. There was no way he would be making the ride and might not manage to appear again for the rest of the festival. That local kid, Trigger Gumm, was due to make his jump in Evel's honour the next day, and Robbie doubted if his father would even make that. I ran back to the crew, waiting by the side of my bike, and told them the news. I had learned, too, that the parade would still go ahead, but without Evel. How could they cancel it now? Robbie would lead it in the truck. Evel would not be there.

We filmed a bit of stuff as the announcement was made public. The bikes fired up and began to move off, Robbie Knievel at the head of the parade in his father's pickup. I decided not to ride. Without Evel, there seemed to be no point. I rode my bike out of the queue and parked it on the forecourt of a nearby store selling lawnmowers and waterproofs. And I stood on the sidewalk and watched the hundreds of bikes set off. The news of Evel's condition had not filtered back very far along the line and, as the riders passed, they grinned and waved and shouted Evel's name, unaware that their hero was laid up in a hospital, a fragile, ailing old man.

We gathered the crew and walked off to a nearby coffee house to talk things through, make plans and check the kit. Later, as we headed back towards the waiting van and my bike, we found ourselves among a dense crowd milling around outside a hotel on a corner near the point from which the parade had left earlier. Something was happening, clearly. We learned that Evel had been scheduled to turn up and give a talk at an event at the hotel. And, despite not making the parade, he had turned up at the hotel later in the day as planned. Now he was about to leave again. I spotted a car pulled up outside the hotel's entrance. Robbie stood by the car's open door, leaning a muscled arm on the frame. I recognised other faces, too, in the small group around him. The crowd knew Evel was there; they pressed towards the hotel, hungry for a glimpse of their hero, I guessed. That hunger made all the sharper by his failure to appear earlier in the day. I wondered if it was genuine concern for the man's wellbeing that etched itself across their tense faces, or a less caring but no less human desire to find out what was going on, to walk up to exciting, unfolding events and be part of them.

The group near the car straightened suddenly, heads straining towards the hotel's wooden doors. Evel came out. He was being helped on either side and I recognised immediately the massive frame of Gene. Evel's head was dipped low; he looked like he was hung between his two minders. He looked up then, his scraggy neck straining forwards and his thin, tight lips compressed beneath his sharp nose. His face told of his illness now, he was more fragile than before. His head dropped again as he made the last few yards to the car, half dragged, half walking. The crowd drew towards him and I went with them. People shouted his name, shouted encouragement, applauded him for making it back again. I, too, shouted his name, just once. And I found myself hoping he would look up as he reached the car and recognise me. He didn't. His minders helped him in, taking extra care with the oxygen tubes and tank. He lifted a thin arm and waved weakly through the passenger window. I was close to the car as it pulled away, his head turned towards me and I again hoped that he might recognise me. I knew the cameras were rolling now, Ben and Ian sensing that there might be useful footage about to present itself. Evel waved a thick-veined hand again and a small, calm smile rested across his face. The car drew away through the crowd. We were booked to see him again the following day and maybe he would make it.

We had been working now for some days and there was an unspoken sense in the air that we were due a bit of relaxation. A night out. After the hotel sighting of him that afternoon, Ben Devlin had called to reconfirm our interview with Evel for the next day and, yes, it would go ahead, though a later start was planned. So if we were going to have a night out at all, this would be it. We took cabs into town and asked to be dropped wherever people went for a drink. We found an Irish bar. It was tiny. Slotted into a narrow space between two proper, full-sized stores, it was like half a building. Inside, the bar ran along the length of one wall. It was punctuated by the brightly coloured, smooth handles of the beer taps and backed by racks of whiskies, their downturned necks plunged into the clear bowls of optics with their little black pouring taps making crosses below. An old television with a dusty screen like the bottom of a fruit bowl stood towards the end of the bar near the door and, at the other, a small microwave oven stood next to an old-fashioned manual cash register. It was a noisy place. There were as many people in there drinking as could fit in and their voices were strident and full, unleashed by fast-swigged beers and hot shots of whisky. The narrow span of the building made the room seem taller than it was and the voices and the clash of glasses echoing around it added to that sense. As the door swung to behind us, I saw pinned to it handwritten notes of cars and garden equipment for sale and homes needed for unwanted pets.

## Cue Ball

Ben Devlin was grinning a devilish smile already. This was the sort of bar where the one emotion that wouldn't flash through your mind as you exited face first through the window with a pool cue up your arse was surprise. I half expected a proper, old-school bar fight to break out before we bought our first drink. We stood out rather badly. Ben Devlin and Nigel led the way, their accents, clothes and posture betraying all of us immediately as strangers to this bar, this town and this country. In my mind, a sudden and immense silence descended in the place as Ben Devlin, in his clipped English tones, asked what beer the barman might recommend. In reality, though, the huge man stood behind his bar like a friendly trawlerman at the helm of his boat, smiled broadly through the crashing noise of his happy customers and made his suggestion. We all nodded our agreement and he set about the business of pouring our six beers into six plain glasses. We huddled towards the bar to pick them up, breaking our group into two bunches to fit around a girl sitting at the mid-point of the bar on a tall stool. As we drank greedily at the first of what we all knew would end up being a lengthy chain of beers, we each looked around the narrow bar. Stuffed animals and posters decorated the walls punctuated by ugly gaming machines and a CD juke box. The girl on the stool was drunk. She looked at us and said something. Her voice was shrill and slurred. There was aggression in it, too. Her eyes darted around us, probably struggling to find focus on this pack of new arrivals with their unfamiliar accents. She turned back to the bar quickly, too quickly, and began to lean perilously far out from her stool. The lean increased – she was going to fall. She had one of those faces that look older than its owner. She was probably young, mid-twenties maybe, but the years and, I guessed, the booze and perhaps other, more sinister substances, had etched themselves on to her skin, leaving it sallow and greasy and marked by small creases. Her hair was yellow and dull. And she fell off the stool to land hard on the bar-room floor. We helped her back on to her stool and regrouped.

We had more beers. And then more. We grew braver and explored further, making our way to the back of the room where it widened substantially. It turned out to be an L-shaped building and in the broadest part of it, in the elbow of the L, we found a pool table. No one was playing and we wondered why. We didn't want to break some local etiquette and risk leaving by the window, but we were keen to play. We had befriended the barman now and asked him if we could use his pool table.

'Got no cue ball, guys. Sorry. No use at all.' He shrugged his massive shoulders and smiled again. This struck us as wrong, that a place such as this one, equipped with every cliché of the trad- itional sleazy American bar, should not be able to grant its happily drunk punters an opportunity to shamble around a pool table and enhance their beer buzz with a game of pool, was a terrible, terrible thing. We were all feeling the beers now and I found myself telling the barman just how terrible this was. A tragedy, in fact. We loved this pub, I explained, we thought it was great and that this pub and all the people in it – who we loved, too – should not have a cue ball for their pool table was a thing of such sadness that it made us all, well, really, really sad. He, in turn, told us that it had just vanished one day and he hadn't got round to getting another.

'Aha. Well, don't you worry.' I leaned my elbow in a shiny puddle of beer on the smooth-topped bar and raised a finger to signify an important announcement was underway.

'Because we shall get you one.' I raised an eyebrow. 'Yes, we shall,' I added sombrely and looked around at the crew and grinned. 'We want to play pool. There's no cue ball here. There's only one answer. We shall have to get them one.' Most of our group smiled back at me and carried on their conversations.

I leaned back, elbows resting on the bar. The pool table stood behind them, empty and ignored. The sorry sight only fired me up all the more to resolve the cue ball problem and see that table lively and splashed with colour as it should be. Ben Devlin and Nigel agreed with me. They too felt that we should do something and, sensing a chance for fun, declared that they would join me on my mission. And the mission was simple. We stood together at the bar to make our plans, taking long pulls of our cold beers. We would steal one. Someone stole the cue ball from this bar and that was an affront to its dignity and standing in the community. And so we three would steal one back. We would find another bar with a pool table and relieve it of its cue ball. The poetic symmetry with which we would then be rebalancing the situation had us almost delirious with pleasure and pride at our cleverness.

We drained our glasses, told the rest of the group that we would be back, promised to return bearing a cue ball, and we left. Once outside, our fervour cooled slightly. We looked up and down the broad street. On either side it was flanked by busy bars, all much bigger than ours. And people flowed in and out of them, gathering in groups by the open doors to talk and smoke and drink in the warm night, spilling out into the street on corners, joshing and pushing and play-fighting. Voices were raised in shouts of laughter, of anger or of protestation and echoed up and down the street between the tall buildings. Big, quiet groups of sturdy adults swept along the pavements to bars hidden deeper in the town's centre. We were going to be killed, I was sure. But I was sure, too, that this was something we had to do: a test of manhood, a challenge. Nigel and Ben Devlin felt the same and we set off, peering through windows to find a pool table. The first few places held nothing for us. We tried to imagine what external features might betray a bar with a pool table inside. And we decided that really stylish places were actually less likely to have one. They wouldn't give space to something as basic and simple as a pool table. So that made our quest a little simpler by narrowing down the options. We looked up and down the street. There weren't any really stylish places; they all looked rough and rugged with their simple doors and signs in primary colours.

## *Extras in a* Smokey and the Bandit *Movie*

We needed different criteria. Big, then; a bar with a pool table in it would have to be big. They take up a lot of room, pool tables, more when they're surrounded by players and their beery mates egging them on. Although the one with which we had become so enamoured and for which we were setting out now on this perilous mission was less than half the size of even the smallest we found on the street. Nevertheless, we moved towards a sizeable looking place down the street on a corner. It had broad windows with dirty venetian blinds standing vertically in them and a plain door set into the very corner of the building at an angle like a canted corner on a table leg. That, we decided, was the place. We walked in. There was a crowd, but it wasn't full to bursting like some. The drinkers lined the walls mostly, standing and talking, their beers clutched in big hands in front of them.

They were older in here than in some we had checked. Most looked to be in their mid-thirties or older. This was not a kids' pub, then, it was a proper drinkers' bar. Many wore dirty baseball caps. I saw cowboy boots and steel toe-capped rigger boots lurking under straight-legged jeans. If ever there was a place that needed a pool table, this was it. We moved towards the bar and saw straight away that, yes, it had a table. It stood parallel to the bar itself, under a broad light with a green shade suspended from the tiled ceiling. The cues were racked along its sides and the cue ball stood in the centre, looking small in the stark light of the overhead lamp. The music was American and old-fashioned. There was just one small problem. Our plan, as far as it had gone, had featured us ordering beers in whatever bar we found a pool table, waiting patiently for our turn to play and then, at some point in our game, lifting the ball and disappearing into the throng with it, as though we had finished our game in the usual way. But no one was playing. In fact, no one was standing within ten feet of the table. We looked around the room. Every wall, every inch of the bar itself, was lined with drinkers, mostly male. Not one was playing pool, but nearly everyone in there was facing the table. They could have been waiting for a ritual sacrifice to take place on it. I looked back to the table. We were some distance from it now, halfway towards it from the bar. The cue ball stood white, stark and impossibly precious under the fluorescent lights like a huge diamond on a plinth under the gaze of a network of security cameras and lasers.

'Right. Tricky this, then,' I muttered sideways to the guys and we all took a swig of our fresh beers. 'Not sure we're gonna be able to pull this off.' I looked again at the customers. 'At least, not without being killed.'

Nigel and I exchanged glances. Clearly, this was one cue ball that would be staying at home tonight and not coming out to play with us. We would have to find another target. But where? I was forming the thought that perhaps we might be better facing the truth, admitting that we had got carried away and, yes, drunk, and be men about it now and face the shame of trudging back without our promised prize, when I looked across at Ben. He was working his way towards the table and grinning at us manically. Fearful of what might be about to happen, Nigel and I walked after him, trying to look casual. We stopped short of actually whistling and scuffing our feet on the lino, but it was a close thing. Hard eyes followed us across the room.

Ben leaned against the table now, still grinning. He had his hands behind his back and I guessed from the small movements of his shoulders and chest that those hands were reaching around behind him.

'What the hell are you doing?' I smiled as I said it, keen not to draw the attention of the crowd around the bar. Ben just smiled back and raised his eyebrows.

'Bloody hell,' I directed my words at Nigel now. 'He's going to try and do it.'

Nigel returned my fixed smile. He has children and a mortgage. I have children and a mortgage and so does Ben. We work in telly, we film stuff and then go home to our families to talk about their days at school. We watch TV at night with our wives. What we don't do is get the shit kicked out of us in redneck bars for stealing cue balls under the noses of extras from a *Smokey and the Bandit* movie.

'Oh Christ, Ben, you'll be killed.' I smiled again and nodded my head now, trying to look like we were enjoying friendly banter at the pool table. Maybe people would think we were just shy and wanted to stay away from the crowd. Maybe we'd each end up tied to fallen tree trunks, being invited to squeal like little piggies. Ben was leaning further back now and I risked a glance behind him. He couldn't reach the ball; it stood in the glare of the lights, a foot away from his grasp.

'Ben, you'll never do it. It's not worth it. Let's find another one. For God's sake.' I couldn't keep up the pretence of having an ordinary conversation now. I have been in fights in bars, in the distant past, and they are not very nice. They weren't very nice in my late teens, and they sure as hell weren't likely to have got any nicer as I approach my forties. Nigel was still smiling. He's not an easily scared man, Nigel, and I guessed that a large part of him would be enjoying the thrill. Although I suspected, too, that he was worried about how this might end. His face confirmed it. And then Ben straightened, eyes alive with excitement, and moved away from the table. There was a door to the left of the bar in front of us. That was the nearest way out. I didn't dare ask what he had done. I didn't dare look at his hands, but from the way he brought them in front of him and clutched his arms across his stomach now, I guessed he had the ball and was trying to hide it in his folded arms. We walked. We didn't run. But we walked pretty bloody quickly. And we didn't look back.

We cleared the door and hit the street, turning left to head up the hill and back towards where we had started. We were not going to make it. I braced for the shouts, waited for things to be thrown, waited to be chased up the street by a baying mob holding baseball bats and nooses. Nothing came. We were still walking fast, our feet hitting the wide pavement hard as we headed up the gentle slope.

'Holy shit.' I spoke first, my face still screwed up and my eyes half closed with tension.

Ben held up his hand and cupped in it, half covered by his fingers and half of it exposed to the neon lights of Butte's main street, was the curved, white, flawless dome of a cue ball. And he threw back his head and laughed loud and long into the night sky.

'You fucking maniac, Devlin.'

'You lunatic. How? Why? Why didn't you just leave it? You're bloody nuts.'

And we all spoke at once. We shared our feelings, our fears, our guesses as to what fate had awaited us if they had caught us. We half ran, half skipped back to the Irish bar and our waiting friends.

When we got there, we slammed the ball on to the wooden bar top. It hit with a sharp explosion that rang round the room like a gunshot.

'One cue ball. Now, can we use your table, please?'

Ben's grin was too wide for his face now. The barman grinned back. He didn't ask questions. He knew that another barman in Butte would be explaining to his customers that, no, they couldn't play pool tonight because there was no cue ball. He didn't know yet which bar it would be, but I guessed that he would find out soon enough. We gathered round the table, racked up the balls and placed the cue ball in the D with reverential care and we played pool as we breathlessly recounted our adventures and our leader's lunatic bravery. I have the ball still. Ben presented me with it months later when we finished editing the film. It was a kind gesture. On it he has written 'Butte '07'. I keep it in my office and I smile every time I see it. I never could play pool.

## Down to Business

The crowd was there to see Trigger Gumm make his jump. They milled about in their hundreds and bayed and shouted and called out under their baseball caps from behind high wire fencing. We were there to film them watching him, to film Trigger himself as he jumped a fleet of cars on his bike and, most importantly, to talk with and film Evel Knievel in an environment as familiar to him as any office. This was our biggest and best chance to step briefly into Evel's world of showmanship, daredevilry and danger. Evel would not be jumping anything today or ever again, but he was the man who put motorcycle jumping on the world map and could rightly be said to be the inspiration behind this and every other large-scale motorcycle stunt since he first pulled on his star-spangled cape and amazed audiences at county fairs. He hadn't arrived yet, though.

We recorded an interview with Trigger Gumm while we waited. Stern-faced with small, uncomplicated eyes and the build of an athlete, he turned out to be not an especially bright and chatty individual, young Trigger. But then sparkling wit and incisive debating skills are not and never have been the prerequisite of the motorcycle stunt jumper. We paced the jump, walking from the mound of earth on which Trigger would land back to the foot of the take-off ramp itself. We walked up the ramp's narrow boards to the lip from which Trigger would launch himself and as we walked we spoke about the stunt. He was aware that, yes, things could go wrong and, if they did, he might well be hurt or worse. I got a sense from him that he was also well aware that this was his best shot at chasing fame and riches and he had calculated the risks involved and felt them to be acceptable. There were, inevitably perhaps, some strong links with Evel Knievel's story in Trigger Gumm's tale. I wished him all the best and hoped very much to be able to congratulate him in an hour or so.

We were walking the line of wire fence, filming the tense crowd, when Evel arrived. He was driven in the huge SUV and as he approached us I saw the familiar face leaning out of the window towards us. He looked even angrier than usual. And he was. He had seen our cameramen and ordered his driver to take him towards them. He roared at them to get out, to get away from the ramp, to get back behind the fence. He shouted that we could not film there. No cameras. This was a dangerous place. We had no right to be here. I had not seen him this angry; he was gripped by a fury that drove his frail body to move faster and more violently than I had seen in our week with him. The crowd immediately behind us was quietened by his rage; they studied Ben and Ian and their big TV cameras. I stepped up to the SUV.

'Evel, it's us. We're supposed to be here.' He looked confused for a moment. He didn't recognise me. 'We're making the film about you. Really sorry you were bad yesterday. We missed you on the ride.'

I used the soft, calming tones of a nurse. Or someone petting a cat.

'You tell us where we can go, Evel, and we'll go there.'

His confusion cleared, he looked at me calmly, his face still flushed in thin, broken lines from his anger.

'He can film there, but you make sure he stays behind the tape in front of the fence here.' He pointed a long, shaky finger at Ben, who stood casually with his camera resting on the ground next to him. 'No closer than that, okay.'

'Thanks, Evel. We'll stay right here out of the way. Hope it goes well today. Thank you.' And his car swept him away, following the line of the fence past the waiting cars and the landing ramp.

It was getting close to jump time. The crowd had grown as big as it was going to get now and a few thousand people were crammed in behind the fence. Children filled the front rank, kids much like the ones who had watched Evel Knievel thirty-five years earlier. It was time first for the razzamatazz and showmanship. A fat man in a fringed leather jacket climbed the landing ramp and stood on top of the mound of carefully sculpted earth breathing through thick lips. He carried a microphone trailing a thin cable. He lifted the mic to his florid face and music piped up from tinny public address speakers. He sang a song about America being great. It was awful and the crowd lapped it up. As the song reached its frenzied climax of loyal patriotism, three fighter jets streaked overhead, their jet roar following in their wake a second behind them and their vapour trails marking their path across the sky directly above Trigger Gumm's take-off ramp. It was all very American indeed.

I wondered what would happen next. And I wondered, too, just what we were all there to see. Was the crowd gathered to watch a man exercising skill and judgement in carrying out a demanding and challenging feat, or were they all there just in case there was blood? And if there was blood, if Trigger Gumm made a mistake and landed on the road to smash his young body to bits in front of the men, women and children gathered around, what would have been achieved? And what would that do to the people in the crowd? Trigger would never be making the jump if the crowd were not there to witness it. And to pay him for the privilege. And so some of the responsibility for what happened must rest with the crowd. With those of us watching. I looked at the beaming faces of the children lined up by the fence and I wondered if they really understood this strange show they were taking part in. And I wondered, too, just when Trigger would do it. How would we know when he was about to jump?

I heard a crackle from the PA system and turned to the left to see Evel Knievel walking out to the flat ground where the cars that Trigger would jump were arranged in careful rows. He raised the microphone to his mouth and made a brief speech in praise of young Trigger Gumm. He spoke about how hard it was to be a motorcycle jumper and he spoke of the immense challenge to Trigger in this jump and the danger he would be facing. The crowd responded with cheers and applause for Evel. And quickly for Trigger, too; he rode out now, his dirt bike snapping and snarling noisily as he sped alongside the ramps and the cars, pulling wheelies. This was all part of the show. He wore the obligatory cape. His crash helmet was more modern than any Evel ever wore and it gave the crowd a better chance to see their hero's brave face as he paraded up and down next to the ramp off which he would very shortly launch himself into the air for our amusement.

I looked back over the audience. The youngsters at the front gripped the wire fence with their small, pink fingers, their faces straining to catch Trigger as he rode past. The adults behind them clapped and cheered. This was a ritual, one that had in various forms been carried out for millennia: one person doing something dangerous for the entertainment of many. And the many responded to the one today in time-honoured fashion. I wondered again when the jump would be made. I hoped the crew were ready to catch it when Trigger made his leap. Of course they would be; they always were. And the noise from the crowd changed. It wasn't a full-on cartoon gasp, but the cheering and the clapping quietened and grew thin and sparse and I heard a thousand sudden intakes of breath. I spun round to see Trigger already midway between the two ramps in the air. He had done it. At least, he had started it.

The bike and Trigger were briefly silhouetted against the blue sky, still streaked with the snowy trails from the jets. In a fraction of a second, he had finished it, landing on the dirt mound, the bike's long-travel suspension absorbing the impact more smoothly and efficiently than the boneshakers Evel rode could ever have managed. The crowd cheered, clapped and whooped. He didn't crash, he didn't die. He wheelied up and down now, the bike's sharp barks lost in the noise from the crowd. If there ever was a bloodlust among them, it was expelled now in a great chanting, roaring shout. Three days later, sitting in the sun taking a breather before another filming session, I read in the local paper that Evel was not happy with Trigger's jump. He condemned it for falling short of the distance Trigger had claimed he would clear. He spoke of his disappointment. His comments made me sad. They chipped away a little bit of the magic.

## *And They Never Forgave Him*

As my week with Evel drew to its close, we made sure we had everything we would need for the film. There was one last interview to record. It was with the man who held the key to Evel's eventual fate. Sheldon Saltman was Evel's publicist, his PR man. He helped Evel shape his public image as a defender of family values and virtue, as a brave daredevil and an all-American hero. He also wrote a book, published in 1977, called *Evel Knievel on Tour.* In it, he spoke of Evel drinking and hinted that he had abused his family. Evel did not like this. He believed that Sheldon had slighted him and risked tarnishing his wholesome image. So he went to the Twentieth Century Fox studios where Shelly worked and, despite his own arms still being in plaster from his most recent accident, used a baseball bat to shatter his PR man's left arm and wrist.

I flew to LA and spoke to Sheldon about the events of thirty years earlier and recorded an interview about the saddest chapter of all in a remarkable life. After the attack, as Sheldon recovered in hospital, Evel's world crumbled about him. Having built his legend and his fortune around an image as a wholesome, American family hero, he had pulled down that image in the most immediate and complete way. Not surprisingly, his career, founded on PR, came to a sudden end when he took a baseball bat to his PR man. He couldn't have done anything more certain to lead to ruination both of his career and his wealth. It all disappeared overnight. He staggered on for a while, but his image never recovered. Who really cares if a man can clear a few buses on a motorcycle? The achievement is and always was irrelevant. It was the legend people wanted, the hero, not the results. They wanted someone who threw himself into the teeth of danger for them, who was never scared, who got hurt but got better again. And they wanted someone who stood up for decent family values, who stood against the drug-taking and hippy lifestyle that America so hated. And Evel, having created that character, took him away again and they never forgave him.

Back in Butte, Evel Knievel Days were finishing. Visitors had packed up and gone home. Banners trailed quietly from posts, the fairground rides and market stalls were dismantled and tidied away. I had one remaining appointment with Evel, but before I went to meet him he had asked me to do one other thing. He told me to visit the Butte stonemason and take a look at what was stored in the yard there. I rode over on the bike, the crew following in the van. I walked around the outside of the small, single-storey building where the stonemason worked. It was a cooler day, the sky grey and reserved. The building stood in a broad car park with only my bike and the crew van in it. Around us, in every direction, the beautiful Montana countryside retreated into the distance and held off, leaving us marooned in a sea of grey tarmac that lay flatly without the shimmering heat hazes of recent days to add an exotic air. To one side of the stonemason's building stood a high, wire security fence. It guarded a narrow yard. I peered through the mesh, my gloved fingers gripping the thick wire. I saw a water tank, an old workbench and neatly stacked piles of new red bricks. At the far end, propped against the wall, was a large, pale stone tablet. The words on it read: 'Words to live for. Faith. Health. Education. Love. Work. Honorability. Dream. Amen.' I knew that I would find it there, I knew what to expect – I had researched it. And I knew, too, that Evel hoped the stone would be erected somewhere in his hometown when he had gone. He had paid for it himself and was rumoured to be prepared to pay for its erection in the town. He wanted to make sure the legend he had created would be remembered. And he was content to pay for the memory's preservation as he had been prepared to pay for the creation of that legend in his own blood and pain. I wrote the words down on a scrap of paper. I would ask Evel about them when we met later in the day.

## Dreams

We were to meet Evel at the Butte Golf Club. As I pitched the Harley on to its stand and removed helmet and gloves, I looked around at the car park with its ranks of golf players' cars. Row upon row of neat, conservative, unobtrusive station wagons and people carriers filled it. Beyond it was yet another low-lying, neutrally styled brick building with a red tiled roof and white painted window frames. This was not the sort of place I had expected to be meeting a childhood hero. We walked to the back of the clubhouse and waited. I heard the now familiar hiss and click of Evel's oxygen tank before I turned to see him arrive, walking slowly around the corner towards us, a woman supporting him by his arm. She was younger than him, with the utilitarian, practical build of middle America topped off by a mound of bottle-blonde hair. Her face was kind but strangely defensive. She was nervous of us. Evel introduced her to us as his second wife, Krystal. The two of them loved golf, a passion they indulge in together as often as possible. By rather sharp contrast, I loathe golf for its fussy, middle-class pretentions, its designated parking spaces, its clubhouse rules and its unforgivably awful clothing. I was disappointed that Evel Knievel, the lionhearted, fearless gladiator himself, had been seduced by the pastel-hued charms of golf and was happy to spend his retirement among the trolley draggers. Of course, I had forgotten that Evel does things his own way.

'Right. You follow us.' He barked his command and leaped into the passenger side of a golf cart with surprising agility. Krystal jumped in next to him, hit the throttle and their green trolley cart shot off. We looked at each other, heads flicking from one to another; this was not what was supposed to happen. Ben Joiner just grinned. He could sense that what he had perhaps anticipated as a pretty boring interview to record at a golf club might just turn out to be more interesting. He hoisted his camera up on to his shoulder and grabbed a golf cart. The rest of our group did the same, jumping into two other carts. And we set off after the legend. Now this was more like it. The fairway, or freeway or whatever golfists call the grass around the holes and flags, flashed by on either side and Evel's cart stayed resolutely in the distance ahead. And then I could see that he had stopped. As we drew closer, I saw that Krystal was out of the cart and lining up for a shot on the first tee. Or hole, or pocket or whatever. Evel wasn't going to play today; he sat in the cart and watched his wife settle herself for a swing. She took the shot. We pulled up alongside just in time and I jumped out.

'Evel, hi. Great to see you,' I was panting as though I had run rather than driven in the cart. I walked round to the side of his buggy. Ben chased after me, Jeff making ready to hook up the sound kit and record the interview.

'We just thought that we could have a little chat about . . .' And they were off again, flashing past where we stood and shooting across the green. I spun round and ran back to my cart. I looked up to see Ben Joiner gripping his sides with laughter. As things deteriorated further into chaos, he loved it all the more. I stamped on the little plastic accelerator pedal and hared after him. It dawned on me that we were probably the first film crew to get drawn into a high-speed golf cart chase across the Butte golf course in pursuit of Evel Knievel. And I decided that Ben was right; this was great fun.

We spun along narrow tracks between hedges, burst into clearings, spotted our quarry and shouted from cart to cart as we hurtled after him. Whether it was luck, driving skill or some devious piece of customisation, Evel Knievel's golf cart was just faster than all of ours. Every time we caught up, every time I jumped out and ran up to Evel, his wife would just be wiggling her backside prior to taking the shot, there would be the sharp click of club against ball and she would be back in the cart and on the throttle just as I pitched up alongside. Evel smiled throughout. He never showed it, never gave a hint that he was doing this to us deliberately, but I suspected he knew full well what he was about. This was our last meeting and he was showing us young pups that Evel Knievel could still give them a run for their money, even if he needed the help of his young wife to do it.

We did corner him eventually. At the last hole, Evel halted the cart and agreed to talk for the final time. I sat in the cart next to him. He looked small in his neatly pressed golfing clothes. We spoke about his career, about it ending. He spoke about the house he had commissioned to be built overlooking the golf course. It was beautiful, the best in Butte. The wrought-iron gates bore his initials and the gardens went on forever. He had sold it, of course, when his career crumbled. He lived in Florida now. And he didn't want to talk about that. I looked into his face as we spoke. He looked more relaxed than I had seen him before; still old, still fragile, but less explosive, somehow gentler. I asked him about the stone he had sent me to see at the stonemason's yard. It was difficult to look at it, I told him, because I knew him now and it was hard to look at that blank space where the final day of his life would be carved when it arrived. I pulled out the note I had made and asked him about the words etched on the stone and if he would add any more. And he said that, no, he would not. I asked him what was the most important thing of those he had listed. He didn't have to stop and think. He drew in another breath, the oxygen tank clicking and hissing behind him. His pale blue eyes looked away briefly as he spoke.

'Dreams,' he said. 'Follow your dreams.'

We shook hands; his was thin and cold in mine but still strong. I never saw him again. I was surprised when he died. I guess I didn't think he would. But he did and the legend he created will live on. It has to, he made sure of that. He paid for it to.

# ACKNOWLEDGEMENTS

The adventures in this book all have one thing in common; they none of them were undertaken alone. And so I want to thank every friend and member of every crew I have worked with over the last year for their patience, forbearance, professionalism and, very occasionally, generosity in the bar afterwards. It really is a team business, making telly, and there is absolutely no room to carry dead weight. Every member of that team, whatever their role, is crucial to its success. So it's fun, but sometimes terrifying too. So thanks all, here's to the next trip. And see you in the bar afterwards.

And so here they are, dragged for once in the limelight, though they'll all skulk off and do something more interesting as soon as you stop looking at their names . . . .

Producers – these are people who do all the hard work in the office and often don't even get to come out and play in the field. Pat Doyle; Grant Wardop; Rowland French; Ben Devlin; Ben Gale; Rebecca Mills; Tony Moss; Gemma Addison. Series Producer – The Big Boss, Andy Wilman. Directors – people who wake up in the morning and for whom everything immediately starts to go wrong: Nigel Simpkiss; James Bryce. Production managers – they manage us. Just imagine . . . : Susie Cooper; Laura Matthews. Production coordinators – they coordinate us . . . Again, just imagine: Sara Hulme; Elena Christodolou; Michelle Clinton; Louise McDonald; Colleen Hannah. Production runner – does all the actual work: Pete Holton. Cameramen – mad, all of them: Casper Leaver; Jay Kennedy; Ben Joiner; Chris O; Iain May; Simon Wagen; Ian Kellet. Minicam – it all works well, until we get involved: Jonathan Thursby; Gary Boulter; Martin Davidson; Doug Krispin. Sound recordists – they spend their lives tied to cameramen, who are all mad: Darren Tate; Ryan Chandler; Pete Cowasii; Russell Edwards; Kiff McManus; Jeff Meese; Dan Chapman. Film Editing – fiddly and dine in the dark: Darren King; Chris Muckle; Clyde Kellett; Colin Peters. Researchers – they do all the work: Gavin Whitehead; Glynn Wood.

Thanks also to: Jeremy Clarkson, James May, Zog and Jill Ziegler, Jonathan Vizor and to Michael Dover, Alan Samson and Susan Lamb at Orion for the gentle nagging, the guiding suggestions and the final burst of, let's be honest, less than gentle nagging. Thanks to Luigi Bonomi for helping me through the writing and to Paul Lyon Maris for getting me the things to write about in the first place.

Thanks too to Katrina Tanzer, my assistant, for making everything happen. Always. And thanks to Mindy, Izzy and Willow for letting me go out to play and never complaining when I'm late back in for my tea.

Photographs © bbctopgear.com: 14 (top); Ben Devlin: 18, 19 (bottom), 22, 23, 24, front endpaper; Freakingnews.com: 19 (top); KNS News: 11; Iain May: 1,2,3,4,5,6,7,8, back endpaper; Jonathan Thursby: 9, 10, 11, 12, 13, 14 (bottom), 15,16,17 (bottom); William Thompson: 20.

Every effort has been made to acknowledge the correct copyright holders and the publishers will, if notified, correct any errors in future editions.

# INDEX

A38 road 169, 170
Abba 107
aircraft, Twin Otter 47, 48, 53
Airport Shopping Dare 50, 51
Albinoni 173
*Aliens* movies 30
Amazon, River, competition 123–124
amphibious vehicle project 138–155
    Channel crossing attempt 138,
        142–155
    the crossing 145–148
    France, arrival in 148–155
    Richard's diary 146
Amundsen, Roald 16
Anderson, Pamela 175
Andress, Ursula 151
Apache gunship helicopter 12
Arctic explorers 7, 16 *see also* McNair,
    Matty
Arctic Ocean 21
Aston Martin DB9 8
Attenborough, David 123
Austin 134
Austria, training for Polar race in 9,
    10–16
*Auto Trader* 111

badgers, honey 122–123, 124,
    125–126
Bangles, The 173
baobab trees 119–120
Bartlett (sled dog) 24, 71, 103
Bathurst Island 91, 94
*Beano* 123
bears, polar *see* polar bears
Beatles, The 173
bees, African 122–123
Bellamy, David 123, 124
Ben (cameraman) 112–113
Billericay 160
Birmingham 9, 124, 197, 207
    Shirley 205
*Blackadder* TV series 77
Blind Boys of Alabama, The 173
Bluetooth 224
BMW motorcycle 110
boat, inflatable 183–184
boots, Arctic 30
Boris (BMW motorcycle) 110
Botswana 108
    drive across 108, 110–137
        and vice president of Botswana
            114, 115–116, 117–118

Botswana—*contd*
 briefing 112–113
 completed 137
 crocodile 136, 137
 Kubu Island 119–120
 mending Oliver 126–130,
  131–133, 136
 microlights 114–115, 116
 preparations 118–119
 Richard's diary 120–121, 131,
  136–137
 river crossing 133–135, 137
 salt flats 113–114, 119, 120–121,
  131
 tourist with comb-over 122,
  124–125, 126
 wildlife 121–123, 124–125–126,
  130–131
 vice president of 114, 115–116,
  117–118
British Bulldogs 46
business cards 5–7
Butte, Montana 196, 197–199, 202,
  203–205, 210, 211, 212
 celebratory ride around 217,
  235–236, 237–238
 chilli sauce saleswoman in 236–237
 cinema manager in 215–216
 drinkers' bar in 243–246, 247
 Evel Knievel Days festival 196–197,
  210, 212, 217, 235–239,
  247–251, 252
 Evel Knievel's house in 256
 Irish bar in 239–242, 246–247
  girl in 240–241
 salesman in 210, 211
 Silver Bow Drive-in movie theatre
  206–209
 stonemason in 252–253
Butte Golf Club 253–256

Butte Shooting Club 197, 200–202,
  206

cable cars 10
Cadillac convertible 208, 209
Caesar's Palace Fountains, Las Vegas
  206, 207, 209
cars, naming 108–110, 181 *see also*
  *individual entries*
Channel, English 138, 141, 142, 144,
  145–147
Cheltenham 87, 123, 160, 161, 165,
  168, 169, 175, 178
 supermarket 162, 163, 164, 165,
  166, 168, 172
Cheltenham to Ledbury road (B4213)
  138, 156, 157, 170–171, 172,
  174–175, 176–179
 house on 175–176
Chitwood, Joe 205
Christie, George 218–219, 220, 224,
  225, 226, 227, 228–234
 wife of 234
Clarkson, Jeremy
 amphibious vehicle project 139,
  140, 141, 142–143, 145, 146,
  149–150, 151, 152, 155
 in Botswana 112, 117, 118, 119,
  120–121, 129, 131, 133, 135
 race to Monte Carlo 8
 race to North Pole 8, 9
  in the race 71–72, 73–74, 94, 103
  in Resolute Bay 61–63
  training 15, 16
 race to Oslo 8
coat, caribou 32–33
Cooper, Tommy 48
Cornflake (Honda motorcycle) 110
*Cosmopolitan* 51
Crash (Hell's Angel) 230, 231–232,
  233

Dan (friend/relative) 53
Davis, Dr Ian 'Doc' 76–77, 78, 83, 84,
    85–86, 87, 95–97, 99, 105
Denver, John 30
Devlin, Ben 193, 194, 201, 205, 211,
    216, 219–220, 221, 228, 231,
    239
  and the cue ball 240, 242–243,
    244–245, 246, 247
Disney film 108
dog sled, race to North Pole with *see*
    North Pole, magnetic, race to
dog sled, training to drive 17, 21,
    22–27, 28–30, 31, 41–42
dog team race, Iqaluit 35–41, 42–46,
    47
dogs, sled 23–25, 26–27, 28–29, 31,
    37, 38–39, 40–41, 45, 71, 107
  during race to North Pole 81,
    83–84, 91, 92, 98, 103
  handling 39
Dover 141–146
  White Cliffs of 147–148

Eastbourne 117
Eastnor Castle estate 133
Edinburgh 203
*Encyclopedia of Nature* 119, 122, 123
'Eternal Flame' 173
Evel Knievel Days festival 196–197,
    210, 212, 217, 235–239,
    247–251, 252
*Evel Knievel on Tour* 251–252
Evel Knievel wind-up toy 193, 194,
    197–198, 210–211
explorers, Polar 7, 16 *see also* McNair,
    Matty
'Eye of the Tiger' 16

Ferrari 108–109

festival, 'Tunik Time' 31–32, 33–35
Fiat convertible (LaBamba) 110
Florida 196, 256
Ford Mustang 108–109
Ford XB Falcon GT351 version 116
Forest of Dean 9
France, coast of 147–150, 151–155
French-Canadian couple in Arctic 31
fridge, Smeg 190
frostbite, effects of 11

Gary (Thursby's right-hand man) 136
Gaz (Arctic specialist) 76, 78, 83, 84,
    85, 86, 87, 89, 95–97, 99
Ginster's meat pasty 160
Glacier Mint adverts 11
Gloucester 179
Gloucester bypass 160
Gloucestershire, flooding in (2007)
    138, 156–158, 160–191
  Richard's journey from London to
    Cheltenham 159–163
  Richard's walk from Cheltenham
    to home 163–173, 174–180
    and blue saloon driver 178–179
    and the Zeiglers 156–157, 180–191
golf 254
golf club, helicopter arrival at 117
Greenland 17
Gribble (teddy bear) 21, 29
Gumm, Trigger 210–211, 237,
    247–248, 249–251

Hammond, daughters of Richard 67,
    103, 109–110, 181 *see also*
    Hammond, Willow
Hammond, father of Richard 27–28
Hammond, Mindy 21, 53, 67, 71, 103,
    235
  and Gloucestershire floods 158,

Hammond, Mindy—*contd*
  162, 163, 166–167, 176, 179,
  181, 182, 183, 184, 235
 naming cars etc 108, 109–110
Hammond, Willow (daughter) 158,
  167, 171, 177, 179–180 *see also*
  Hammond, daughters of
  Richard
Harley-Davidson motorcycles
  227–228, 231–232, 235
 Road King 197, 198–201, 207, 212,
  215, 217, 231–232, 235, 237,
  252, 253
   ride to meet Hell's Angels leader
   on 218–221, 224, 225–226
*Hawaii Five-O* 187
Heathrow airport 32, 208
helicopter, Apache gunship 12
helicopters, Coastguard and RAF
  160–161, 171–172
Hell's Angels 212, 217–219, 220, 224,
  226, 227, 229, 232, 233, 234
  *see also* Christie, George
 and Evel Knievel 217–218, 233, 234
 motorcycles 226–228, 231–232,
  235
 Ventura chapter 218
Hollywood 234
Honda motorcycle 110
honey badgers 122–123, 124, 125–126
'Hot, Hot, Hot' 173
hunter, polar bear 64–66, 68, 69


Ian (US cameraman) 201, 202, 205,
  239, 248
igloo-building competition 33–35
Igluik 49, 53
Imbruglia, Natalie 16
Inuit-inspired artwork 32
Inuit people 65, 93

iPod Nano 166, 171, 172, 173,
  174–175
iPod roulette 106–107
iPods 106, 173–174
Iqaluit, northern Canada 17–20, 30,
  31–32, 33
 airport 17–18, 48–52
  travellers at 49–51
 dog team race 35–41, 42–46, 47
 school 33
 'Tunik Time' festival 31–32, 33–35
Ivan (Zeiglers' next-door neighbour)
  187–188, 189


Jay (camera assistant) 14, 15
Jean Pierre (French-Canadian lodger)
  31, 45, 47
Jeff (US soundman) 201–202, 205,
  211, 231, 255
Jenny (friend/relative) 53
jet car crash 219, 233
jobs, cool 4
Joiner, Ben 196, 201, 202, 205, 211,
  232, 239, 248, 249, 254, 255
*Jurassic Park* 97, 99–100


K2 (sled dog) 71
Kalahari Desert 121
Kennedy Space Centre 110
King, B.B. 173
Knievel, Evel (Bobby)
 and attack on author of book about
  him 251–252
 career ends 252
 death of 192–193, 256
 documentary about 192, 193–256
  at drive-in movie theatre
   206–209
  encounter with farmer on
   Harley ride 222–224

film crew in Irish bar 239–242
final meeting with Evel 253–256
first meeting with Evel 197–203
Harley ride to meet Hell's
    Angels leader 218–223,
    225–226
interview with Evel's PR man
    251, 252
meeting with Evel in cinema
    213, 214–217
motel meeting with Hell's
    Angels leader 218–219, 220,
    226, 228–235
search for cue ball 241–246
tour of Butte with Evel 203–205
early days 205–206
at Evel Knievel Days festival 237,
    238–239, 248–249, 250, 251
followers of 209–212, 215–217
gravestone 253, 255
and Hell's Angels 217–218, 233,
    234
house in Butte 256
in retirement 196
Wembley Stadium crash 213–214,
    216
Knievel, Krystal 254–255
Knievel, Robbie 196, 237, 238
knives 58–59
Kubu Island 119–120

LaBamba (Fiat convertible) 110
Lake District 55, 162–163
Lancia Beta 112, 118, 119, 120, 129,
    133
Land Rover 108, 109, 111, 158 see also
    Range Rover
diesel (Lollipop) 177–178, 181, 182,
    183, 184, 185
4.6–litre V8 181, 189

Series III station wagon 111
Land Rover Monthly 91
Las Vegas, Caesar's Palace Fountains
    206, 207, 209
Leatherman 39, 113
Ledbury to Cheltenham road (B4213)
    138, 156, 157, 170–171, 172,
    174–175, 176–179
house on 175–176
Livingstone, Ken 139
Lollipop (Land Rover) 177–178, 181,
    182, 183, 184, 185
London Marathon, shin splints
    training for 167–168
Lotus Esprit 150–151, 155
Lyke Wake Walk 88–89

Maglite torch 128
Makgadikgadi Pan salt flats 113–114,
    119, 120–121, 131
Manchester 111
Marlboro 147
Marvin (sled dog) 24–25, 71, 92
May, Iain (cameraman) 15, 152
    drive across Botswana 114
    race to North Pole 70, 75, 76, 77,
        78, 80–83, 90, 93, 94–97,
        99–100, 106
May, James
    amphibious vehicle project 140,
        142, 143, 145–146, 147,
        149–150, 151, 152, 153, 155
    attributes 9
    in Botswana 112, 114–115, 118,
        119, 120–121, 129, 133, 135
    race to Monte Carlo 8
    race to North Pole 9
        in the race 71–72, 73–74, 78, 94,
            103
        in Resolute Bay 61–63

May, James—*contd*
  training 15
  race to Oslo 8
McNair, Eric 17, 19
McNair, Matty
  achievements 17, 44
  bungalow 18–21, 30, 31, 36–37,
    47
    lavatory use in 19–20
  dog sled training 17, 21, 22–23, 24,
    25–26, 27, 28–29, 30, 31,
    41–42
  igloo-building competition 34,
    35
  local dog team race 35, 36–38,
    40–41, 42–43, 44, 45, 46
  in the race 70, 71, 72, 75, 78, 79–80,
    81, 82, 83, 84, 86, 91, 94, 97,
    98, 102, 107
McNair, Sarah 17, 19, 20, 47, 75–76,
    78, 82, 83
Mercedes-Benz 112, 118, 119, 120,
    129, 133
  SLR 8
microlights 114–115, 116
Moleskine notebook 52, 166
Montana 193, 196, 200, 220, 253 *see
    also* Butte, Montana; Knievel,
    Evel, documentary about
Monte Carlo, race to 8
Morgan 108–109
*Motorcycle News* 166
motorcycles, Hell's Angels 226–228,
    231–232, 235
motorcycling 220, 224–225
Motorhead 173
motorways
  M4 159–160
  M5 161, 163, 165, 168
  M50 18, 177, 178

Nelson, Admiral Lord 152
Nissan Micra 159
Noah (bush mechanic) 129, 130, 132
North Pole, geographic, first ever all-
    female expedition to 17
North Pole, magnetic, race to 8–107
  aircraft pickups 104, 107
  beard shaving competition
    105–106, 107
  boots 70
  dog sled training 17, 21, 22–27,
    28–30, 31, 41–42
  final preparations 67–69
  flight to Resolute Bay 52–54
  instructor 61–62, 63, 64
  at Iqaluit airport for flight to
    Resolute Bay 48–52
  Jeremy and James win 73, 103
  last night in 107
  local dog team race 35–41, 42–46,
    47
  planning 16–17
  in Resolute Bay 54–61
  Richard's Arctic explorer's journal
    52–53, 64–66, 67–68, 74–75,
    90–92, 97
  Richard's race 72–104
    first day 72–75, 78–84
    first night 83, 84–88
    second day 88, 89–102
    final halt and preparation for
      aircraft pickup 103–105
  sledging team 75–77
  the start 69–72
  tent 61–64, 83, 84, 104
  toileting 74–75, 90–91, 96, 101
  training 9–16
  the truck 59, 70, 71–72, 78, 94, 102,
    103
notebook, Moleskine 52, 166